BILLERS, BANNERS AND BOMBAST
THE STORY OF CIRCUS ADVERTISING

CHARLES PHILIP FOX

and

TOM PARKINSON

PRUETT **P** PUBLISHING COMPANY
Boulder, Colorado

Library of Congress Cataloging in Publication Data.

Fox, Charles Philip.
  Billers, Banners and Bombast.

  Bibliography;p.
  Includes index.
  1. Advertising—Circus. I. Parkinson, Tom
1921— . II. Title.
HF 6161. C424P37. 1982   659.1'97913 82-16561
ISBN: 0-87108-609-3

First Edition
1 2 3 4 5 6 7 8 9

Printed in the United States of America.

The authors thank Ringling Bros. and Barnum & Bailey Combined Shows, Inc., for permission to reproduce in this book advertising material involving circus names they own. Those names are:

Ringling Bros. and Barnum & Bailey Circus
The Greatest Show on Earth
The World's Greatest Shows
Barnum & Bailey Circus
Ringling Bros. Circus
Sells Floto Circus
Hagenbeck-Wallace Circus
Sparks Circus
John Robinson Circus
Al G. Barnes Circus
Buffalo Bill's Wild West
Adam Forepaugh-Sells Bros. Circus

Special acknowledgement is made of the great assistance given by the Circus World Museum, Baraboo, Wisconsin, through Robert L. Parkinson, chief librarian and historian, and Greg T. Parkinson, endowment director, of this fine institution.

The authors benefitted materially from the special aid given to them by James Strobridge, Andrew Donaldson Jr., Harry Anderson, Gene Baxter, Fred D. Pfening Jr., Rick Pfening, Jim McRoberts, George Gallo, Richard Flint, and many others.

Front Endpapers: Left, Nothing was more typical of circus posters than the clowns, whether they were unnamed generic faces, or recognizable jesters such as Pat Valdo, Lou Jacobs and Felix Adler. **Authors' Collection. Right,** Animals, too, were continuing favorites of poster printers and viewers alike. Sea elephants, gaping hippos and gorillas were among them, but none could equal the frightening appeal of a snarling tiger. **Authors' Collection.**

Back Endpapers: Left, Adding a brave trainer brought new dimension to wild animal posters. Intrepid trainers, Beatty and Jacobs among them, peopled such posters for all the significant shows. **Circus World Museum. Right,** In irreverant references to their bosses, billposters called these the nut bills. But everyone else called them portraits, and the biggest shows used many of them. They depicted integrity and helped convince the public that theirs was a show to see. **Authors' Collection.**

Dedication

This book is dedicated to those who advertised the American circus—printers and artists, unbounded bill writers and innovative press agents, paste-splattered billers and hard-pressing car managers, proud general agents and lowly programmers. The authors hold personal admiration for many of them and for four in particular who epitomize this loyal legion that moved ahead of circuses which they rarely saw.

F. Beverly Kelley worked advertising and publicity miracles for Ringling, Hagenbeck, Cole and Dailey. He brought a flair and a nobility unmatched in the business.

Harry Anderson, third generation to operate the Enquirer show poster plant, continued a professional and family heritage that had begun in the earliest days of dominance by Cincinnati craftsmen in this demanding trade.

F. A. Boudinot, first as a young programmer and finally as general agent of the Greatest Show on Earth, typified the Advance, its demands and its loyalties, always battling for the show as he did when he led its opposition wars.

R. M. Harvey recorded long service as general agent for circuses and provided a lively linkage between the historical curiosity of the authors and the fabulous earlier era of Ben Wallace, James A. Bailey and Jerry Mugivan.

We salute them and those with whom they worked.

Contents

CHAPTER 1

The Terror

The Terror Is Coming.

O ne hundred fifty-six cities on as many mornings woke up to that warning. Previously prosaic walls, windows, and signboards were newly illuminated with scarlet posters that seemed to scream the words.

The Terror Is Coming.

Those towns comprised Ringling Bros. and Barnum & Bailey's spring route and the summer-fall tour of Al G. Barnes-Sells Floto Circus.

The terror was Gargantua the Great, Ringling's angry gorilla. Gargantua's threatening arrival comprised the opening phase of an outstanding advertising campaign. As an institution, circuses always could be counted upon for innovative and effective advertising. The 1938 Ringling campaign, particularly its Gargantua teaser phase, shines out as one of the most successful. It was registered in a disastrous circus season that almost wiped out this institution; a sudden recession demonstrated that the Great Depression was not over after all. Many circuses and other businesses collapsed, but Gargantua's mentors marched on.

The campaign was not particularly large or costly or different. But it was tremendously effective. Everyone within range came to know about "The World's Most Terrifying Living Creature." Advertising accomplished its assignment well. Just as with Barnum's Jumbo, Hagenbeck-Wallace's Clyde Beatty, Ringling-Barnum's Ubangi savages, and today's Gunther Gebel-Williams, circus advertising proved its power. We know of JoJo, the dog-faced boy, of Annie Oakley, Emmett Kelly, the Siamese twins—and Gargantua—because of circus advertising. We know the circus as an institution and various circuses by name all because of the ads. Hundreds of circuses have played tens of thousands of one-day stands behind the style of advertising that is identified with and practiced by the American circus.

Ringling's campaign marked a revitalization of the circus and its return to family control. John Ringling North acquired Gargantua and then added Frank (Bring 'Em Back Alive) Buck, famed animal importer and safari commander. The show also featured Terrell Jacobs' wild animals and an opening pageant called "India," forerunner of North's series of outstanding spectacles.

The advertising and promotional campaign was executed by in-house experts. Roland Butler, a curmudgeon with a pixie touch, prepared the newspaper advertising, direct mail pieces, and poster art. F. Beverly Kelley and Frank Morrissey handled radio publicity. Arthur Hopper was in charge of outdoor advertising. Frank Braden and Gardner Wilson assembled material for local

New Yorkers had no idea what was afoot when their city blossomed with announcements of The Terror in March 1938. The puzzle would continue when the signs were augmented to read "The Terror Is Coming." This display was at 69th Street and West End Avenue. **Fred D. Pfening Jr.**

Farther uptown it was the same story; this was at 148th Street and Park Avenue. The Terror was everywhere but the explanation was nowhere—until Ringling Bros. and Barnum and Bailey Circus took another step in its huge teaser campaign and identified The Terror as its own Gargantua the Great. The innovative ad campaign was a major success. **Fred D. Pfening Jr.**

Curiosity was great, but even with Terror signs across the street from Madison Square Garden, Ringling's New York home, few linked the ads to the circus until the show was ready to spring its surprise. By then, everyone was talking about The Terror. It would be the same in every town on the route. **Fred D. Pfening Jr.**

publicity efforts and generated the national publicity in magazines and news services.

Gargantua glowered from every ad. Butler laid out a wide variety of newspaper ads and prepared a sixteen-page courier featuring Gargantua and Frank Buck along with dozens of additional attractions. Ballyhoo for the courier claimed a circulation of two million copies, and it probably actually rounded out to that total.

It was with posters that the circus accomplished the most. Already the Ringling show was using an array in some 102 styles and sizes. For the new season it would add more. One showed Frank Buck atop an elephant at the head of a sumptuous procession of oriental and circus grandeur. Another was for Terrell Jacobs' black leopards, and both posters came in several sizes. At the top of the line were two styles of lithographs to introduce the gorilla. One was an upright showing Gargantua, his massive arms upraised, charging through the veldt. In the other, the horizontal, a huge Gargantua grasps a hapless native hunter in one hand, while the victim's fellow tribesmen retreat in haste. Powerful posters, they heralded "The Largest Gorilla Ever Exhibited," "The World's Most Terrifying Living Creature." The art and lithography were done by the masterful Strobridge Lithographing Company.

New also was the Terror piece, used in a teaser campaign devised by Arthur Hopper. Under his plan, a brigade of billposters hit each town three weeks ahead of the show to put up posters that read only "The Terror." The teaser was taking shape. Two weeks out, another group posted the second half to make each stand read "The Terror Is Coming." At least in New York, the engagement was long enough to permit a third phase in which

Sparking Ringling's initiative in 1938 was its brand new attraction, Gargantua. There was an assortment of startling new posters to herald this frightening feature, among them this one-sheet. The show used every advertising and publicity medium to make Gargantua's name a household word, an overnight triumph for circus advertising. **Authors' Collection.**

At each city on its route, the circus circulated this sixteen-page courier by the thousands. With Gargantua on the cover, it proclaimed additional circus features inside—one more step in the multi-media ad campaign. **Authors' Collection.**

each stand of paper was amended to read "The Terror Is Here! Ringling Bros. and Barnum & Bailey Presents Gargantua the Great."

The combination of newspaper, radio, and outdoor campaigns, augmented by local and national publicity, achieved its aims.

But there were complications. This was an era of freewheeling labor power. A new union made up largely of circus baggage stock drivers struck the show. Even Gargantua was brought to a halt. The mighty Ringling circus went back to winter quarters. The advertising crews out ahead of the show had posted Terror paper and Gargantua posters along with all the other advertising in another dozen towns that would not see The Terror that season after all. Later, twenty-five cars of Ringling features and equipment joined Ringling's subsidiary, the Al G. Barnes-Sells Floto Circus in South Dakota. Included were Gargantua, Frank Buck, Terrell Jacobs, and the advertising men and materials for continuing the massive campaign.

Now the promotion staff not only was selling a new product in Gargantua, but also was faced with the task of changing show names, changing brands. It was as if Cadillac were selling a new convertible and then suddenly it was Buick's car to sell. Butler and Company were up to the task. New billing proclaimed "Al G. Barnes-Sells Floto Circus Presenting Ringling Bros. and Barnum & Bailey's Stupendous New Features." The press and radio material was amended. A new edition of the courier came forth. Date sheets and the date strips used in connection with pictorial lithographs were amended to carry the new title. From July onward, Gargantua glowered for Barnes-Sells Floto.

Arthur Hopper's teaser ads were compacted for one-day stands. At each town, the first ad said "The Terror Is Coming." Regular pictorial and dated billing for the show appeared at the same time. The effect still was powerful. Youngsters in Illinois and Wisconsin were bug-eyed the day that their town was posted by the circus billers.

Circus advertising procedures can be translated into terminology more meaningful to space buyers, media representatives, and ad agency personnel. The Ringling show, in the last throes of its tented era, hired an agency to prepare and place its advertising, and

When troubles beset the parent Ringling-Barnum circus, principal features were moved to a subsidiary, Al G. Barnes-Sells Floto Circus. The Ringling promotion staff converted the campaign to Barnes-Sells Floto and went merrily along—teasers, Gargantua and all. **Authors' Collection.**

On Ringling in New York or Barnes in any Western town or any circus anywhere, advertising was massive and effective. "Billed like a circus" became a superlative among other advertisers. When Barnum & Bailey billed Paris in 1902, a newspaper complained the entire city had been turned into a "garish display." Each flag on the map represents a Barnum & Bailey billboard, so the city was indeed bright with a blanket of circus lithography. **Ringling Museum of the American Circus.**

later, as an indoor attraction, it retained an agency for part of the work of implementing an entirely different kind of promotional system. With that exception, circus advertising has been an in-house production. Shows retained their own copy writers and space buyers but called them bill writers and contracting press agents. They added artists and billposters and some specialists that ad agencies do not know about—banner men, programmers, and press-agents-back. Printing houses functioned somewhat like ad agencies when they submitted poster layouts for sale, but perhaps as often they carried out job printing assignments brought to them by circus agents.

Typically, circuses for nearly two hundred seasons have taken on one of the toughest advertising assignments—the hard sell of a product available only on a single day. It was quite different from the usual assignment of selling a product that is available in many places for a long time. It was more challenging than the local merchants' "Dollar Days" in that there was no opportunity for residual value in ensuing weeks.

The circus faced a three-way marketing task: title, date, and feature. It had to implant an awareness of the date so that customers would reserve it. It had to convince the public that this was a quality concern—that the circus name, or title, assured high standards. Third, it had to convince the public that it offered a worthy product—that this season's features set this circus apart from other shows and other years and consequently could not be passed by.

Oddly, the philosophy of circus advertising relied nearly as heavily on the absence of the circus as it did its presence. Its fifty weeks of silence were nearly as important as its two weeks of action. Each circus tried to find markets that it and other shows had not overplayed in the past so that the territory was fresh and the attraction was novel. Then came the blitz campaign, with strong factors of excitement, uniqueness, and urgency. Theirs was not a chore of breaking a national campaign simultaneously in 150 or 200 markets, but rather the launching of that campaign 150 times in as many days to reach those markets. The resulting circus campaigns probably were at least as effective as most advertising efforts carried out by standard organizations with more common procedures.

But many of the goals, if not the procedures, were the same for circuses as for regular advertisers. They used print and broadcast as well as outdoor advertising. Each show emphasized brand name—the circus title—and hoped for recognition if not recollection. It stressed new products in the form of this year's novel attractions and big features. Circuses have a great history in direct mail technique and its equivalents through the use of heralds and couriers. The shows long have understood the effectiveness of promotions, tie-ins, and free coupons. They have utilized local sponsors in some instances and such devices as free admission to farm ladies or reduced prices for children, knowing as a result that whole families might attend.

Challenged by a negative thought—"If you've seen one, you've seen them all"—circuses adopted two procedures well before general advertising discovered them. One is the declaration that the show is "bigger and better than ever"—the showman's equivalent of offering not just Cheer, but in fact New Improved Cheer. Simultaneously, in direct competitive situations the circus disparaged Brand X by free use of giant posters reading "After the Minnow Comes the Whale" or "Wait for the Big Show." Moreover, most circuses never have backed away from head-to-head competition that included unfavorable, even scurrilous, remarks about their rivals.

Skilled general agents of major circuses made a science of selecting markets—designating towns in which their show would spend each valuable day. They considered every factor of demographics, season, economics, and competition in routing their circuses. Sometimes they picked a different assortment of cities within their usual territory. Occasionally, they would abandon all familiar places and embark on a season in an entirely different part of the country. It was as if they were selecting test markets, identifying at least 150 markets in which to invest a year, or dumping all familiar markets and offering the product in as many new places.

Certainly the circus utilized the advertising industry's later concept of saturation. On a given day, the force of circus agents descended upon a city to buy expanses of newspaper space and runs of broadcast time. They were the inventors and masters of every art in the outdoor advertising business, almost literally wrapping up towns in their advertising paper, posting paper in such volume as to make the "100% showings" of latter-day billboards seem insignificant by comparison. In cities that might count from 50 to 100 billboards as a full showing, circuses frequently would post outdoor advertising in all sizes and shapes to total 15,000 to 20,000 sheets. Using that billposters' unit of measure, this was enough paper to fill from 626 to 833 standard twenty-four sheet billboards. Circuses invented saturation advertising.

The pressures on circus personnel to produce results were as great and perhaps as quickly measured as with advertising managers and agencies in other more prosaic fields. If the general agent's decisions about territory and season proved wrong, the show could collapse in a matter of days. If he and the show owner did not see sufficient advertising as they reached each town, the advance car manager's head was on the block. Producing tear sheets for ads and publicity was the only system of job security for press agents. The lithographer who could not achieve a "Main Street showing" with posters in the windows of principal stores was soon to be looking for new employment. The whole system was out of business unless, in one day and every day, the advertising department placed a campaign that would result in sufficent business on another single day two weeks hence. It was as demanding as an ad agency's holding an account or an ad manager's producing results at the cash register.

It was not by passive luck that circus business has survived nearly 200 seasons. It is no coincidence that when the age of advertising dawned, it was the circus that boosted it over the horizon.

Circus posters were taking on a more familiar form by 1852, when J.H. and F.F. Farwell printed this one for Johnson & Co. The show's agent wrote the name of the town and the date on each poster. The Farwell plant was one of several show printing houses on New York's Spruce Street. **New-York Historical Society.**

CHAPTER 2

The Show Printers

A circus usually spent more for advertising than for any other single part of its operation. For most of show history, posters were the most important and voluminous form of advertising, while heralds and couriers meant more print orders in the millions. A circus might eat up more than its own weight —elephants, tents, train and all—in the tonnage of printed matter it bought annually.

Little wonder that show posters constituted one of the principal elements of the entire printing industry for many years. Not surprisingly, numerous printers specialized in meeting this demand. As might be expected, an alliance between each circus and its poster printer was critical to any measure of success.

Circuses developed many advertising techniques used later by others. Shows made the kind of purchases that encouraged printing firms to invest in more presses and new methods.

In typical operation, a circus ordered posters in many sizes and styles. Its printer produced the inventory and shipped out to the show's advance advertising department the daily assortments of paper requested—literally millions of sheets of exciting advertising in massive stocks of pictorial posters, heralds, and couriers.

Show print specialists also took on the quick-service, short-run printing challenge of furnishing the show with date sheets—those straight letterpress posters, each with the name of a town and the date on which the show would play there. These printers dealt with beautifully lithographed pictorial pieces on one hand, and on the other with garish giant red type and even six-foot numerals for the dates . . . "One Day Only, Jacksonville, May 21." A circus dealt in superlatives, so its printer moved easily from ordinary 36-and 72-point type to 5,184-point supertype for impressing the day of the month upon everyone who came within a city block of the date sheet.

A set of date sheets was good only for one day and one town, so there was no room for error or delay. Since circuses moved every day, the printer's customer was in a new spot for each delivery. So the shipping was as complicated as the printing requirements. Copy for date sheets made the show printer a center of sensitive information about circus routes. He took care to keep the confidential tour details away from rival shows. Each circus guarded its advance route jealously and kept it secret as much as possible so that others could not gain competitive advantage. Woe to the show printer who got his routes mixed up, who left a list around the shop for a rival showman to read, or who leaked towns and dates to a competing show.

As a circus prepared to go on tour, it ordered paper for the season, and that supply was stacked up by the printer, then shipped out as the circus called for it. The lithographer printed all the paper in the winter and invoiced the circus as the posters were used during the summer. The show might complete its billposting of final towns in

THE
ELEPHANT,

ACCORDING to the Account of the celebrated Buffon, is the moſt reſpectable Animal in the World. In Size he ſurpaſſes all other terreſtrial Creatures ; and, by his Intelligence, he makes as near an Approach to Man, as Matter can approach Spirit. A ſufficient Proof that there is not too much ſaid of the Knowledge of this Animal is, that the Proprietor having been abſent for ten Weeks, the Moment he arrived at the Door of his Apartment, and ſpoke to the Keeper, the Animal's Knowledge was beyond any Doubt confirmed by the Cries he uttered forth, till his Friend came within Reach of his Trunk, with which he careſſed him, to the Aſtoniſhment of all thoſe who ſaw him. This moſt curious and ſurprizing Animal is juſt arrived from *Philadelphia*, on his Way to *Boſton*.—He will juſt ſtay to give the Citizens of *Providence* an Opportunity to ſee him. He is only four Years old, and weighs about 3000 Weight, but will not come to his full Growth till he ſhall be between 30 and 40 Years old. He meaſures from the End of his Trunk to the Tip of his Tail 15 Feet 8 Inches, round the Body 10 Feet 6 Inches, round his Head 7 Feet 2 Inches, round his Leg, above the Knee, 3 Feet 3 Inches ; round his Ankle 2 Feet 2 Inches. He eats 130 Weight a Day, and drinks all Kinds of ſpirituous Liquors ; ſome Days he has drank 30 Bottles of Porter, drawing the Corks with his Trunk. He is ſo tame that he travels looſe, and has never attempted to hurt any one. He appeared on the Stage, at the new Theatre in *Philadelphia*, to the great Satisfaction of a reſpectable Audience.

☞ The Elephant having deſtroyed many Papers of Conſequence, it is recommended to Viſitors not to come near him with ſuch Papers.

*** A Place is fitted up for him (ſuitable to receive genteel Company) in a Store back of the Coffee-Houſe ; where he will remain till the 8th of *July* only, as he is to be at *Cambridge* at the approaching Commencement.

Admittance, One Quarter of a Dollar—Children, One Eighth of a Dollar.

Providence, June 27, 1797.

Printed by Carter and Wilkinson.

October or November. Not until after that would the printer be paid for the last order. Thus, the show printer was in fact carrying the show almost all year for at least part of the paper cost. Perhaps in January or February he would print stocks of posters for the coming season and again wait until fall to get paid for the last part of it.

At the season's end, the printer gave the show an inventory of the paper that was still in stock—"on the shelf." The show's agent took this into account when ordering quantities or varieties of posters for the ensuing year.

Thanks largely to circuses, though with a nod to patent medicines and a few others, the most prominent form of advertising for decades was the poster. Advertising historians note that "the spirit of P. T. Barnum pervaded outdoor advertising" after the Civil War. Eventually, billboards replaced posters, the difference being that posters were usually smaller bills pasted at random on nearly any wall or fence and gave rise to the old warning "Post No Bills", while billboards were panels constructed especially for displaying signs. For random posters, called daubs, dimension was not particularly important. Size was determined first by the size of the bed on the printing press and by the size of the woodcuts. Later, the dimension was restricted to the size of the lithograph stone that a man can handle readily, and this became the norm. Eventually, a unit of measure called a "sheet" was standardized at twenty-eight by forty-two inches—the size of lithograph stones.

A half-sheet was twenty-eight by twenty-one inches; a two-sheet was forty-two by fifty-six inches; three-sheets and four-sheets were made up of horizontal one-sheets stacked on top of each other. Thus, a three-sheet was forty-two by eighty-four inches. Six- and eight-sheets were multiples of three- or four-sheets.

As advertisers other than circuses began to use billboards in national campaigns, the need for standardization increased. In 1912, the industry established the twenty-four-sheet as standard for billboards. The frames were twelve by twenty-five feet, allowing for a mat of white paper around the advertising material. In recent times, advertisers have designed paper to fill the entire panel, using a thirty-sheet with no mat. While such big posters may once have been done on as many pieces of paper as there were sheets

A "poney," "lama." "Kentucky panthers' were good music on the Jewish cymbal and violin were promised by this 1826 menagerie poster. It includes blank spaces where the agent was to write in the time and place for the local appearance. **American Antiquarian Society.**

New printing developments made possible this poster, measuring more than eight feet high and three feet wide. It proclaims the National Menagerie of 1833, where the hyena cries instead of laughs and the elephant has strange toes if the artist is to be believed. **The Whaling Museum**.

in its size, usually they were printed on fewer pieces, and "sheet" was only a unit of measure.

Circuses ordered lithographs in half- and one-sheet sizes. They ordered two-sheet, three-, four-, six-, eight-, and nine-sheets. Lithographs also came in twelve-, fifteen-, sixteen-, eighteen-, twenty-, twenty-eight-, and thirty-two-sheet units. Occasionally there were forty-eight- and sixty-four-sheets. First the W. W. Cole Circus and then Forepaugh-Sells and the Buffalo Bill show used lithographs of 100 sheets and more.

To fit narrow window spaces there were posters known as panels in both half- and one-sheet sizes. Streamers were one-sheet high and from two- to twenty-eight-sheets wide. These were printed with the circus title and were spread across the top of large stands of pictorials. Buffalo Bill once used a streamer that was forty sheets, or 140 feet wide, proclaiming "Buffalo Bill's Wild West and Congress of Rough Riders of the World Just As Presented at Chicago's World Fair."

Because posters were ordered in quantities, the printers were able to keep their prices low, and this encouraged circus owners to use greater amounts of the colorful paper.

The William P. Hall Shows ordered paper from the Great Western Printing Company in 1905 and paid a half cent for a half-sheet, two cents for a one-sheet, and twelve cents for a three-sheet lithograph. When it ordered paper from Riverside Printing in Milwaukee, a one-sheet cost three cents, a three-sheet, ten and one-half cents and a twenty-four sheet, eighty-two cents.

The Strobridge Lithographing Company in 1909 invoiced Barnum & Bailey five cents for each one-sheet, thirty cents per eight-sheet, seventy-five cents per twenty-sheet, and $1.20 for each thirty-two sheet. In 1918, one order for 20,000 sheets (ranging from 108 twenty-four-sheet posters to 4,220 one-sheet posters) cost Barnum & Bailey $2,043.49. In 1930, the Erie Lithographing Company was still charging five and one-half cents per sheet and one dollar for a twenty-sheet poster.

In 1938, Robbins Bros. Circus bought paper from Erie. Their twenty-sheets cost one dollar each; a fifteen-sheet, seventy-five cents; nine-sheet, forty-five cents; and three-sheets, fourteen cents each. The show also bought large quantities of one-sheets, half-sheets, and date sheets in the same period. A year later, Ringling Bros. and Barnum & Bailey Circus was using posters in 102 different sizes and subjects from Erie Lithographing Company. A fraction of that list included the following:

24-sheet	portraits bill
20-sheet	tent interior
20-sheet	wild animal scene
18-sheet	crouching tiger
16-sheet	Pallenberg bears
16-sheet	unloading trains
16-sheet	Wallenda wire act
15-sheet	lion head and title
12-sheet	black panther
8-sheet	giraffes
8-sheet	Dorothy Herbert on rearing horse
4-sheet	Terrell Jacobs lion act
3-sheet	seal act
2-sheet	clown and title
1-sheet	portraits
1-sheet	Gibson knife act
1-sheet	Clyde Beatty and lion
1-sheet	clown and donkey

The partnership between circus and printer was paramount every day throughout the season, year after year. It continues

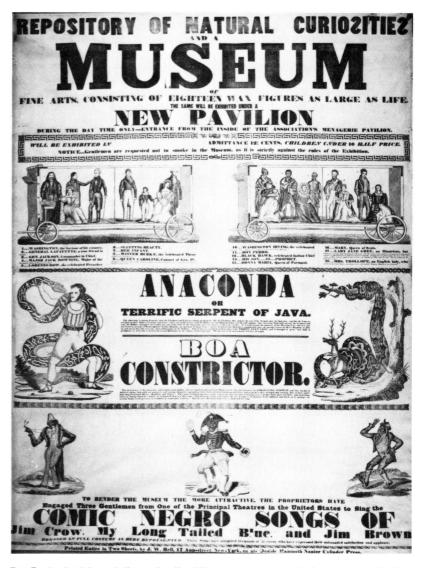

The Zoological Association advertised its wax museum and giant snakes with this large poster of 1835. Show printer Jared W. Bell was so intent upon the great size of posters from his brand new press that he overlooked the reversed letters in the top line. The museum was an offshoot of the Association's menagerie. **Circus World Museum.**

with both operations today as shows use posters, window cards, and mailing pieces. It began at the very dawn of American circus business and before some major printing methods saw the light of day.

As printing technology developed, circuses played a key role. Pioneer shows were major customers of the printing industry and continued as both businesses grew. Picking up with posters and handbills, two age-old items from fifteenth-century Europe, circuses used everything that the printing industry could devise and effectively pressured for more. Posters developed into the sophisticated outdoor advertising industry. Handbills evolved into newspapers on the one hand and direct mail advertising on the other. Show printing was one of the earliest specialties in the printing trades, and some of the early leaders in graphic arts specialized in circus printing.

For all the self-sufficiency attributed to circuses, the shows were dependent on outsiders for printing. It was perhaps the only, and certainly the greatest, area for which they went to outsiders, to towners. There was a dependency on railroads, but usually some other form of transportation could be made available. There was no substitute for printed advertising, and circuses could not do the printing themselves. This brought about the close alliance between not only the circus and printing as industries, but also between individual circuses and specific printers. With a little circus alliteration showing through, a battle-scarred old circus agent, W. E. (Watseka Bill) Franklin, declared that "Printing, Parade, Performance" were the essential elements of circuses. He might have added "Portability," but he was correct in that every show leaned heavily on the printing trade.

This poster for Levi North's Circus of 1855, a one-sheet printed in green on tan, was done by Farwell, Purcell & Co. on a steam press. Such woodblock posters would continue in wide use for some years, although the first lithographs were beginning to appear on circuses. **Circus World Museum.**

Early Beginnings

Mr. Poole, an equestrian and forerunner of the American circus, advertised in 1786 with bills printed by Carter—who just might have been John Carter, once an apprentice in the print shop of Ben Franklin and later a partner in Carter & Wilkinson, Providence, Rhode Island. Carter & Wilkinson printed broadsides for advertising the first elephant in the country in 1797. Meanwhile, John Bill Ricketts introduced the first full circus to America in 1793 and referred from the outset to his printed bills. Pepin & Breschard, arriving from France in 1807, quickly peppered Plymouth, Massachusetts, and all ensuing towns with green posters depicting an equestrian bounding lightly on horseback while waving two American flags. In 1822, Jonas Booth installed the first steam-powered press in America, thus multiplying production and reducing the cost of his posters. Show printing, along with books and lottery tickets, was the backbone of the Booths' business for three generations.

Manufacture of the Hoe press on Napier's cylindrical principle brought more potential for show printers. Little handbills were augmented by new posters six and eight feet tall. This required the printer's coordination of several sheets that would be pasted together and posted as one design. There also were larger presses for single sheets. A lot of circus posters were coming off the presses by 1833, when a New Hampshire editor noted that circuses were operating on "a new plan . . . [using] large bills measuring seven or eight feet in length . . . with cuts representing the lion and the monkey."

Richard Hoe and Company delivered a new Napier press to Jared W. Bell, New York, who almost immediately was producing posters in excess of six by nine feet for the 1835 circus season. These were produced in four sections and assembled later. For the Zoological Associations that year, Bell turned out six-and-one-half-by-five-foot posters advertising, among other things, the "anaconda serpent of Java." Bell seems to have been influenced by his circus connections. His credit line on the poster reads, "Printed entire in two sheets by J. W. Bell on his double mammoth Napier cylinder press." If "double mammoth" sounds like a circus, it is little wonder, for many people of the time were

G.F. BAILEY & CO'S
CIRCUS & MENAGERIE.

HIPPOPOTAMUS.

Sarony, Major & Knapp turned out this lithograph for the G.F. Bailey circus of 1867. While lithographs began to appear on the 1840s and were numerous in the 1860s, most circuses used wood-block posters until the 1870s. **Circus World Museum.**

investing in menageries and circuses. Even Hoe, the press manufacturer, was a stockholder in the Zoological Institute, which operated this and other touring shows.

Illustrations had been used from the first, but the mahogany woodcuts were difficult to make and costly to buy. Newspapers, shows, printers—everyone used them sparingly. Examination of the columns of the *Hartford Currant* in 1793 suggests that it had only four cuts. One was for the local bell foundry, others of a horse and a house, both readily adaptable to many advertisers

15

but in fact rarely used. The fourth, showing a Windsor chair, was used in turn by the several furniture makers who advertised. Other printers and their customers were equally sparing with illustrations.

But Joseph Morse took care of all of that. He found a way to replace costly mahogany with inexpensive pine that was both easy to get and simple to carve. The use of illustrations burgeoned. Morse also devised a technique for gluing several blocks of pine together to make much larger illustrations.

When Morse developed pine blocks, he was experimenting primarily to achieve multicolor printing—a development of equal importance to the trade. "I was the first man to use the pine board for show cuts," he recalled. "I first introduced the use of colors and cut the tint blocks for them on flat, smooth pine boards. Very soon I found that I could use pine for the black print also."

By 1840, the Booths already were identifying themselves as show printers. They, like Bell and others in the field, were using many of the new Morse pine block cuts. Suddenly, things could be illustrated easily.

Back when Ricketts was showing Philadelphians and New Yorkers their first full circus, something important was happening to printing in Munich. Alois Senefelder, son of a court actor to the king of Bavaria, became a dramatic author and actor himself. But upon watching the printing of his play, Senefelder determined to be printer instead of playwright.

VAN AMBURGH & COS GREAT GOLDEN MENAGERIE.

A PUPIL OF THE GREAT VAN AMBURGH THE ORIGINAL AND ONLY
GREAT SUBDUER OF WILD ANIMALS.

Another early lithograph depicted this mixed bag of a man and beasts on the Van Amburgh Menagerie of 1868. The art probably had been in use since Van Amburgh himself was with the show. But by this printing, he had departed and the type announced some unnamed "pupil" would handle the subduing. T.W. Strong was the lithographing firm. **Circus World Museum.**

McConnelsburg
June - 19.

HOWES'
LONDON CIRCUS! HIPPODROME!
AND SANGER'S
ENGLISH MENAGERIE OF TRAINED ANIMALS.

McConnelsburg
June 19

BEDFORD, JUNE - 21

BEDFORD, JUNE - 21

James Reilley, Engraver and Decorative Steam Job Printer, 12, 14 & 16 Spruce St., New York. Largest Show Bill Printing Establishment in the World.

Woodcuts could include great detail and finesse. This was a product of the James Reilley print shop for Howes' London Circus of 1873. Adding the individual town and date was still a problem. Sometimes the agent wrote the information in longhand, as with the "McConnelsburg, June 19" here, while others used crude date stamps, as with the "Bedford June 21" on this poster. **Circus World Museum.**

He had to learn to engrave lettering in reverse on copper plates. But copper was costly, so he practiced on a flat stone used earlier in preparation of ingredients for ink. He covered the stone with the wax ink used in copper etching, and the wax was removed in the shape of desired letters or artwork. But soon he considered eliminating the copper and printing directly from etched stone—not a totally new idea. Once his mother needed to make a laundry list hastily while the laundress waited, but there was no paper. Alois wrote the list on his stone in an ink that he had concocted. Later, he put acid on it to see if it would etch the exposed portion

of stone and leave the inked part in relief, or elevated. That it did. Thus, in 1796 he invented the ink and the mechancial means to print from stone—printing from an inked surface that could be either raised or lowered from the initial stone surface—either relief or intaglio.

Next, he found a way to transfer existing printing from paper to stone to new paper. That led to means for printing from existing paper pages to new paper pages. Both of these were chemical rather than mechanical processes. They took him to the next step—finding that stone could be treated so that portions covered with a

COLE'S SOUTHERN CIRCUS AND MENAGERIE.

Another beautiful example of the woodcarvers' craftsmanship, this W.W. Cole Circus poster not only introduces the idea of attaching a separate paper bearing the printed date and place but also measures 28 by 42 inches, the size that would be established as the standard one-sheet. **Circus World Museum.**

WILL BE SEEN IN SAXBY, DUNBAR & CO'S INTERNATIONAL CIRCUS.

Business for the 1872 Saxby, Dunbar & Co. show was pretty good in the mind of the poster artist for the Gibson & Co. Steam Lithographic Press. But he was realistic enough to include a lemonade butcher working the seats. One-ring shows some time placed a single tent pole in the center of the ring. **Library of Congress.**

Both woodblock and lithography are capable of great detail and expression. One relies on a painter, the other on a carver. Lithography achieves shadings by the artist's skills with brush and paint. Woodblock depends upon how much surface the carver cuts away. Removal of less wood makes a darker imprint; removal of more brings a lighter shade. Different shadings result as the carver leaves lines that are wider or narrower, more or fewer, checked or solid. Woodcuts transfer ink from whatever part of the wood surface has not been removed. In contrast, lithography picks up ink from a stone surface which prints a slightly grainy texture not unlike that made by crayon or pencil. This enlargement is from a woodblock of the John B. Doris Circus, 1883. The lithography detail is from an 1899 Buffalo Bill poster. **Library of Congress, Authors' Collection.**

fatty soap would take ink, while those parts treated with water would reject ink. In 1798, he perfected this method of stone-printing by chemical means.

"I took a cleanly polished stone, inscribed it with a piece of soap, poured thin gum solution over it, and passed over all with a sponge dipped in oil color. All the places marked with fat became black at once. The rest remained white....Wetting the stone after each impression and treating it again with the sponge produced the same result each time....It made no difference now whether the design was worked in relief or intaglio, as good impressions could be obtained even when the drawing was perfectly level with the surface of the stone....I had invented and discovered the entire art. Everything rests on the same principle:

ink of wax, soap, etc.; then gum, aquafortis or another acid...[and] further, oil varnish or lampblack."

This was lithography. The word comes from Greek terms meaning "stone" and "writing." One could draw on stone with a greasy material, wet the rest of the stone, and subject it all to ink. The greasy or fatty material would accept ink, the wetted areas would not. Paper pressed against the stone would be imprinted in the shape of inked areas, while wet space printed white.

From 1793, Senefelder had been working with the court musician, publishing the latter's symphonies, works for clavier and flute, and other music. Even his early inventions produced superior sheet music, but lithographed sheet music was still a better printing job. This continued to be an early use for lithography. It

Courier Co. designed this one-sheet in 1877 so the same art could be utilized by any number of circuses. In such stock paper, the top line could be changed to name other riders and the bottom line could substitute another show's name. Van Amburgh added the imprint of town and date. **Circus World Museum.**

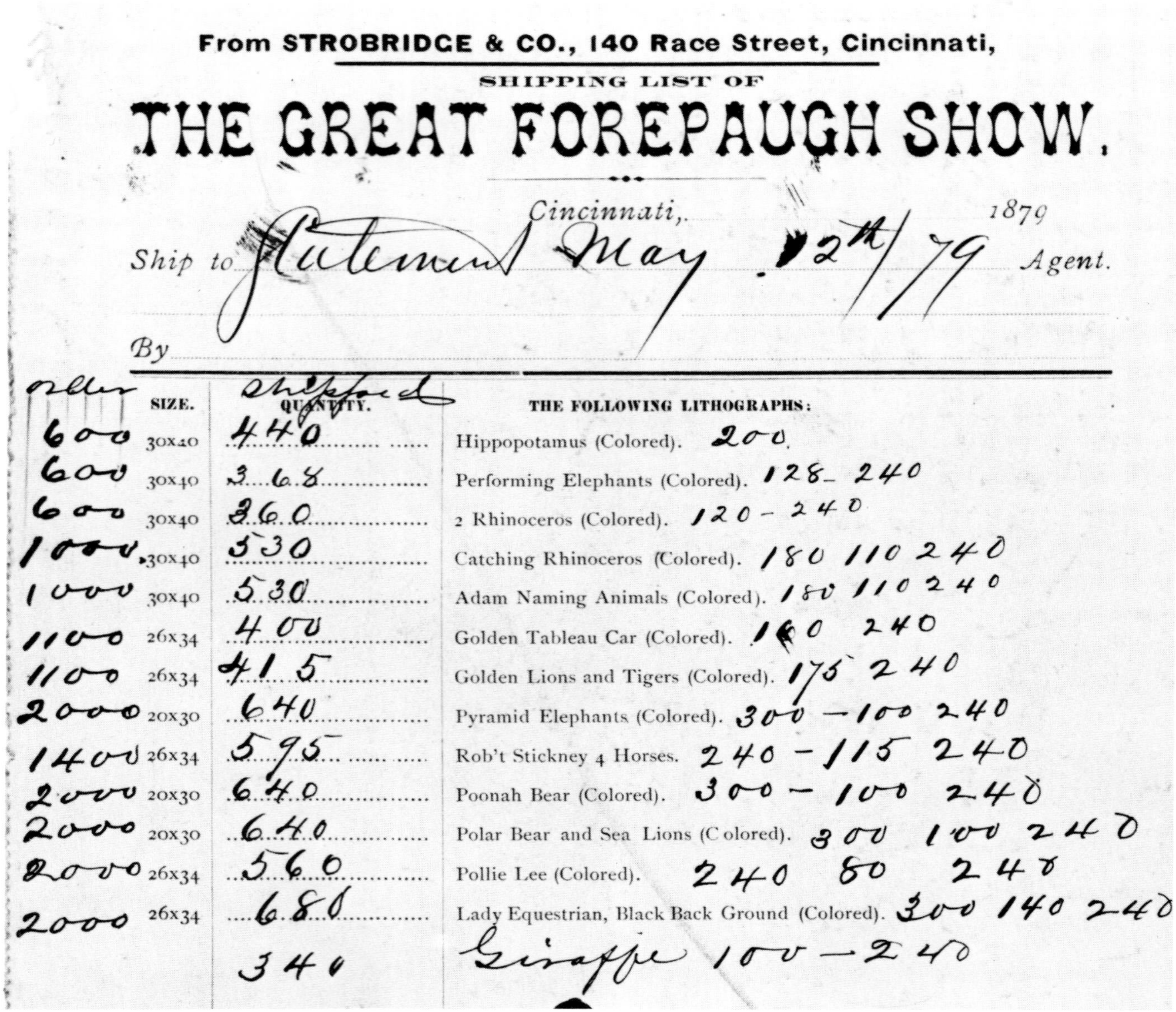
From STROBRIDGE & CO., 140 Race Street, Cincinnati,

SHIPPING LIST OF

THE GREAT FOREPAUGH SHOW.

Cincinnati, 1879

Ship to Statement May 12th/79 Agent.

By

Order	SIZE.	QUANTITY. Shipped	THE FOLLOWING LITHOGRAPHS:
600	30x40	440	Hippopotamus (Colored). 200
600	30x40	368	Performing Elephants (Colored). 128 240
600	30x40	360	2 Rhinoceros (Colored). 120 - 240
1000	30x40	530	Catching Rhinoceros (Colored). 180 110 240
1000	30x40	530	Adam Naming Animals (Colored). 180 110 240
1100	26x34	400	Golden Tableau Car (Colored). 160 240
1100	26x34	415	Golden Lions and Tigers (Colored). 175 240
2000	20x30	640	Pyramid Elephants (Colored). 300 - 100 240
1400	26x34	595	Rob't Stickney 4 Horses. 240 - 115 240
2000	20x30	640	Poonah Bear (Colored). 300 - 100 240
2000	20x30	640	Polar Bear and Sea Lions (Colored). 300 100 240
2000	26x34	560	Pollie Lee (Colored). 240 80 240
2000	26x34	680	Lady Equestrian, Black Back Ground (Colored). 300 140 240
		340	Giraffe 100 - 240

By the 1870s, the Strobridge Lithographing Co. was an important factor in the business. By this document it was billing the Great Forepaugh Show for more than 7,000 lithographs. Strobridge also was selling then to John Robinson, P.T. Barnum, Howes, and the Cooper & Bailey Show, among others. **Circus World Museum.**

also was used for art in "the style of Rembrandt" and to illustrate church booklets.

First experiments were made with Kellheimer stone, but soon the quarry near Kellheim was exhausted, and Senefelder switched to Solenhofer stone. It was a lucky turn that the experimenter lived near the proper stone; lithographers for decades to come would declare that only Solenhofer stone would serve the purpose.

In his biography and textbook, published in 1817, Senefelder stated that one could print material in several colors by using a separate stone for each color. He provided recipes for blue and red inks but noted that there was a problem with green. Better, he said, to print first in blue and then overprint in yellow to arrive at green in the end. Thus, he anticipated not only multicolored lithographs of some years later, but also the process color work of today. He saw great promise for stoneprinting: "In the future," he wrote, "true paintings will be produced by its means." He was predicting inexpensive duplication of art and the appearance of such chromolithographs as those of Currier & Ives. Those "true paintings" also would include millions of circus posters.

Again, his writing noted that lithography in 1817 had spread to Frankfort, Paris, Berlin, "even Philadelphia." Indeed, Americans were importing Solenhofer stone and following Senefelder's process. Since lithography then was slow and costly, it was not immediately snapped up by shows and show printers, but there were pioneers. G. and W. Endicott, New York, was producing lithographed circus posters in the 1840s. Welch & Mann used one in 1846; Raymond & Waring had another in 1848. By the middle 1860s, both the Lent and Mabie circuses had lithographs along with their other posters. But pine block printing still dominated. Even seventy-five years after Senefelder, printers saw

The Donaldson Lithograph Co. of Newport, Ky., was among the many prominent lithographers serving circuses from the Cincinnati area. The office wing in the foreground was the site for many meetings affecting circuses—sometimes dickering over art and prices, sometimes deciding to foreclose for overdue accounts. **Donaldson Lithograph Co.**

In this Donaldson plant, artists drew new posters directly on Kellheimer stones. This large staff of artists was putting the basic black outlines on stone for Great Wallace Circus posters of about 1902. Such "black" artists were the elite among lithograph artists. On multiple sheets, a different black artist handled each section of the poster separately. Ties and vests were the order of the day. The stones rest on sturdy wooden frames that can be rolled about. **Donaldson Lithograph Co.**

In another wing the color department held forth. Some artists worked on stones that would add blue to the final poster, some handled stones for the red or yellow portions. Sample portions of the project were placed alongside the artist as a guide to the final product. As each color stone was completed, proofs were taken for approval. The current poster is a multiple sheet depicting somersaulting riders. The man seated at the second stone is working from photographs of an equestrienne he will add to the art on the stone. **Donaldson Lithograph Co.**

In the press room the final product was pulled together. The young pressman at center stands near the bed of the Hoe press in which the flat stone is placed. The press combined the inked stone with the rollers to imprint each sheet with a new color. Each of four press runs added another color to the paper. The press in the rear would work with a different color than the one in the foreground. At the left rear a man inks a proof press with a hand roller. The c-shaped tool on the pillar is a scraper for cleaning ink from the leather rollers on the press. **Donaldson Lithograph Co.**

Prim young ladies in the bindery room pasted parts of multiple sheets into vertical sections of a size billposters could cope with. Other workers folded the big posters in a standard way so billposters would know how to unfold them in sequence. These women are working on paper for Cozad's California Dog & Pony Show. The big posters are for an act with a pyramid of five concentric circles of performing ponies. The scene seems overly posed, since the paper is in no logical sequence on the table, nor are the paste pots in easy reach. **Donaldson Lithograph Co.**

no advantage in junking their massive stocks of woodcuts on every conceivable subject in favor of possible replacement on stone.

Blooming of Color

Meanwhile, color capabilities were perfected for both systems. For pine blocks, the design was drawn on wood with India ink, then unwanted parts were carved away, leaving the design in black. The printer pulled additional proofs with which to make a duplicate block for each color. On one, the artist indicated which parts ultimately would appear in red, and a wood-carver cut away all the rest. The process was repeated for each color, and each block was used in turn to apply its color to the eventual poster.

By 1847, color printing was a reality, and circuses were the prime users. Bell probably was the first to print in color; he did a five-color poster of the Raymond & Company band chariot with a ten-horse team, all shown in red, gold, blue, green, and black. A variety of type faces appeared in colors. All of that was surrounded by thirty-four black-and-white woodcuts of animals and birds. The finished product was six feet high.

Crane & Company's Great Oriental Circus ordered a color poster from G. and W. Endicott for the 1849 season. Edward Purcell, another show printing specialist, produced a stunning full-color poster that season for R. Sands & Company. Still another New York show printer was the Sarony firm (sometimes called Sarony & Major), which did color work for the big Spalding & Rogers and Sands, Nathan circuses, among others, in the 1850s.

As woodblock posters of four colors and more became common-place, they carried a beauty and printing sophistication that seems amazing today. A typical pine block poster was produced by the James Reilley house for the Howes Great London Circus in 1873. It began with a solid base of putty-colored ink as an under-coat over which the colors and design were added. The color blocks were yellow, blue, and red. Each had its share of the design, carried in angled lines, slashes, or hash marks. Lines of one color might be printed next to, between, on top of, or apart from the others to gain design, shading, added colors, and art effects.

Lithography also began with the black drawing, sometimes on paper but, in the case of experts, directly on stone. With proofs on more stones and with artists for each color, the process was completed. The system is not unlike modern color printing in which so-called color separations are made from the original color design; a separate negative represents the area to be covered by each color. In all of the processes, skilled printers could get different shades or tints of a single color or numerous additional colors. With as few as four plates, they could achieve nearly unlimited variety of color by use of overlapping plates and the consequent mixing of colored inks. The fundamental colors were black, yellow, blue, and red, or, more specifically, black, yellow, cyan, and magenta.

With either woodblocks or lithography, the so-called "black" artist, who did the full basic illustration, was counted the most important. Other artists might be assigned to the yellow, blue, or red portions. Assignment of the black work also depended upon the special talents of an artist. One might be particularly good with cowboys and Indians, another might specialize in wild animals, clowns, or lettering. On multiple sheets (the larger sizes), a different artist did the black work on each section in order to speed up production.

In 1872, the Barnum circus overwhelmed its competition by use of giant color posters made from huge woodblocks. Other shows followed quickly with large color posters. By that time, at least thirteen concerns were describing themselves as show printers, and a printing journal estimated that they did $1.5 million worth of work yearly for circuses—big money in the 1870s. Even the modest shows were spending $10,000 or more, and others were buying $50,000 worth of show posters each season. In 1891, Ringling Bros. alone was spending more than $100,000 yearly with the Courier Company. By 1894, the Donaldson directory listed sixty-three show printing companies.

Several of these originated with the job printing departments of various newspapers. In Chicago, the Journal Job Print became the John B. Jeffrey Show Print Company. There were the Detroit

Free Press Show Print and the Philadelphia Ledger Show Print. In Buffalo, New York, the job printing division of the *Buffalo Courier* grew into the Courier Company, which claimed to be the largest of all show printers. Charles M. McCuen and later George Bleistein headed up that company, which entered the show printing field via its engraving department. Later, it cut back on engravings in order to produce woodblocks and then lithographed posters. The *Cincinnati Enquirer* did circus work in its job printing department but sold that phase of its business to H. J. Anderson, who continued the operation as the Enquirer Job Print. Today it is called the Enquirer Show Printing Company.

By the late 1870s, lithography was taking over, and woodblocks were considered passe. Not everyone made the switch. Samuel Booth & Sons, for forty years a show print company, failed to make the transition and eventually faded from the scene. Henry Anderson's Enquirer Show Print switched over to lithography long enough to do a spectacular series of posters for Buffalo Bill's Wild West, with Tom Tully as artist. In the early 1900's, however, Anderson concluded that there still was business to be had in the letterpress and woodblock field; he dropped lithography. Nearly a century later, his grandson and great-grandsons continue as the principal suppliers of circus paper. Their posters still include several made from 1890 woodblocks as well as a full line of paper reproduced by modern photo offset and letterpress methods.

The transition from pine blocks to lithograph stones was illustrated by the Barnum show's inventory of surplus equipment. In 1875, it had four lithographed posters and seventy-two woodcut posters to dispose of. In 1883-84, it used 152 lithographs and offered 145 woodcut designs for sale. Lithographs now were more economical, and their inks withstood the weather much better. Showmen agreed that lithographed posters were superior in beauty and effectiveness. They preserved the artist's work to a greater degree. The colors were more brilliant, and the blended colors were far more varied, softer, and more natural.

Lithography had become popular and profitable in more than the circus field. Nearly every home had framed chromolithographs—colored pictures—on the wall now. Many of the firms that did circus work also printed these military scenes, religious views,

Another Strobridge file recorded progress in drawing each poster. This sixteen-sheet tiger was originated by Harry Ogden on December 23. Other workers—Jones, Koehne, and Beach—finished their parts by January 14. In addition to black artists there were specialists for animal detail, lettering and other portions. **Circus World Museum.**

reproductions of oil paintings, portraits and other inexpensive art. Even the one most famous of all today, Currier & Ives, solicited circus work. Napoleon Sarony did panoramas of cities and patent medicine labels as well as show posters. Gibson & Co. was big in valentines and Easter novelties. The Endicotts printed covers for sheet music along with pioneering in circus color work. Strobridge did church printing and military scenes along with bonds and diplomas. About the only major lithographer of the time who hasn't been linked somehow with circus work was Louis Prang, who initiated the American Christmas card business instead.

Frank Leslie's Illustrated, a picture news journal, utilized woodblocks for those illustrations. In order to gain speed and better

An original design was done first in black in reduced sizes. A proof was completed with watercolors and submitted to the show for approval. This version was lined to indicate how it would be divided into sections as a twelve-sheet. Andrew Donaldson, Jr., general manager of the Strobridge plant for many years, explained that a photographic slide of the original was projected on a wall in twelve-sheet size. Portions of the projected art were traced in crayon and pressed onto stone, giving the black artist an outline to follow. Black artists assigned to this project were Rudolph F. Kure, Lewis H. Keneerly, and Charles H. Elmes. The first edition of the poster was printed for the 1914 season, another was to be done for 1915. **Jim McRoberts Collection.**

Ringling Bros. asked Strobridge to revise an existing poster for 1915. The baseball elephants became tango elephants and three herds became five. The name of the black artist working on each three-sheet section is noted on the file card. The new version was printed on December 29, 1914. **Jim McRoberts Collection.**

publishing deadlines, Leslie perfected a system by which several artists could work on different woodblocks which ultimately would be combined into a single view. It was the same concept that show printers used in creating giant-sized posters. Leslie's Civil War scenes, in particular, were much sought after. One of his artists, Matt Morgan, switched to the Strobridge Lithographing Company in 1878. Using experience from Leslie's, Morgan put Strobridge into the manufacturing of multiple-sheet lithographs. Other businesses earlier had followed the circus lead in utilization of smaller lithographed posters, and now Proctor & Gamble commissioned Strobridge to produce a twelve-sheet to advertise its soap. Artists and other employees of the Strobridge plant posed, in 1883, for that scene.

With circus campaigns as their guide and inspiration, other businesses began to think of advertising in national dimensions. Quaker Oats was among the first. The trademark dates from 1877, but little more occurred until new owners took over in 1882. They hired K. B. Newell, the first person apart from circuses and patent medicines to be called an advertising manager. He launched a circus-style national campaign that included billposting, large newspaper advertisements, new logos, and a deluge of novelties mailed like circus couriers. Boys delivered Quaker Oats handbills as they had distributed circus heralds before. In 1891, Quaker Oats dispatched a fifteen-car train from Iowa to Portland, Oregon, to introduce the product to the Pacific Northwest. It was like a circus train, complete with a former circus press agent hired to arrange publicity stops in many cities along the way. The blitz campaign in Portland was like nothing so much as a routine circus saturation effort. It created a huge demand for the product, just as its forerunners built the irresistible urge to see a circus. Thereafter, business and industry continued to adopt circus methods for the new field of national advertising.

In the hey-day of circus lithographs, most were printed in four or five colors, using a separate stone for each color on each sheet, or typically ten stones for a two-sheet. The Adam Forepaugh Circus continued use of woodblock posters later than most. However, in 1881 the Avil Printing Co. of Philadelphia produced a Forepaugh one sheet which printing experts today say has fourteen distinct colors. This indicates the use of fourteen stones for

separate colors rather than the overlapping or mixing of colors with fewer stones.

William H. Donaldson was apprenticed in 1857 to Middleton, Wallace & Company, the forerunner of Strobridge Lithographing Company. At that time he was the only man in the pressroom who spoke English. Several German pressmen learned their English from his version with a Scottish burr.

Donaldson, with pressman Henry Elfs, formed his own company in 1863. By 1872 he had a steam-powered press and four years later had six such presses. In 1900 the Donaldson Lithographing Company moved to Newport, Kentucky, where it continued until the 1930s. Meanwhile, Donaldson's son, William, Jr., in Cincinnati launched a trade paper, *The Billboard*, to carry news of billposters. Since they worked for shows including fairs, circuses and theaters, *The Billboard* evolved into a general show business trade paper and continues today as the bible of the music trade. In 1906, Donaldson launched four more publications. Three failed, but he sold the fourth, *Signs of the Times*, which continued as a journal of the sign industry and in 1981 celebrated its seventy-fifth year.

Strobridge of Cincinnati

Among the greatest show printers was the Strobridge Lithographing Company in Cincinnati. Hines Strobridge joined Middleton-Wallace in 1854. The others eventually dropped out, and the business became Strobridge & Company by 1867. About that time, the firm did its first circus work—posters for the Dan Rice show. In the 1870s, Strobridge printed for its Cincinnati neighbor, the John Robinson Circus, and late in that decade the firm filled an order for 5,000 copies of an eight-color lithograph for Cooper & Bailey Circus. They first did work for the Barnum show in the 1870s.

Strobridge produced lithographs of the finest quality. Another of its assets was its commission salesman, A. A. Stewart, covering the show field. Originally, he was paid 15 percent of the gross receipts that he generated, but Strobridge directors decided that he was making too much money out of the gigantic circus orders and cut him back. Ultimately, he was paid 10 percent of the first $250,000 and 2½ percent thereafter. At that time, Strobridge was selling about 2.5 million sheets per year to circuses and an equal amount for theater attractions. In 1877, the company installed steam presses that could make 2,600 impressions per day. About 1905, the company proposed to switch from stone presses to rotary presses with zinc plates, but its German craftsmen resisted. Circuses were chief among the few national advertisers; now others began to take interest. As Strobridge's role in national advertising developed around 1910, it hired Howard Sharp, foreman at U.S. Printing & Lithographing, to bring the old craftsmen and new presses into productive combination. Sharp was still with Strobridge in 1938 to draw the original artwork and then print the Gargantua paper.

In February 1911, Barnum & Bailey advised Stewart and Strobridge of its needs for the coming season. There were thirty-four sizes and designs of paper. Included were 2,000 copies of a thirty-two-sheet parade poster, and another 5,000 one-sheets for the parade. They ordered great quantities of posters featuring portraits of Bailey and Barnum—2,600 copies for a twenty-eight-sheet version, 3,000 sixteen-sheets, 3,000 three-sheets, 5,000 one-sheets, and 5,000 half-sheets. In all, the show bought 121,600 posters totaling 1,474,800 sheets.

During World War I, Charles Ringling feared that a shortage of flour would limit the amount of pasting that his billposters could do. He told Nelson Strobridge, that, as a result, they might have to use more window posters and tacked banners. He anticipated a new spectacle for 1917 requiring a number of new posters. Strobridge then was furnishing the show with wall work in editions of 3,000 posters at four and one-half cents per sheet.

Strobridge recalled James A. Bailey as a "liberal advertiser, not extravagant or foolish or a tightwad . . . He believed in spending money to advertise, but his partner, Barnum, was the greatest advertiser. Barnum used bizarre ideas and got people to talk about him. Bailey, on the other hand, believed in letting people know things as they were. There was no humbug about Bailey."

Strobridge supplied great quantities of circus advertising when Barnum & Bailey toured Europe and again for Buffalo Bill's Wild West European tours. More recently, after the Gargantua paper, Strobridge did a special piece for the 1939 Man in the Moon act.

After Ringling-Barnum approved this original art in 1928, artists would complete the shading of letters and Erie would procede with manufacture. **Circus World Museum.**

However, the act fell during the Madison Square Garden engagement, so the paper was destroyed. After that, the Ringling show

Enquirer Printing Co. developed this unconventional poster for Buffalo Bill's Wild West in three drafts. In the second, portraits of various Rough Riders are moved to the wreath around Cody's picture. The show's title and the "Cody Calendar" line were transposed, surprisingly relegating the title to minor position, and giving the other line choice position. In the third draft of the watercolor version, the lettering has been completed and the newer photograph of Buffalo Bill is in place. It was not Cody, but James A. Bailey, a partner in the show, who approved Buffalo Bill posters. **Circus World Museum.**

proposed posters designed by Norman Bel Geddes, but Strobridge declined the work. It may have been because the show was behind in its payments, but circus veterans like to think that it was because the lithograph firm declined to put its name on the unorthodox colors and designs involved in the new posters. The McCandlish firm in Philadelphia got the order. F. A. Boudinot induced Strobridge to take a Ringling order for three new posters in 1954, the last of a long association.

A concentration of plants made Cincinnati a world center in lithography, with many skilled artisans from Germany and elsewhere. Gibson & Company was a Cincinnati pioneer. The Russell-Morgan Company, highly regarded by showmen, grew out of a job printing shop in Cincinnati in 1867 and later became the United States Lithography Company. One of the founders was John F. Robinson, of the circus family, and Gil Robinson later was president.

There were other close associations between circuses and their printers. John Dingess, general agent for several shows in the 1850s and 1860s, dealt with MacBriar & Sons, another Cincinnati lithographing firm, and Dingess married a MacBrair daughter, thus helping to gain business for the printers and easier credit for whatever show he steered at the time.

The firm of James Reilley, New York, sometimes known as Cleary & Reilley, was associated with the many showmen known as the Flatfoot Party who headquartered around Somers, New York. In the 1870s, Reilley was supplying paper for such outfits as the Great North American Circus, the Van Amburgh Menagerie, and Howes Great London Shows. In 1870, it sold its stock of pine cuts to the Jeffrey firm in Chicago. Both had been printing woodblock posters for the Forepaugh Circus, and Jeffrey continued that practice.

Credit by the Season

The casualty rate among circuses was astronomical. Many failed, and others periodically found it difficult to pay their bills on time. Understandably, this had a great impact on the show printing business. Because orders for paper were large, the shows usually

Finally, the lithograph is produced, complete with the 1899 calendar on which the show date for each city would be indicated with an X. Bailey's responsibilities for the Cody show included operation of the advance department. **Circus World Museum.**

33

THE GREAT VAN AMBURGH CO'S NEW GREAT GOLDEN MENAGERIE, CIRCUS AND COLOSSEUM.

HYATT FROST, MANAGER.

HIPPOPOTAMUS HOG.

Matt Morgan

Strobridge & Co. Lith. Cincinnati

THE FIRST AND ONLY ONE EVER IN AMERICA.

Will Exhibit at GALENA.

Monday, SEPT 27

spent—or owed—most at the show printer. Seasonal aspects of both businesses led to some of the problem. During the winter and spring, printers produced most of the season's posters and warehoused them until each circus began to send in its orders. The circus paid for posters after they were used. Thus, the printer incurred most of his cost in the winter and recouped the money only week by week during the summer. Not until late fall would he receive payment for the final portion of the circus season. Then it was nearly time to put up cash for winter printing again. A trade paper in 1894 said that any show printing company needed substantial capital and had to be a good judge of men, since some showmen were not good credit risks. At issue was not the intent of show owners, but the amount of business that they drummed up. For the printers, supplying winter credit for summer payment was expected of a business tied to the seasonal nature of circuses.

When business was poor and a show fell behind, it was easy for the printer to go along in the expectation that business would improve. Under the same conditions, circus personnel would work without pay in hopes of pulling through. A railroad, however, would refuse to move a circus without advance payment; that step often precipitated a show's collapse. A show printer did not want to alienate an important, though delinquent, customer. If he shut the circus off from its paper supply, the show stood little chance of continuing business or catching up with its debts. Even so, the time could come when the printer would be forced to seize the circus to protect his claim.

Thus, it was not unusual that Howes Great London should owe the Reilley printing firm a substantial sum. To prevent control

Wart hogs were billed under a wide variety of far-fetched names. This one not only enjoyed favorable billing but also has its portrait done by a well-known artist. Matt Morgan signed the piece, although it was unusual in circus art for the originator to do so. **Chicago Historical Society.**

by other creditors, Reilley took over the Howes show and later induced James A. Bailey to purchase it.

Strobridge found itself on both sides of the credit teeter-totter. In 1882, W. C. Coup Shows were much in arrears and about to collapse, so Strobridge attached the show and forced a sale. Five years later, in opposite circumstances, Strobridge itself was short of cash to finance winter work of printing and storing tons of posters in anticipation of spring sales, so it borrowed $50,000 from circus owner W. W. Cole. Simultaneously, in that 1887 season, the Doris & Colvin Colossal Shows fell behind in its payments, and Strobridge had to wait for a court-appointed receiver to pay the balance. There may have been several show accounts in arrears that season; twice Strobridge asked for more time on the Cole note.

Business for Norris & Rowe Circus was bad in 1909 and was no better after three weeks in 1910, so the Donaldson Lithographing Company attached the show. At its sale in June, circus owner Walter L. Main was among the principal bidders. It developed that he was acting for Walter Shannon, a partner in the defunct Norris & Rowe, who still hoped to save that circus. However, the sale was set aside, probably because Shannon could not come up with the money to cover his bids, so the show was sold again in August.

Ten seasons earlier, the Donaldson Company had foreclosed on the J. H. LaPearl Circus, which was swallowed up by the Great Wallace Show in the process. Donaldson and Wallace had more than one association. The Norris & Rowe sales had taken place at Wallace's quarters. Separately, Wallace moved his poster

Only occasionally were circus posters produced from photographs rather than drawings. This one was done by Maxwell Frederick Coplan, who also was doing other work for the show at the same time. The girl is Kitty Clark, a favorite performer in the 1940s. **Authors' Collection.**

RINGLING BROS AND BARNUM & BAILEY CIRCUS

THE GREATEST SHOW ON EARTH

purchases from the Courier Company to Donaldson and subsequently asked Donaldson to print three Wallace bills from old Courier artwork. When the Courier Company sued Donaldson for copyright violation, a court ruled that copyright was available only for "works of art" and that circus posters did not qualify, thus denying the Courier claim. The unique decision, however, was overturned by the U.S. Supreme Court, and Donaldson had to pay up.

Seizing and selling a circus might help a printer's overdue accounts, but it usually created another problem. There still was a stock of imprinted paper and now no circus to match up with it. Even if a solvent showman simply decided not to tour again, the printer could be stuck with piles of paper imprinted with the title of the discontinued show. Sometimes a show printer could induce a new circus to use such an abandoned title for which there was paper on the shelf. Showmen on short bankrolls sought out these old stocks of paper and changed the name of their own shows according to what bargain paper was available.

The original Hugo Bros. Circus closed after the 1915 season, leaving a supply of paper. So J. Augustus Jones renamed his show and used the leftover posters in 1918, and the King brothers used the last of that paper on their show as Hugo Bros. about 1921. Floyd and Howard King changed the name of their early show as one and then another supply of old posters was used up. Earlier, they expended leftover stocks of paper imprinted for Sanger European Circus, and later their show became M. L. Clark & Sons.

The Cole Bros. title experienced similar switches, and one circus writer claimed to see a jinx on the name, especially for the lithograph outfits. Circus owner Martin Downs, along with the Walker Lithograph Company, made up the Cole Bros. name for his 1906 season and continued its use through 1909. The former Coulter circus became Cole Bros. in 1912, using the abandoned paper, but it folded after long suffering, and the Walker lithograph house found itself giving the title to J. Augustus Jones for a show in 1916. Jones's Cole show did so well that it printed more posters. Jones promptly died, so Cole Bros. paper was available when John Pluto decided to open a circus in 1926. Supplies of Cole posters existed at more than one printing house when Floyd King needed a new name for his show. It became Cole Bros. for 1929 and 1930, whereupon it folded and became the property of the National Printing Company. All of these were small circuses. A large show formed in 1935 selected the Cole Bros. title for other reasons, but the agent, Floyd King, knew that Cole posters were on the shelves of several printers. The new show used up those aging posters and also fell heir to the plates with which to print more. That Cole Bros. continued for fifteen years. Meanwhile, in 1938, it opened a second unit, called Robbins Bros. Circus because posters were leftover from an earlier show by that name.

Poster Artists

Several artists became identified with circus poster production, despite the division of black work among various parts of multiple sheet posters and the further subdivision between black and color artwork. Paired up with Matt Morgan at Strobridge was H. A. Ogden, a recognized artist in several fields and producer of the basic design of nearly all Barnum & Bailey posters. Another Strobridge artist was Emil Rothengaten, who sometimes signed his work as E. Roe or just as E. R. Harry Bridewell was in the Strobridge coloring and lettering department. Adolph and Otto Rimanoczy, father and son, were brought from Europe by Strobridge because of Adolph's well-known skills with portraits. He did many of performers and show owners.

Charles Livingston Bull, an animal artist with a fine reputation, did magnificent work for Ringling Bros. Circus. About 1915, Strobridge printed his polar bear and crouching lion pieces as well as a leaping tiger design that turned out to be one of the most famous circus posters of all time. Despite, or because of, his renown elsewhere, Bull's name did not appear on any of his circus lithographs.

Although some artists were known in the trade, signing their work was the exception rather than the rule. In 1929, the name Colby appeared on a few Ringling posters of an unusual fantasy-like style. An artist named Ashbrock made a poster featuring

twenty-four black liberty horses for Ringling Bros. and Barnum & Bailey Circus around 1930.

In that period, the Erie Lithograph Company had the services of Verne Meyer and Joseph Hornik, both specialists in drawing horses and wild animals. An Erie man with a Strobridge background, Joe Schermerle, was particularly adept at drawing Indians and wild west scenes. An artist named Kannely signed a drawing of a white-faced clown on a Ringling poster. In the same decade, artist Hap Hadley drew a striking poster of Ringling's Ubangi savages.

Ringling's 1941 posters by Norman Bel Geddes and E. McKnight Kauffer included their initials on posters for the "Holiday" spec and the elephant ballet. Their most outstanding work was a poster for Alfred Court's animal act. Lawson Wood, especially known for his playful monkeys on *Collier's* magazine covers, signed two monkey cartoon posters for Ringling in 1943. Bill Bailey signed all of the posters for which he was commissioned, including an interior of the Big Top, the Liberty Bandwagon, and a new leopard act.

Forrest Freeland produced Ringling posters for Unus and his one-finger stand, juggler Frances Brunn, and the Alzanas high-wire artists. All were signed with his initials. Freeland went on to do similar special paper for the Clyde Beatty Circus, Cristiani Bros. Circus, and the Beers-Barnes Circus in the 1950s.

Whether circus posters were copyrighted varied through the years, as did copyright legislation. Because Gibson & Company copyrighted early circus work, its samples have been preserved at the Library of Congress. Sells Floto copyrighted a particular series of posters in 1919. George Christy copyrighted posters printed for his Christy Bros. Circus in 1925 by the Riverside Printing

Richard Jester, a member of the show staff, designed this one-sheet for the circus in 1979. The bottom portion was blank to allow for imprinting local information about the engagement, much as shows and printers had done a hundred years earlier. **Ringling Bros. and Barnum & Bailey Circus.**

BEAUTIFUL PLUMAGED BIRDS

From all parts of the World, to be seen in the Grand AVIARY DEPARTMENT of

Montgomery Queen's California Menagerie, Caravan and Double Circus.

But there was another way. The phenomenon of stock paper dates back to the very beginning of show printing and continues in the 1980s. In stock paper, the pictorial portion and perhaps some generalized wording are printed, but no circus name appears. There is only blank space where a title—any title—can be added later. The printer prepares such posters in substantial quantities to cut costs and increase efficiency. He lists each style of stock paper in his catalog. Circuses, often small ones, can order from this supply

Company. It was unusual for the show to handle copyright. More often, the printing company obtained such protection, even if it involved artwork actually owned by one of its clients. In a flurry in the 1940s, Ringling Bros. and Barnum & Bailey Circus copyrighted a series of lithographs. After a hiatus, that circus resumed the practice and now is highly protective, not only of its copyrighted posters, but also of any other material from the long inactive show titles which it owns. Ringling is especially protective of its slogan, perhaps the best in all of advertising—The Greatest Show on Earth.

Special and Stock

Principal circuses used so-called special paper, that which was designed especially for them—each show with its own art and title included. Some shows went further to create posters that named and depicted individual performers. It was a mark of distinction for a performer to be the subject of special paper.

COLE'S SOUTHERN CIRCUS AND MENAGERIE.

SIMSPORT, SATURDAY, FEB. 11

COLE'S NEW GREAT SO ...USICAL BRIGADE.

and have their individual titles imprinted in the open space. Many shows order the same stock art; only the circus name is different from order to order.

In the woodblock era, there were both stock and special posters. Artwork was costly, and many shows preferred to use ready-made pine blocks at lower rates. The concept of stock paper switched readily to lithography and again to photo-offset techniques.

A printer would offer typical circus designs in his stock assortment—an animal act, clowns, acrobats, bareback riders, tents. They came in various sizes, and a showman could select his entire season's supply and have them imprinted with his name and sent to his advance department. The risk that another show with the same type of art might play the same territory and post nearly identical paper was not too great, and the only alternative was the more costly special paper.

Some of the early work produced by Gibson was stock paper. The Courier Company offered stock in the 1870s and 1880s. Strobridge sold stock paper in the 1890s. Riverside Printing Company was noted for especially high-quality lithography in stock paper. Many others also were in the business.

In 1899, Donaldson Lithographing Company sold four-color paper in stock designs at forty-two cents for a six-sheet, sixty-three cents for a nine-sheet, and eighty-four cents for a twelve-sheet. There were many subjects, among them trained horses, chariot races, and Japanese acrobats.

The Erie Lithographing Company had dozens of designs in a catalog of stock circus paper. Prices ranged from five cents for a one-sheet to ninety-six cents for a twenty-four sheet. Imprinting the title cost more. By 1930, Erie was charging nine cents for an unimprinted one-sheet. Central Show Printing Company of Mason City, Iowa, in 1936 charged sixteen cents for a one-sheet with the title included. Enquirer charged $1.50 for a nine-sheet in 1972, with cross-lining extra. Imprinting a title on stock paper was called cross-lining. Many tented and indoor circuses of the 1980s bought their paper from Enquirer's assortment of stock posters. By this time, stock paper was the rule, and special circus paper was a rarity.

The Riverside Printing Co. offered this stock piece to smaller shows. Each buyer could have his own show title imprinted in the space at the top. The perch pole art was routine enough to fit nearly any troupe. **Authors' Collection**.

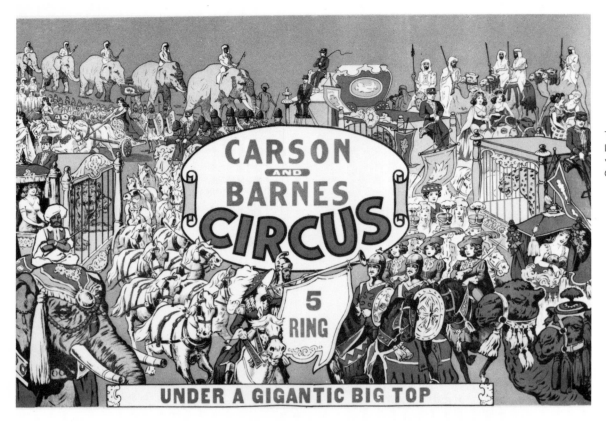

The Enquirer Printing Company manufactured large quantities of this art work and sold them to various shows, including the Carson & Barnes Circus of 1979. **Enquirer Printing Co.**

Circuses changed printers, sometimes switching every few seasons. Part of it was a matter of price, service, and competition. Part of it was because certain agents favored particular printers and took the business with them as they moved from show to show. Buffalo Bill, for example, began with the W. J. Morgan firm of Cleveland. Later, that show's work was done by A. Hoen & Company of Baltimore, which had been producing quality show printing since 1835. The Cody show next went to Courier of Buffalo, then Enquirer of Cincinnati, and finally Strobridge of Cincinnati. The moves coincided with changes in agents or ownership.

Similarly, Ringling Bros. patronized Hoen as well as Riverside, a Milwaukee firm of sixty-one years' operation. Ringling also bought from the Chicago Show Printing Company in the 1890s, and when Ringling leased the John Robinson show in 1898, the Robinson account was moved to Riverside as well. While spreading its orders around, Ringling Bros. ordered a substantial proportion of its paper from Courier Company of Buffalo. In February 1901, for example, the Courier Company accepted a Ringling order for 1,000 pieces of a forty-eight-sheet poster showing a baby elephant. Twenty-five days later, the calf died and Ringling canceled the order. Courier, hoping to salvage the business, suggested that the animal be stuffed and displayed as Barnum had done with Jumbo. But that paper never was produced.

In contrast, two years later, Ringling Bros. Circus geared up for combat with Barnum & Bailey. Courier amended existing poster designs. It doubled a run of sixteen-sheet excursion bills, making it 4,000 copies, and added 2,000 copies of the sixteen-sheet portrait bill. In addition, Ringling ordered 3,600 pieces of a six-sheet parade bill; 3,600 copies each of three-sheets depicting the menagerie, circus, spectacle, and big show; 6,300 copies of a special one-sheet; and 7,200 copies of another. Courier had forwarded a color sketch for a proposed thirty-two-sheet "Jerusalem" spectacle piece as well as a new three-sheet depicting a crusader and a six-sheet of a lady bareback rider.

But five years later, the Courier Company would realize that business with circuses was not necessarily smooth. Strobridge's salesman, A. A. Stewart, was the middleman negotiating Ringling's purchase of the Barnum & Bailey show from the Bailey estate. At the time, the bulk of Ringling's printing business was with the Courier Company. But terms of the sale apparently required that both Barnum & Bailey and Ringling Bros. shows buy all of their lithographs from Strobridge. Stewart had not forgotten where his responsibilities and advantages reposed.

Charles Ringling carried out the terms of the agreement. In September 1908, he notified the Morgan Lithography Company of Cleveland that he would be unable to negotiate with them because "we have closed a contract with the Strobridge Co. for all of our lithography for 1909, this deal being a part of another and larger deal of great importance to us and involving much besides the printing." Then, in January 1909, Charles Ringling advised George Bleistein that despite their long association and high personal esteem and great satisfaction, Ringling would not be placing any print orders with the Courier Company that season. Obviously, this was a shock to Courier, especially so close to the new season.

Ringling told Stewart that some of the printers felt badly that Strobridge was doing all of their lithographs. "So be it," said Stewart. "And some of the showmen are not altogether satisfied that you've got the two shows."

Pages from the stock paper catalog of the United States Printing and Lithograph Co. indicate some of the varieties from which a show owner could select his own assortment for imprinting with his show name. **Circus World Museum.**

RINGLING BROS AND BARNUM & BAILEY
COMBINED
THE WORLDS LARGEST
AMUSEMENT INSTITUTION

GENERAL OFFICES
NO 221 INSTITUTE PLACE
CHICAGO ILL

WINTER QUARTERS
BRIDGEPORT CONN

Sarasota, Florida, Feb. 29, 1928

My dear Mr. Lowe:

I am sorry I had to hold the sketch of the 100-CLOWN BILL for a few days, however I am returning it to you tonight.

It is difficult to tell about this bill in black and white, as it is a new idea for us, and I want to make it one of the most novel bills we have had, and I want to ask you to again submit this sketch in colors.

We must eliminate the Jewish clown head, as many of our patrons have taken offense at anything which might be termed an attempt to ridicule or burlesque the Jewish race. We do not want to show a Jewish clown face at all.

There is a repetition of the clown Policeman, but I know you can readily substitute another clown face for one of these.

We must get as much of the jovial appearance to the faces as possible, and I think your artist has done very well. However, wish you would suggest to him that we are making a special effort to get an unusually novel bill out of this, and to add as much comedy as he can to the faces.

I have decided to have a 16-SHEET made of this, as I think it shapes up better in the lay-out.

I shall send you an under-line for the bill a little later on. I have also decided to omit the words: "COMBINED SHOWS" and used the line: "100 CLOWNS" as indicated below.

use lines   1 0 0   and eliminate "Combined Shows"
             CLOWNS

Hoping to receive the colored sketches of Circus Interior and 100 Clown Bill at your earliest convenience, I am

Yours very truly,

John Ringling

Mr. J. R. Lowe,
Erie Lithographing Company,
Erie, Pennsylvania.

John Ringling picked up the banner after Mister Charlie's death and followed through on the details of each new poster. His 1928 letter to J.R. Lowe of Erie orders some changes in the proposed art. Unexpectedly, he cut short the show's title in order to say "100 Clowns." **Authors' Collection.**

The final result appeared as a one-sheet in Fort Wayne and other cities on the 1928 route. By then, the artist had contrived to come up with 100 different clown faces without offense to anyone. **Circus World Museum.**

Attention to Detail

If circus posters developed and retained an appeal all their own, it was because circus men took an active role in the finished product. True, artists like Harry Ogden were circus specialists, but they learned from troupers what it took to sell circus tickets and to distinguish circus posters from others. When lithograph companies submitted art for proposed posters, show owners or their agents reacted in more than a passive way. Often, they simply rejected a proposal. When Ben Austin submitted a Rothengaten watercolor of lions, tigers, and leopards for a Sells & Downs poster, Willie Sells responded, "Cannot use the sketch—will not want general animal bill." He would suggest some other circus subjects instead. Willie knew specifically what he wanted on posters.

Buffalo Bill himself paid little attention to poster detail, while James A. Bailey passed judgment on every piece of Barnum & Bailey paper. Charles Ringling took a similar interest and did not hesitate to demand changes at late stages. In 1912, Strobridge produced a line of new paper for the Ringling spectacle—"Joan of Arc." W. H. Horton wrote to Nelson Strobridge to say, "Mr. Charles Ringling is very much disappointed with the spectacle paper generally. He mentions one bill in particular, the 28-sheet Coronation Procession. This bill has a broken title line, as you know, part of the line in the usual colors and the remainder in

43

white. This will have to be changed on all of the bills that you have not already pasted . . . You will remember Mr. Ringling often has mentioned the fact that he did not want any of the paper at any time with the title broken in colors, as this always gives the appearance of two bills and detracts greatly from the strength of the paper."

That was not all. Horton said that the costumes on the left side were too dark and that the whole poster gave an "indistinct and poor appearance from a short distance, making it altogether a very poor proposition." And most of all, "Mr. Ringling does not like the small number of people represented in the spectacle bills, as the numbers are not at all in keeping with title and caption lines."

Nelson Strobridge responded to his best client as one might expect. Part of the title line was in white because of the background on which it was placed. Whether to go against the general rule had been a topic of a "convention" among Strobridge artists, and they had decided that the white version would carry farther in daylight and be more readable in the half-light of evening. But: "We have given instructions for red to be over-printed at once on

Portraits of the distinguished owners often were added to pictorials. Courier created such a series for Ringling Bros., each with a different scene but all with the portraits. **Gary Schamberger Collection.**

The Calhoun show printing plant produced an unusual series of posters for the Forepaugh show when it introduced wild west features. Usually a show's title would be much more prominent. Buffalo Bill objected when the Forepaugh show got into the wild west theme. **Circus World Museum.**

all that have not been pasted, 2,000 out of the 3,000 print order. We are very sorry we guessed wrong in this case and wish to assure you it was not done carelessly."

Strobridge was at a loss regarding other criticisms. "There is no answer we can make," he said. "We thought we had made the greatest line of spectacle printing that had ever been done."

Even that did not end the exchange. Mr. Charlie himself picked up on the matter of population in the poster. "There are about 25 faces shown in this bill, all told, and in the Ballet bill, if you will count the faces, you will see about the same number. When the sketch of the Ballet came to Baraboo, [I wrote] asking that rows of girls be shown in the back of the bill to give the idea of great numbers. This was not done . . . . These bills are not what they should be. I have not seen all of the bills on the other subjects, but

I hope that when we see them all on the fence that they will be up to your usual high grade of work."

Strobridge replied that he had not counted the faces: "It is not necessary; I get your point that there are not nearly enough. Another season, I trust we shall meet with better success. We put the work on stone just as it was called for in the sketches. Please do not think we are disposed to take lightly what you say, for we are very much concerned. The full significance of your letter has not failed to be appreciated."

So even the mighty Strobridge had to go back to the drawing boards. And even a circus king counted the house in crowd scenes on his posters.

Probably this attention to detail and ability to change for better effect is why drawings were presented and photography did not

45

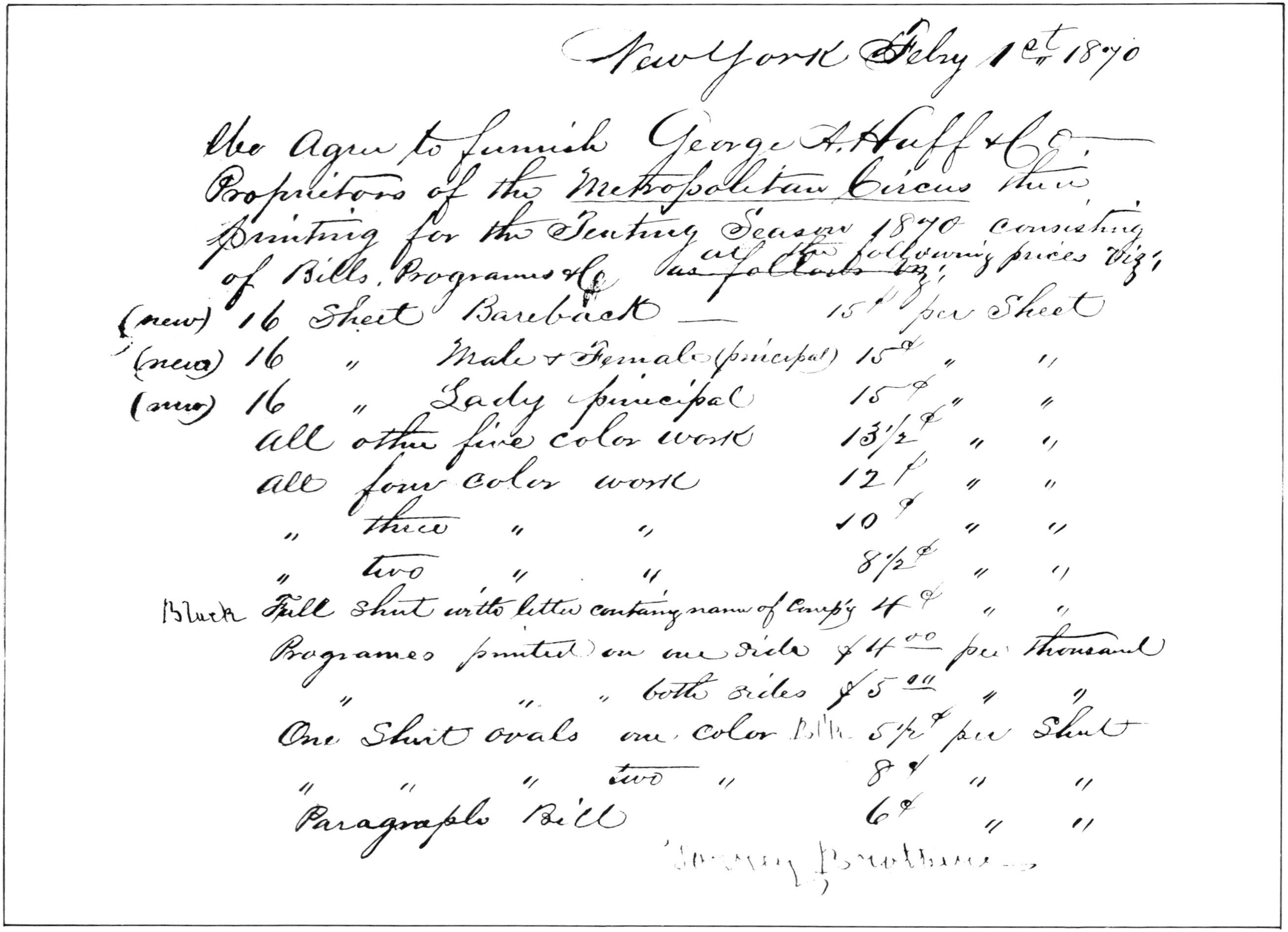

New York Feby 1st 1870

We Agree to furnish George A. Huff & Co.
Proprietors of the Metropolitan Circus their
printing for the Tenting Season 1870 consisting
of Bills, Programs &c as follows at the following prices viz;

(new) 16 Sheet Bareback ____ 15¢ per Sheet
(new) 16 " Male & Female (principal) 15¢ " "
(new) 16 " Lady principal 15¢ " "
All other five color work 13½¢ " "
All four color work 12¢ " "
" three " " 10¢ " "
" two " " 8½¢ " "
Black Full Sheet with letter containg name of Comp'y 4¢ " "
Programes printed on one side $4.00 per thousand
" " " both sides $5.00 " "
One Sheet ovals one color Bills 5½¢ per Sheet
" " " two " 8¢ " "
Paragraph Bill 6¢ " "

Torrey Brothers

Torrey Brothers, another New York show printing house, quoted 1870 prices for the George A. Huff & Co. Metropolitan Circus. Some five-color work cost 13.5 cents per sheet; three colors cost ten cents. Black one-sheet title bills came in at four cents each. A new sixteen-sheet of bareback riders was $2.40 per copy. **Illinois State University.**

		EDITION	SHIPPED	ON HAND
Giraffe	1-sheet upright	10,000	3,000 *525.00.*	7,000 *.075.*
Giraffe	½-sheet upright	20,000	6,000 *525.00.*	14,000 *.0325.*
Giraffe	3-sheet upright	2,000	500 *570.00.*	1,500 *.38*
Clown	1-sheet upright	10,000	3,000 *665.00.*	7,000 *.095.*
Clown	½-sheet upright	20,000	6,000 *665.00.*	14,000 *.0475.*
Leaping Lion & Tiger	1-sheet upright	10,000	3,000 *595.00.*	7,000 *.085.*
Leaping Lion & Tiger	½-sheet upright	20,000	6,000 *595.00*	14,000 *.0425.*
Hippo	½-sheet upright	20,000	4,800 *608.00.*	15,200 *.04.*
Tiger Head	½-sheet upright	20,000	4,800 *608.00.*	15,200 *.04.*
Tiger	½-sheet flat	20,000	4,800 *532.00.*	15,200 *.035.*
Lion	½-sheet flat	20,000	4,800 *532.00*	15,200 *.035.*
Hippo	1-sheet upright	10,000	3,950 *465.00*	6,200 *.025.*
Tiger Head	1-sheet upright	10,000	3,950 *465.00.*	6,200 *.025.*
Tiger	1-sheet flat	10,000	3,800 *434.00.*	6,200 *.07.*
Lion	1-sheet flat	10,000	3,800 *434.00.*	6,200 *.07.*
	5-sheet streamer	1,000	500	500 *.75*

8,218.00

375.00 Omitted

With this tabulation, McCandlish Lithograph Corporation inventoried the paper it had printed, shipped or stored for the Ringling show as of May 1950. **Authors' Collection.**

lend itself to the circus projects very well. Some shows tried using photos instead of drawings as the starting point. Sparks Circus had some in the 1920s, and there have been other isolated cases along the line, including Dailey Bros. in the 1940s. When Ringling added a mate for Gargantua in 1941, it was impossible to photograph the two gorillas together, for their affair was totally in the minds of press agents, and the two animals were incompatible. Nor did the show do the poster in original artwork. Separate photo portraits of the two gorillas were pasted together in a fine composite

that made them appear as friends, if not lovers. The press agents also enhanced the photo to give M'Toto a more curvaceous figure. This illustrates why there were few other photographic posters. Photos were too rigid. Drawings could be more dramatic, and press agents could use artistic license to make elephants bigger, girls more beautiful, lions meaner, clowns funnier—and gorillas cozier.

This is not to say that photography was forsaken entirely. Circuses just preferred artwork as original material. But in later

To augment lithographs, some shows used window cards—quarter-sheet posters on stiff card stock. The Ringling-Barnum "circus kings" card was among the most dignified circus paper and was used in the 1930s. Others include Sells Floto 1920, Barnum & Bailey 1915, Ringling clown 1924, Robbins 1925, Ringling McCoy 1936 and Ringling leopard 1965. **Authors' Collection.**

years, printers made much use of photo-offset lithography, a process in which a color photo is taken of the artwork, and color separations are made photographically. Color filters do the work that once was accomplished by the color artists and black artists of the pine block and stone eras.

Lithography from the first was an offset printing process, as opposed to the letterpress or relief processes. Modern photo-offset lithography became cheaper and satisfactory. But it lacked the superior quality of those posters produced on stone or zinc engravings. It could not reach the degree of expression, the finesse, the

delicate touch that has been achieved only by fine artists working with stone.

By the 1950s, the demand for posters had begun to wane. The surviving shows used fewer varieties of posters and fewer numbers of each. For one thing, there were fewer places to put them. Circus men complained that commercial billposting firms placed permanent billboards where circus daubs formerly could be had. Newspapers, radio, and television made massive inroads as effective means of advertising and circuses turned to them. Even architecture conspired against circus posters; new buildings included few blank walls on which show paper could be placed and fewer windows in which the one-sheets and half-sheets could be located. The so-called Lady Bird Act, advocated by the wife of President Johnson, outlawed signs and signboards on federally subsidized highways. Environmentalists lacked appreciation for billboards, even those carrying the fine artwork of Strobridge, Enquirer, Erie, or Globe.

In the 1950s, the Neal Walters Poster Corporation, using aged type, plates, and presses from a Kansas City show print firm, was supplying most circuses. Enquirer and Globe also were among the most active. Their orders came from Clyde Beatty Circus, King Bros., Al G. Kelly & Miller Bros., and others. But already, Mills Bros. Circus had eliminated the use of outdoor advertising.

Ringling-Barnum used fewer posters and correspondingly fewer billposters. When the show converted to indoor operation, it also changed promotional systems. The old operation was replaced by the use of promoters, and whether outdoor advertising was to be used was left up to each promoter in his own towns. He could order Ringling paper from supplies on the shelf.

It was about 1976 that Ringling-Barnum changed another aspect of advertising theory. Instead of using an overwhelming variety of posters in gigantic quantities, it would hereafter use a single design for each tour. This was a widely accepted procedure in the general advertising business—use one design at a time, perhaps switch to a new one when a new campaign was begun. Thus, Ringling-Barnum came to use a new poster design with each new production. That meant a new poster for the Blue unit one season, the Red unit the next. Each used its poster through a two-year routing cycle. The poster art was similar, if not identical, to the art used at the same time for newspaper advertising.

As an indoor circus, Ringling also eliminated the use of separate date sheets and the date strips that had been pasted to pictorial posters since the beginning of circus billing. In the new form, a one-sheet poster included blank space for imprinting the town and date within its own dimensions, rather than adding another piece.

Other circuses from about 1960 onward used assorted poster designs but in much reduced quantities. Almost all of these now were stock paper with individual titles added. The remaining show printing houses, however, were turning to the old designs. By photo-offset, they were duplicating art from long-ago shows for use by the current circuses. Old lithographs borrowed from Fred. D. Pfening, Jr. by Floyd King were photographed and duplicated by Acme Show Print of Hugo, Oklahoma. Enquirer also offered stock paper from old designs. Among other companies still in the game were Globe Poster of Chicago, which also was doing twenty-four sheets for the Ice Capades, the Harlem Globetrotters, and other shows. Its stock circus paper found favor among Polack Bros. and other indoor circuses sponsored by the Shriners, the police, and local clubs. In the 1960s, Ringling used old shelf stock inherited by the Diamond Match Company. Back in 1905, Courier, Erie, Donaldson, U.S. Litho and others had joined in a single holding company, Consolidated Litho, but continued as if they were independent. Later they were reorganized as the United States Printing and Lithographing Company, and in 1959 it all became part of Diamond International. As Ringling produced new paper thereafter, it usually was done by National Printing, of Houston.

Whether it was National and Enquirer in the 1980s or Jared Bell and Edward Purcell 150 seasons earlier, the process was basically the same. Show printers produced quantities of distinctive circus paper and stood by for instructions from their traveling clients.

Executive suite for the circus advertising department was a gaudy railroad car fitted up as home and office for the show agents and billposters. The advertising car for the W.B. Reynolds Circus of 1894 had a frilly skirt to hide the wheels. **Authors' Collection.**

Bright paint and big lettering made the Gentry Bros. bill car stand out in any railroad yard, serving as a billboard itself. For the crew's picture, the car manager rated a chair and the paste-maker/chef wore his white-coat badge of office. **Gene Baxter Collection.**

CHAPTER 3

The Advance

Turn in that charcoal gray for a noticeable check or plaid with a lion's claw fob. Strike that BBD&O to make it RB&BB. Drop the Madison Avenue address and pick up the mail at the general delivery window in six different towns each week.

For circus advertising was handled quite apart from any agency stereotype or big-city format. There were no chrome suites in a glass high-rise, but, instead, scrolled and scarlet railroad cars, wheeled offices operating each day in a different city.

If anyone approximated an account executive, it was the show's general agent, whom others might term vice-president, marketing and vice-president, traffic. His operation was in-house. There was no agency—except the dummy corporation set up to claim agency discounts. His media buyer was called a contracting press agent. For a staff, he had not promising young MBAs, but mostly grizzled billposters in paste-spattered bib overalls. Circus advertising was a workaday procedure.

That rolling office for the advertising department was a railroad coach designated as the advance car, or bill car. There might have been a rolltop desk at some winter quarters farm, or in a corner of the show printer's plant, but the true command post for circus campaigning was aboard the bill car.

Once, the advance department consisted of a man on horseback with oversized saddlebags. Later, he had a two-horse bill wagon. At the peak of circusing, there were three, and perhaps even four, advertising cars ahead of some circuses. In more recent times, a semitrailer and several station wagons filled the role.

The circus general agent mapped out a season's route of perhaps 150 to 200 towns. To him, they were good towns and bad towns; fresh towns, filler towns, feeder towns, and towns you made because they were railroad division points or county seats. The agent filled two key roles—contracting and advertising. Months ahead, he sent a contracting agent to each city to schedule the railroad moves for the entire circus, buy groceries in February for a distant June exhibition day, rent the show grounds, contract for feed, and wrangle over the price of a city license. That was part of the circus advance department, although not advertising. No public word about the show's coming would be revealed until the time was ripe.

Then the agent turned loose his crew of billers on their crimson cars, and they set about to eliminate all blank space—by the generous application of brilliant circus advertising.

The advance car usually was a combination passenger and baggage unit out of regular railroad service. The baggage end accommodated tons of poster paper, stacks of date sheets, and such tools of the trade as brushes, paste buckets, barrels of flour, and cartons of tacks. In the passenger half, seats were replaced by storage cabinets with work-space tops. Overhead were bunks. At the far end was a little office for the car manager and similar space

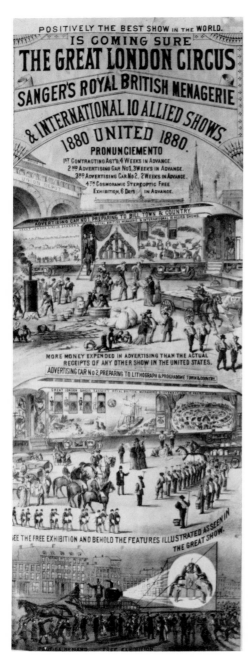

In each town the crews fanned out to fill their various advertising missions. In this poster, the Great London Show of 1880 advertised its advertising crew, illustrating how they worked from the advance cars to place posters, date sheets, heralds and couriers throughout the area. **Harold Dunn Collection, Howard Tibbals.**

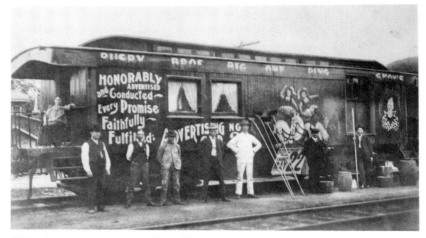

This advance car was one-third of Busby Bros. Circus rolling stock. A baggage car and a sleeper made up the show train itself. Billposters rested their long brushes against the side of the car in 1900 at Carbondale, Ill. **Circus World Museum.**

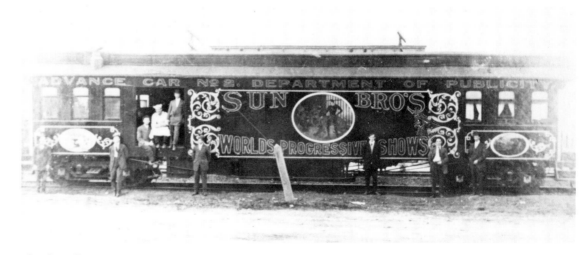

Sun Bros. Circus proclaimed Advance Car No. 2 for its Department of Publicity, but this single car was the whole affair. Circus agents couldn't seem to keep from doubling their numbers, just on principle. **Circus World Museum.**

for the contracting press agent. Often, the bill car had an upright boiler to provide steam, both to cook up kettles of paste and to prepare the billposters' meals.

Usually a circus operated with a single advertising car, although some of the greatest shows had more. That single car might be designated as Advertising Car Number 2 just because circuses liked to deal in bigger numbers. The billposters who called it home simply spoke of "the car," and everyone knew that they were "on the advance" or "on the car," or simply "ahead."

Manpower aboard the car included billposters—who pasted large showings of paper on walls and fences; banner men—who tacked cloth posters high on the sides of downtown buildings;

lithographers—who decorated store windows with posters; and programmers—who distributed heralds and couriers. Each man had his assignment. Some went up and down city streets to place posters; others were sent to the countryside, where they decorated barns or village fences. Others rode local passenger trains to surrounding towns to spread glad tidings that their circus was coming.

With the posters printed and on the shelves, and with the bill cars rolling, the next task was to get them together in the right places. Nothing was left to chance. The circus agents and printers worked closely together. There were endless instructions and countless express shipments.

Before the season got underway, the agent made up a list of

A rare photo of the W.W. Cole Circus shows its advance car on Southern Pacific sidetracks in San Francisco. Typically, the crew would be away from the car during the day. A passenger train is halted at the station beyond the car. The Cole show played San Francisco in 1873, 1880, 1881, and 1884. **Southern Pacific Railroad.**

Some big shows used two or more advance cars. Miller Bros. & Arlington 101 Ranch Real Wild West used from one to three cars at various times. Ladders, brushes and paste buckets were tools of the trade. **Circus World Museum.**

Burr Robbins perfected his advertising poster skills with his circuses, including this 1887 unit, and then quit the road to start a local billboard business. **Authors' Collection.**

posters to be used on a typical day. He specified size and quantity of each variety in the show's poster repertoire. Throughout the season, he instructed the printer to ship given numbers of such daily sets. He also called for the date sheets and in each case indicated where the paper should be shipped.

A show's List 1, for example, designated a mix of circus paper needed to bill a typical town. With shows that had more than one advance car, these predetermined orders were established for each car. Often, there were several such lists, to be ordered in any multiple or combination.

List 1 for the Ringling Bros. advance in 1916 designated two styles of twenty-four sheets and called for nine copies of each. There were four varieties of twenty-sheet posters, and the order included eight copies of each variety. The quantities were the same for sixteen-sheet, twelve-sheet, and eight-sheet posters. There were two styles of fifteen-sheets, six-sheets, and three-sheets, and the order provided for eight copies of each to be sent. They listed only one variety of four-sheet and called for eight copies of it. There were twelve each of both kinds of two-sheets, all for billposting or wall work. List 1 also included 288 assorted one-sheet pictorials, 48 one-sheet title bills, and 48 half-sheets for the window work. That added up to 2,688 sheets for one list to one car. The total ballooned when several lists and two or three cars were accounted for.

The Norris & Rowe Show came out of California behind a deluge of posters distributed from this car. But even these extensive advertising campaigns and a colorful parade back on the show were not enough; the show failed in 1910. **Circus World Museum.**

Barrels of flour for paste-making and other supplies are alongside the Cole Bros. Circus Advertising Car, a bright red model that toured in the 1940s. **Circus World Museum.**

When ordering for a given period, an agent might call for the printer to send twelve or fifteen days' wall work and as much for window work. If there was opposition to wage against another show or a larger city to bill, the agent would call for more paper. In one case, the Ringling agent asked for 100 extra twenty-four-sheets and 2,000 more one-sheets, choosing designs that stressed the show name; in opposition, he wanted to emphasize the Ringling title.

In 1911, when Ringling Bros. Circus was an eighty-four car show playing 143 towns, the allotments of paper to each of the three advance cars and in total made an impressive print order:

Season's Allotment		Daily Allotment Per Car		
		Car #1	Car #2	Car #3
2,000—32 Sheet—Street Parade		5	3	2
3,000—28 " —Portrait & Title		9	5	2
2,000—24 " —General Animals		5	3	2
2,000—20 " —Clowns		5	3	2
3,000—20 " —Elephants		9	5	2
3,000—20 " —Schuman Horses		9	5	2
3,000—20 " —Acrobats		9	5	2
3,000—16 " —Parkers Riders		10	3	2
2,000—16 " —Chariot		5	3	2
6,000—16 " —Portraits		16	11	5
3,000—16 " —Loyal		11	3	2
3,000—16 " —Delno		9	5	2
3,000—12 " —Alex Troupe		8	5	3
3,000— 8 " —Baby Elephant		11	3	2
3,000— 8 " —Mijares Wire		11	3	2
3,000— 8 " —Giraffes		8	5	3
3,000— 6 " —Comedy Horse Act		8	5	3
2,000— 6 " —Hippo		5	3	2
6,000— 3 " —Portrait		20	9	3
3,000— 3 " —Miss Clark		8	5	3
2,000— 3 " —Rhino		5	3	2
5,000— 1 " —Parade		24	—	4
5,000— 1 " —General Animals		24	—	4
5,000— 1 " —Schuman Horses		24	—	4
5,000— 1 " —Portrait		24	—	4
5,000— 1 " —Rhino & Hippo		24	—	4
5,000— 1 " —Giraffe		24	—	4
5,000— 1 " —Loyal		24	—	4
5,000— 1 " —Miss Clark		24	—	4
5,000— 1 " —Elephants		24	—	4
5,000— 1 " —Clowns		24	—	4
5,000—½ " —Baby Elephant		24	—	4
5,000—½ " —Portrait		24	—	4

That amounted to 914,000 sheets, or an average of 6,390 sheets per town. It raises the question of just where one might place 627 posters of all sizes in a typical town.

Louis E. Cooke, a mustachioed extrovert, headed up the advance for Barnum & Bailey, W. W. Cole, Forepaugh-Sells, and other shows in his illustrious, self-publicized career. At one time, he piloted the advance of both Buffalo Bill's Wild West and Barnum & Bailey Circus. That put him in command of six advertising cars and 150 men working about 200 towns. They posted from 15,000 to 25,000 sheets on an average day.

In 1893, Cooke instructed Strobridge about shipping paper to the bill cars. Barnum & Bailey had opened in Madison Square Garden and was holding forth in Brooklyn. Considerably earlier, Cooke's crews had billed New York and its environs for those engagements and for seven additional weeks of largely one-day stands. Now, on April 25, 1893, he dispatched instructions to Nelson Strobridge to ship the following pictorial work to Henry Hedges:

12 days, List 1; 12 days, List 2, to Providence, R.I.
12 days, List 1; 12 days, List 2, to New London, Conn.
 6 days, List 1; 6 days, List 2, to Gardner, Mass.
 6 days, List 1; 6 days, List 2, to Lynn, Mass.
 6 days, List 1; 6 days, List 2, to Biddeford, Me.
12 days, List 1; 12 days, List 2, to Lewiston, Me.

Last of its breed was this No. 1 Car of the Ringling-Barnum advance in 1954. The car now is on display at the Circus World Museum, Baraboo, Wisconsin. **Gene Baxter Photo.**

Henry Hedges was on the Number 1 bill car, due to arrive several days hence at Providence. The twelve-day supply of paper would stock the car for any extra demand and would furnish the sets for stands to be played during the week of June 19—Providence on Monday; Woonsocket, Tuesday; Taunton, Massachusetts, Wednesday; Newport, Rhode Island, Thursday; Fall River, Massachusetts, Friday; and New Bedford, Massachusetts, Saturday. When Hedges arrived in Providence early in May, he would find this stock of paper awaiting him at the express office. Cooke's similar instructions would supply the car with paper for the next

five weeks. The list of towns was significant, of course. The show would play New London on June 26; Gardner, July 1; Lynn, July 6; Biddeford, July 15; and Lewiston, July 22. Arriving in each of those cities about six weeks in advance of the play date, car manager Henry Hedges would restock his bill car in preparation for the ensuing work.

Cooke's instructions droned on. Strobridge was to ship six- or twelve-day sets of List 1, List 3, or List 4 to Alf Piel at the same towns. Piel would be aboard the second advertising car, perhaps a week or two behind Hedges, and he, too, would find bundles of

posters waiting for him—the quantities needed for the towns that followed each shipping point.

The Number 3 car, with G. P. Campbell in charge, would follow the others at the usual interval in the same New England cities. He would pick up posters waiting for him at the express offices, all according to Cooke's instructions.

"With reference to the new 36-sheet circus bill and the 16-sheet leaping horse bill," Cooke continued, "send us enough so that the balance will divide equally in each of the shipments for the remainder of the season . . . If you will be kind enough to advise

Before and during the Railroad Era, many circuses operated their advance departments with wagons. These were the billers' wagons with Burr Robbins in 1877, Whitney in 1888 and Gollmar in 1892. **Authors' Collection.**

me by return mail, stating when the 36-sheet bill will be ready and how many of the jumping horse bills and Barnum and Bailey heads you have now shipped, I will then be able to give further instructions." Cooke, like other general agents and boss billposters, knew exactly how many copies of each poster were expected to be used in a typical city—and what to change for specific cities.

Through most of American circus history, the telegraph was as valuable a business tool as telephones are today. General agents were in constant communication with their bill car managers, contracting agents, press agents and show owners. A telegram had the added advantage of providing a tangible piece of paper with

Later came the Gasoline Age, when truck circuses criss-crossed the country, and motorized advertising departments heralded their coming. Campbell's Circus Car 2 was a show-piece in itself during the 1920s. Downie Bros.' custom semi-trailer, poised at winter quarters for the 1938 tour, featured out-sized lettering and decorative corner posts on the outside, tons of colorful posters on the inside. King's bill car paused at Newport, R.I., in 1954. **Ed Tracy Collection; Circus World Museum.**

the message. It could be held pending arrival, and it could be kept or filed.

Telegraph charges were calculated according to the number of words. General business developed a telegraph style of speaking that omitted some words, hopefully without being ambiguous. Show business went further and developed a code in which a single word could stand for several. Published by W. A. Donaldson, manager of the Cincinnati lithograph company in 1894, the code covered every phase of show business, so anyone could use it to compose a telegram for his needs of the moment. An agent might send this message. "Prim. Embark. Link. Open. Clay. Decent." His show printer would decipher that as follows:

Prim = Send us at once twenty sets of dates commencing;
Embark = June 15;
Link = Printed in blue ink on white paper;
Open = One hundred copies of;
Clay = three-sheet poster lithographed in colors;
Decent = Cannot send money today.

Each party had a book giving the code words and their meanings. The agent paid for telegraphing the six code words. The printer could tell from them that the agent meant the full message of thirty-two words.

"ALL HANDS ROUND!"
4-PAW ADVANCE-CALL
All Parties Engaged for the ADVANCE-CORPS, including
MANAGERS OF ADVERTISING-CARS, SPECIAL AGENTS, BILLPOSTERS AND LITHOGRAPHERS
IN EVERY DEPARTMENT ARE REQUESTED TO REPORT AT
Forepaugh's Headquarters, 1,205 Chestnut st., Philadelphia,
MONDAY, APRIL 2,
In the meantime communicating by mail with ROBERT J. FILKINS, GENERAL MANAGER ADVERTISING.
MR. E. ABT WILL PLEASE REPORT APRIL 9.
1883

ADVERTISING - CAR
FOR SALE CHEAP.

I have in my possession, for immediate sale, a superior and ALMOST NEW ADVERTISING-CAR, which can now be seen at the Baltimore and Ohio Depot, Broad and Prime streets, Philadelphia. It is elegantly and elaborately painted and varnished, outside and inside, and is conveniently and well furnished with drawers, sleeping-car berths, state-room, office and baggage room, steam paste-boiler and modern-planned apartments for paper and lithographs, and the necessary requirements to go AT ONCE ON THE ROAD WITHOUT FURTHER COST.

The car is of unusual length, is built of well seasoned and good material, has the new improved adjustable trucks and axles to change gauge, Westinghouse automatic air and combination brakes, with the latest improvements in all respects. There is not in the business a more valuable or better arranged advertising-car. I have no use for it, and will dispose of it. VERY CHEAP FOR CASH, or will make payments to suit responsible purchasers should they desire time.

JAMES E. COOPER,
1,215 Wallace street,
Philadelphia.
Philadelphia, March 26, 1883.
1883

VAN AMBURGH, FROST, STONE & CO.
ADVANCE-CALL.
ALL PARTIES ENGAGED FOR THE ADVANCE BRIGADES, BILLPOSTERS, LITHOGRAPHERS, PROGRAMMERS, ETC., ARE REQUESTED TO REPORT AT GRAND HOTEL, CONNERSVILLE, IND.
THURSDAY, MARCH 29.
H. B. KNAPP, General-agent.
1883

WANTED.
Two more Billposters, immediately, for WAMBOLD'S CIRCUS AND MENAGERIE. Address I.W. WASHBURNE, Danvers, Mass.
1883

"FALL IN! FALL IN!"
All Agents, Lithographers, Programmers, Billposters and Fence-decorators engaged by us for the coming tenting season are ordered to report at COLUMBUS, O., on SATURDAY, APRIL 7. Advertising-cars will leave on Monday, April 9.
SELLS BROTHERS.
1883

The First to Start and the Last to Close.
THE BILLPOSTERS' PARADISE
WANTED FOR SEASON OF 1883,
100 EXPERIENCED BILLPOSTERS
FOR
W. W. COLE'S GREAT SHOWS.
Highest wages paid to BILLPOSTERS of established and untarnished reputation. No others need apply. Consult your interests and secure a permanent situation. Good reliable men never leave us untilthey became managers. Civil Service system. Promotion according to ability. All present employes remain. Remember, we do not close in the "middle of the season." First-class men now out of work should appreciate this. We shall hang up our Christmas stockings "on the road." Better wages and longer seasons than any other show. The best advertising-cars, best hotels, best printing, and best everything.
10 GOOD CORNET OR BUGLE PLAYERS
also wanted to complete the greatest corps of advertisers in the world. No programmers wanted. Application should be made at once. Address LOUIS E. COOKE, Advance-manager Cole's Circus, New Orleans, La., until Dec. 10. After that date No. 5 Taylor street, Newark, N. J.
1883

COME TO THE FRONT.
ALL BILLPOSTERS AND LITHOGRAPHERS ENGAGED FOR
NATHANS & CO.'S
CONSOLIDATED SHOWS
MUST BE IN GENEVA, N. Y., ON TUESDAY, APRIL 10. Hotel, Tompkins House. Send me your present address at once.
HARRY CORDOVA, care S. Booth & Co.,
201 Centre street, New York.
1883

WANTED FOR
JOHN B. DORIS' NEW MONSTER SHOWS,
50 BILLPOSTERS. 50
None but MEN OF CIRCUS EXPERIENCE, sober and thoroughly reliable. All applications must be accompanied by full information, with whom they have traveled and references. TO TOURISTS AND LUSHERS—Your time would be limited, consequently I do not want you to communicate. Address immediately,
E. H. DAVIS, General agent. Lockbox No. 188, Philadelphia, Pa.
1884

BILLPOSTERS WANTED
THE
Barnum & Bailey Greatest
Show on Earth
Offers best accommodations and opportunities for advancement to
First Class, Sober, Experienced Circus Billposters
Address:
BARNUM & BAILEY,
Bailey Building,
27 East 22nd Street, - - - NEW YORK
1907

WANTED,
Ten Good, First-class
BILLPOSTERS
WITH THE
Barnum-London Shows.
Must be sober, first-class men. Apply with full particulars, W. H. GARDNER, care Goodwin & Henry, City Billposters, Detroit, Mich.
1884

"ARE YOU THERE, MORIARTY?
THEN LET THE BATTLE GO ON."—Lord Nelson.
All Billposters Engaged with Sells Brothers are Notified to Report as Follows:
Those engaged for Advertising-car No. 1 report at Columbus, O., Saturday, March 29. Those engaged for Advertising-car No. 2 communicate immediately with James H. Decker. Members of Sea'd-ing's Brigade No. 3 get marching orders from him. Members of T. T. Bird's Brigade No. 3 communicate with him at Grand Opera-house, Columbus. Those who are not informed regarding which car or brigade they belong with, write immediately. All are requested to write, that we may know whether they will positively report. ALL OTHER PEOPLE ENGAGED ARE INFORMED THAT SELLS BROTHERS' MONSTER 60-CAGE MENAGERIE AND GREAT 4-RING CIRCUS, absolutely, indisputably the largest and finest equipped Circus and Menagerie under the sun, will open its season on WEDNESDAY, APRIL 16, at Columbus, Ohio.
SELLS BROTHERS.
1884

Each winter most circuses advertised in the *New York Clipper* or *The Billboard* for the billposters they would need in the coming season. Most shows offered good accommodations and long seasons while also raising the question of sobriety. In the spring a second ad told the men when and where to report for starting the season's work. The W.W. Cole show claimed a "civil service system" for its crew. Sells Bros. was looking for "fence decorators." **John Van Matre.**

THE STROBRIDGE LITHOGRAPHING CO.

CINCINNATI AND NEW YORK

INVOICE

OUR ORDER NUMBER 71440

CINCINNATI, May 11, 1918

SOLD TO BARNUM & BAILEY, Greatest Show on Earth

THIS SHIPMENT CONTAINS

__12__ DAYS WALL
__12__ DAYS WINDOW

ORD. BY W H   REC'D 5-3   SHIP'D VIA Freight Big Four   PREPAID

To C St Clair, Buffalo, N Y

LIST No. 1

No. of Sheets	NAME OF BILLS	List No. 1 No. Per Day	Quantity	Price Per Copy	Amount		TOTAL	
24	General Animals	9	108	1.02	110	16		
24	Street Parade	9	108	1.02	110	16		
20	Hannefords	9	108	.85	91	80		
20	Aladdin Procession	9	108	.85	91	80		
20	All Lady Acts	9	108	.85	91	80		
16	Portraits	9	108	.68	73	44		
16	Bears	9	108	.68	73	44		
16	One Clown .... 180 Extra	9	208	.68	195	84		
16	Aladdin Assembly .... 180 Extra	9	288	.68	195	84		
15	Lion	9	108	.63¾	68	85		
15	Clowns	9	108	.63¾	68	85		
12	High Jumper ...... 180 Extra	9	288	.51	146	88		
12	Chinese .... 180 Extra	9	288	.51	146	88		
12	Rhino	9	108	.51	55	08		
12	Bagonghi	9	108	.51	55	08		
12	Aladdin Procession	9	108	.51	55	08		
12	Title	9	108	.30	32	40		
8	Giraffes	9	108	.34	36	72		
8	Lady Rider	9	108	.34	36	72		
8	Perch Acts ...... 180 Extra	9	288	.34	97	92		
8	Lion-Tiger-Title	9	108	.34	36	72		
6	Lion-Tiger-Leopard	9	108	.25½	27	54		
6	Bird Millman ...... 180 Extra	9	288	.25½	73	44		
4	Bears	9	108	.17	18	36		
4	Aladdin—Princess	9	108	.17	18	36		
3	Portraits	9	108	.12¾	13	77		
3	Girl, Clown, Bear	9	108	.12¾	13	77		
2	Lady Rider	12	144	.08½	12	24		
2	Lion-Tiger-Leopard	12	144	.08½	12	24		
12	Streamer	7	84	.30		20		
7	Streamer			.17½		00		
	....							
	....							
	....							
	....							
	....							
	....							
	....							
	WINDOW WO							
	Assorted 1 Sheets (16 Kinds)	352	4224	.05½				
	Assorted ½ Sheets (4 Kinds)	88	1056	.02¾	2368	74		
	Freight Charges				54	91		
	....				2423	65		

Pages 61, 62, and 63: Standardized assortments made it easy to order routine quantities of circus paper. The mix for a regular day was indicated; agents could order for several days. Sometimes they called for extra quantities as well. The Barnum show used these standard lists in 1918, each designed to meet the assignment of a different billing crew or to serve special circumstances.

In this case, Strobridge shipped twelve days' worth of List 1, probably to the Number 1 Advertising Car. Each day or town was allotted nine copies of most varieties of posters. This order would stock the car for both wall and window work in upcoming towns across Ohio and into Illinois.

List 2 supplied the billing crew which worked villages along the railraod lines out of each show town, advertising the excursion trains that would operate on circus day. The order included no half-or one-sheets for hanging in store windows, just big posters for pasting on barns, fences and grain elevators.

List 3 provided a different mix for general billing, probably by Car 3. While these three orders were for delivery in Buffalo, List 4 went ahead to Chicago to serve fifteen towns farther along the route. The show would be in Buffalo July 1-2 and Chicago, July 12-14. List 4 probably went to the skirmish car, which ranged far and wide ahead of the show to advertise the circus where ever it might cross routes with a rival outfit or where special effort was needed for some other reason. **Circus World Museum.**

THE STROBRIDGE LITHOGRAPHING CO.
CINCINNATI AND NEW YORK

INVOICE

CINCINNATI, May 21, 1918

SOLD TO BARNUM & BAILEY, Greatest Show on Earth

ORD. BY P W H REC'D 5-3 SHIP'D VIA Freight Big Four PREPAID

TO G S Roddy, Buffalo, N.Y.

OUR ORDER NUMBER 74458

THIS SHIPMENT CONTAINS 12 DAYS WALL -- DAYS WINDOW

LIST No. 2

No. of Sheets	NAME OF BILLS	List No. 2 No. Per Day	Quantity	Price Per Copy	Amount		TOTAL	
24	General Animals	6	72	1.02	73	44		
24	Street Parade	6	72	1.02	73	44		
20	Hannefords	6	72	.85	61	20		
20	Aladdin Procession	6	72	.85	61	20		
20	All Lady Acts	6	72	.85	61	20		
16	Portraits	6	72	.68	48	96		
16	Bears	6	72	.68	48	96		
16	One Clown 120 Extra	6	192	.68	130	56		
16	Aladdin Assembly 120 Extra	6	192	.68	130	56		
16	Tiger Excursion 280 Extra	14	448	.68	304	64		
15	Lion	5	60	.63¾	38	25		
15	Clowns	5	60	.63¾	38	25		
12	High Jumper 100 Extra	5	160	.51	81	60		
12	Chinese 100 Extra	5	160	.51	81	60		
12	Rhino	5	60	.51	30	60		
12	Bagonghi	5	60	.51	30	60		
12	Aladdin Procession	5	60	.51	30	60		
12	Title	5	60	.30	18	00		
9	Excursion 280 Extra	14	448	.38¼	171	36		
8	Giraffes	5	60	.34	20	40		
8	Lady Rider	5	60	.34	20	40		
8	Perch Acts	5	60	.34	20	40		
8	Lion-Tiger-Title	5	60	.34	20	40		
6	Lion-Tiger-Leopard	5	60	.25½	15	30		
6	Bird Millman 100 Extra	5	160	.25½	40	80		
4	Bears	5	60	.17	10	20		
4	Aladdin—Princess	5	60	.17	10	20		
3	Portraits	5	60	.12¾	7	65		
3	Girl, Clown, Bear	5	60	.12¾	7	65		
2	Lady Rider	5	60	.08½	5	10		
2	Lion-Tiger-Leopard	5	60	.08½	5	10		
12	Streamer	2	24	.30	7	20		
6	Excursion Streamer	14	168	.15	25	20		
3	Excursion Streamer	9	108	.07½	8	10	1739	12
	Freight Charges						37	00
							1776	12

THE STROBRIDGE LITHOGRAPHING CO.
CINCINNATI AND NEW YORK

INVOICE

CINCINNATI, May 23, 1918

SOLD TO BARNUM & BAILEY, Greatest Show on Earth

ORD. BY P W H REC'D 5-3 SHIP'D VIA Freight Big Four PREPAID

TO W H Delly, Buffalo, N.Y.

OUR ORDER NUMBER 74459

THIS SHIPMENT CONTAINS 12 DAYS WALL 12 DAYS WINDOW

LIST No. 3

No. of Sheets	NAME OF BILLS	List No. 3 No. Per Day	Quantity	Price Per Copy	Amount		TOTAL	
24	General Animals	2	24	1.02	24	48		
24	Street Parade	2	24	1.02	24	48		
20	Hannefords	2	24	.85	20	40		
20	Aladdin Procession	2	24	.85	20	40		
20	All Lady Acts	2	24	.85	20	40		
16	Portraits	2	24	.68	16	32		
16	Bears	2	24	.68	16	32		
16	One Clown 40 Extra	2	64	.68	43	52		
16	Aladdin Assembly 40 Extra	2	64	.68	43	52		
16	Tiger Excursion 80 Extra	4	128	.68	87	04		
15	Lion	3	36	.63¾	22	95		
15	Clowns	3	36	.63¾	22	95		
12	High Jumper 60 Extra	3	96	.51	48	96		
12	Chinese 60 Extra	3	96	.51	48	96		
12	Rhino	3	36	.51	18	36		
12	Bagonghi	3	36	.51	18	36		
12	Aladdin Procession	3	36	.51	18	36		
12	Title	3	36	.30	10	80		
9	Excursion 60 Extra	3	96	.38¼	36	72		
8	Giraffes	3	36	.34	12	24		
8	Lady Rider	3	36	.34	12	24		
8	Perch Acts	3	36	.34	12	24		
8	Lion-Tiger-Title	3	36	.34	12	24		
6	Lion-Tiger-Leopard	3	36	.25½	9	18		
6	Bird Millman 60 Extra	3	96	.25½	24	48		
4	Bears	3	36	.17	6	12		
4	Aladdin—Princess	3	36	.17	6	12		
3	Portraits	3	36	.12¾	4	59		
3	Girl, Clown, Bear	3	36	.12¾	4	59		
2	Lady Rider	19	228	.08½	19	38		
2	Lion-Tiger-Leopard	19	228	.08½	19	38		
12	Streamer	2	24	.30	7	20		
7	Streamer	4	48	.17½	8	40		
6	Excursion Streamer	4	48	.15	7	20		
	WINDOW WORK							
	Assorted 1 Sheets (16 Kinds)	144	1728	.05½	95	04		
	Assorted ½ Sheets (4 Kinds)	36	432	.02¾	11	88		
½	Foot Ball Elephants - 270 Extra		270	02¾	7	43	850	67
½	Bears - 270 Extra		270	02¾	7	42	18	42
	Freight Charges						869	09

No. of Sheets	NAME OF BILLS	List No. 4 No. Per Day	Quantity	Price Per Copy	Amount		Total	
24	General Animals	5	75	1.02	76	50		
24	Street Parade	5	75	1.02	76	50		
20	Hannefords	5	75	.85	63	75		
20	Aladdin Procession	5	75	.85	63	75		
20	All Lady Acts	5	75	.85	63	75		
16	Portraits	5	75	.68	51	00		
16	Bears	5	75	.68	51	00		
16	One Clown	5	75	.68	51	00		
16	Aladdin Assembly	5	75	.68	51	00		
16	Tiger Excursion	2	30	.68	20	40		
15	Lion	5	75	.63¾	47	81		
15	Clowns	5	75	.63¾	47	81		
12	High Jumper	5	75	.51	38	25		
12	Chinese	5	75	.51	38	25		
12	Rhino	5	75	.51	38	25		
12	Bagonghi	5	75	.51	38	25		
12	Aladdin Procession	5	75	.51	38	25		
12	Title	5	75	.30	22	50		
9	Excursion	5	75	.38¼	28	69		
8	Giraffes	5	75	.34	25	50		
8	Lady Rider	5	75	.34	25	50		
8	Perch Acts	5	75	.34	25	50		
8	Lion-Tiger-Title	5	75	.34	25	50		
6	Lion-Tiger-Leopard	5	75	.25½	19	13		
6	Bird Millman	5	75	.25½	19	12		
4	Bears	5	75	.17	12	75		
4	Aladdin—Princess	5	75	.17	12	75		
3	Portraits	5	75	.12½	9	56		
3	Girl, Clown, Bear	5	75	.12½	9	56		
2	Lady Rider	5	75	.08½	6	38		
2	Lion-Tiger-Leopard	5	75	.08½	6	37		
12	Streamer	5	75	.30	22	50		
7	Streamer	5	75	.17½	13	13		
6	Excursion Streamer	2	30	.15	4	50		
3	Excursion Streamer	1	15	.07½	1	13	1145	59
	Freight Charges						21	04
							1166	63

THE STROBRIDGE LITHOGRAPHING CO.
CINCINNATI AND NEW YORK

CINCINNATI, May 15, 1918

SOLD TO BARNUM & BAILEY, Greatest Show on Earth

ORD. BY P W H REC'D 5-21 SHIP'D VIA Freight Big Four   PREPAID

TO   Ralph W Peckham, Chicago, Ill.

INVOICE
OUR ORDER NUMBER
1154
THIS SHIPMENT CONTAINS
15 DAYS WALL
-- DAYS WINDOW
LIST No. 4

Apart from the biggest shows, most outfits had a single bill car two weeks ahead of the show itself. If the circus was to play Spokane on August 16, the bill car arrived in town August 2, and so on. The bill car's location always reflected the big show's route. If the car was to keep up with the show, it could be in a town no longer than the show was to play the same town. One-day show stands were billed in a single day; there was no time out for rain, no time off. If the show played a big city for two days, the bill car had two days in which to complete its work. If the car fell behind, the manager had to find some way to double up on the billing and catch up on the schedule.

Usually circuses did not play on Sundays, so billers, too, had a day off. But holidays were a special headache to the bill car. The town in which the show would play on July 16 could be billed routinely on July 3, but working a town that would be played on July 17 would be a different story. The lithographers and billposters could not reach store managers or building owners on the Fourth of July to gain access and permission for posting their paper. Therefore, the crew had to double up and bill six towns in five days. Often, this was eased by the car manager's sending a few of the billers to the second town early by regular passenger train. They could get a head start in the second town before the holiday.

Smaller units of billers frequently were dispatched on extra missions away from the car; such a detachment was called a brigade. A brigade might be sent off for days at a time on a different railroad to bill feeder towns. Another might be sent back to a town already posted to repair the showing of paper after damage by a storm. The most frequent was an opposition brigade—men to battle with the similar crews from competing circuses. On some shows, a permanent brigade trailed the bill car by a week and acted in lieu of a second car. Men on a brigade lived at hotels and traveled on public passenger trains, not having a bill car of their own.

Makeup of the crew on a bill car was much the same across many seasons. The John Robinson Circus of 1923 had twelve billposters and seven lithographers, as well as a car manager, a paste maker, and a chef. It also had four billposters and four bannermen as one brigade and a second brigade of four bill posters.

In 1937, the big Cole Bros. Circus had twelve billposters, eight

Monthly billings from Strobridge documented the orders shipped to the Barnum & Bailey advance. While the paper was delivered to a specified city, it usually was intended for use in other towns to be billed a few days later and played two or more weeks later. There was little connection between the named cities and the paper delivered there. **Circus World Museum.**

lithographers, two programmers, a paste maker, a car manager, and a contracting press agent, as well as a boss lithographer and a boss billposter. The brigade had five men, and an opposition brigade was composed of eight men. This show also had a checker-up and two banner pullers.

For the Clyde Beatty Circus of 1947, a typical fifteen-car show, the advance included a car manager, a boss billposter, a boss lithographer, twenty-one billers, a press agent, and a school agent, whose task it was to arrange for classes to be dismissed on circus day.

Al G. Kelly & Miller Bros. Circus, an ad-minded truck show, in 1955 had twenty billers, two bosses, a brigade manager, an opposition manager, a car manager, and two press agents, all working with a supply truck, five panel trucks, and an auto.

Miller Bros. 101 Ranch Real Wild West Show in 1925 had ten billposters, six lithographers, and five bannermen on Car 1; eight billposters on Car 2; and five billposters on Car 3, posting an aggregrate of about 6,000 sheets a day.

When shows had more advance cars, the schedule was expanded, and each car was given specific duties. The first car had the basic billing duty and carried the most men. A three-car advance might schedule one car six weeks ahead of the playing date. Four weeks out, the second car would arrive with more billposters and the first bannermen. Two weeks ahead would be a car with a few billposters, fewer lithographers, and perhaps others; its main job was to reach towns along the railroads and bill special excursions that each line would run to the city on circus day. The second or third car might put extra effort into billing the country routes—grain elevators, country stores, and crossroads sheds—to reach the residents of farms, plantations, and ranches. One or more of the cars was charged with distributing heralds and couriers. The first car brought the contracting press agent, and often the general agent himself was aboard.

With Barnum & Bailey's advance in 1893, Car 2 was thirty days ahead and sent billposters on both town and country routes. Car 3 was fourteen days out and carried lithographers for town window work and billposters to continue farther out on country routes. Car 4, a week ahead, billed the excursions. Barnum &

INVOICE

Empire Poster Printing Co.

Quality Display Printing

429
WEST SUPERIOR STREET
CHICAGO 10

N⁰ 1155

SOLD TO	Ringling Bros. - Barnum and Bailey Circus 139 North Clark Street Chicago 2, Illinois	SHIPPED TO	John J. Brassil Ringling Bros. - Barnum and Bailey Circus New York City, New York

SHIPPED VIA				
F. O. B.	☐ Prepaid ☐ Collect	CUSTOMER'S ORDER NO.	SALES ORDER NO. **13448**	TERMS: NET DATE **March 2, 1954**

QUANTITY	DESCRIPTION	UNIT PRICE	AMOUNT
	MADISON SQUARE GARDEN - Car 1		
	NOW		
48 - 9	Sheet Dates @	$ .98 ea	$ 47.04
36 - 8	" "	.87 "	31.32
36 - 6	" "	.66 "	23.76
90 - 4	" "	.44 "	39.60
180 - 3	" "	.33 "	59.40
180 - 2	" " (Spec.)	.22 "	39.60
2400 - 1	" " (Flat)	.11 "	264.00
2400 - 1	" " (Up)	.11 "	264.00
12,000 - 1/3	" " @	5.46 C	655.20
12,000 - 1/4	" "	3.97 C	476.40
4,800 - 1/2	" " (Flat)	7.94 C	381.12
4,800 - 1/2	" " (Up)	7.94 Cq	381.12
4,800 - 7x21	Dates	3.97 C	190.56
4,800 - Panel	Dates	7.94 C	381.12
	▨▨▨▨▨▨▨		
330 - 2	Sheet Bottoms for 4-sheet	.22 ea	72.60
330 - 4	" " " 8 "	.44 ea	145.20
120 - 4	" " " 6 "	.44 ea	52.80
120 - 18	" Paper Banners	1.96 ea	235.20
	MADISON SQUARE GARDEN (NOW) CAR 3		
24 - 18	Sheet Cloth Banners @	9.78 ea	234.72
180 -	Bottoms to cover bottom half of 9 Sheet CLOTH @	2.445 "	440.10
			4,414.86

WE HEREBY CERTIFY THAT THESE GOODS WERE PRODUCED IN COMPLIANCE WITH ALL APPLICABLE REQUIREMENTS OF SECTIONS 6, 7 AND 12 OF THE FAIR LABOR STANDARDS ACT, AS AMENDED, AND OF REGULATIONS AND ORDERS OF THE UNITED STATES DEPARTMENT OF LABOR ISSUED UNDER SECTION 14 THEREOF.

QUADRUPLICATE

Posters appeared throughout New York City in early March for the Ringling show's 1954 engagement in Madison Square Garden, March 31 through May 9. With such a long run it was feasible to retrace all of the billing and cover the dates with new paper reading "Now." This was the order for printing the "Now" paper. **Circus World Museum.**

From The Strobridge Lithographing Co.,

124-132 CANAL STREET, CINCINNATI, O.

THE LARGEST SHOW LITHOGRAPHING HOUSE IN THE WORLD.

The Barnum & Bailey

GREATEST SHOW ON EARTH.

BOXED——2 DAYS IN A BOX.

Cincinnati, _____ 1893.

Ship to _____ Agent

By _____

No.	Original Order	Size	No. per day.	No. Days this Shipment.	NAME OF LITHOGRAPHS.	No. Days shipped to Date.	Balance Days on Hand.
1	1000	30x40	5	†	Roman Standing Race		
2	4000	30x40	20	†	Columbus Procession		
3	4000	30x40	20	†	Taking Possession		
4	4000	30x40	20	†	Ship Voyage		
5	4000	30x40	20	†	Departure		
6	1000	30x40	5	†	Rhinoceros		
7	1000	30x40	5	†	Horse and Ox		
8	1000	30x40	5	†	Performing Elephants		
9	1000	30x40	5	†	7 Open Dens		
10	1000	30x40	5	†	Trick Ponies		
11	1000	30x40	5	†	Hippos		
13	1000	30x40	5	†	Horse Fair		
14	1000	30x40	5	†	Giraffe		
15	1000	30x40	5	†	Rare Birds		
16	1000	30x40	5	†	Rare Animals		
17	4000	30x40	20	†	Return and Presentation		
18	2000	30x40	10	†	Ground Act, Nelson Brothers		
19	4000	30x40	20	†	Ballet		
20	2000	30x40	10	†	Herbert Brothers		
21	3000	30x40	15		Illusions, New		
22	1000	30x40	5	†	Dog Race		
23	3000	30x40	15	†	Seeing Land		
25	2000	30x40	10	†	5 Hora Act, New		
26	4000	30x40	20	†	Isabel ~~Wearing Jewels~~		
27	2000	30x40	10	†	Brothers, Lamoyne, Aerial		
28	1000	30x40	5	†	Clowns and Animals		
29	1000	30x40	5	†	Trained Stallions		
30	2000	30x40	10	†	Gautier and Loyal		
31	2000	30x40	10	†	Trained Animal Kingdom		
32	2000	30x40	10	†	New Chariot Race		
33	1000	30x40	5	†	Clown Elephant		
34	2000	30x40	10		Barlow and Amphlet		
35	4000	30x40	20	†	Illuminated Fete at Barcelona		
36	2000	30x40	10	†	4 Silbons		
37	1000	30x40	5	†	Melachor Chimes and Calliope		
39	3000	30x40	15	†	Parade No. 1, Nursery Rhymes		
40	2000	30x40	10	†	Male Principal, Barlow		
41	1000	30x40	5	†	Monkey and Donkey		
42	2000	30x40	10	†	Battle Scene		
43	3000	30x40	15	†	Columbus before Isabella at Baza		
44	3000	30x40	15	†	Parade No. 2. Mounted People		
45	2000	30x40	10	†	Lady Contortionist		
46	1000	30x40	5	†	20 Clowns		
47	3000	30x40	15	†	Parade No. 3, Small Chariots		
48	3000	30x40	15	†	Parade No. 4, Hippodrome		
49	3000	30x40	15	†	Parade, No. 5, Open Dens		
50	2000	30x40	10	†	Yucca, Strong Woman		
51	3000	30x40	15		Parade No. 6, Historical		
52	2000	30x40	10	†	Trained Cats		
53	2000	30x40	10	†	Siege of Baza		
54	2000	30x40	10	†	Surrender of Grenada		
55	2000	30x40	10	†	Wm. Showles		
57	4000	30x40	20	†	Oriental Splendors		
58	1000	30x40	5	†	Ladies' Hurdle Race		
59	2000	30x40	10	†	Nelson Family		
60	2000	30x40	10	†	Ronaldo, Aerial Gymnast		
61	1000	30x40	5	†	Men's Jockey Race		
62	1000	30x40	5	†	Man and Horse Race		
63	1000	30x40	5	†	Monkey and Poney Race		
64	2000	30x40	10	†	Miss Allen, Equestrienne		
65	4000	30x40	20		Black Orang Outang		
66	1000	30x40	5	†	Japanese		
67	2000	30x40	10	†	Ouda, Wild West		
69	4000	24x32	20	†	Barnum Portrait		
70	1000	30x40	5	†	Funny Acts		
71	4000	30x40	20	†	Landing		

Barnum & Bailey's List 1 of 1893 itemized seventy-one one-sheet lithographs, and it appears the show ordered sixty-six of them for use in New York. The circus ordered printing of from 1,000 to 4,000 of each style and allocated from five to twenty copies of each to each town. **Circus World Museum.**

Tom Dailey apparently was stocking his Number 2 Car for an opposition battle in Kentucky during 1910. For opposition against other shows, a billing crew would use lots of portraits and title bills, emphasizing its show's name and owners over those of the rival outfit. **Circus World Museum.**

Bailey's Car 1 was for opposition. It might be months or hours ahead of the show's appearance, according to the whereabouts of competition or any emergency that might require them to repair paper or even change the route.

Traveling apart from the cars might be more press agents, perhaps special brigades, and probably a checker-up—the man who came along just before the show day to determine both that the billers actually posted the paper that they claimed they had and that the property owners had not taken it down.

Ringling Bros. and Barnum & Bailey discontinued its Number 3 car in 1928. It used two advance cars through 1940, then carried on with one car until the end of 1954. This was the last use of a railroad car for circus advance work. It used correspondingly fewer men and less paper. In 1941, the McCandlish Lithograph Company shipped ninety-one sizes and styles of paper to the Ringling car. Ten years later, the variety was reduced to eighteen. By 1979, Ringling-Barnum was using a single style in three sizes. At Denver, the show used 200 copies of the one-sheet, 50 of the thirty-sheet version, and a quantity of window cards. The emphasis had switched to radio, television, and newspapers. Other circuses also had cut back on billing; they employed one or two men and modest quantities of date sheets and stock paper. Fewer places would permit the wall work, and even window work was hard to square. The billposters themselves were a vanishing breed.

But through most circus seasons, the quantities of paper posted were incredible. The Hagenbeck-Wallace Circus of 1934 posted 28,898 sheets at Boston, 22,881 in Philadelphia, and 101,108 in Chicago. In 1892, Topeka, Kansas was decorated with 24,000 sheets of posting for Ringling Bros. Circus. Under average conditions, a show might expend from 5,000 to 8,000 sheets per day. If the going was rough or the potential was great, a circus could put 15,000 to 20,000 into a town. It all varied by the size of the show and the town.

An advance department did not come cheap. Most general agents for medium-sized circuses reserved for it a substantial portion of the daily expenses. R. M. Harvey figured that one-third of the show's costs ought to be for the advance. Floyd King liked to

SUperior 7-9089

Empire Poster Printing Co.

Quality Display
Printing

429
WEST SUPERIOR STREET
CHICAGO 10

N⁰ 1312

SOLD TO	Ringling Bros., Barnum and Bailey Circus 139 North Clark Street Chicago 2, Illinois
SHIPPED TO	John J. Brassil Ringling Bros., Barnum and Bailey Circus General Delivery Montgomery, Alabama

SHIPPED VIA

F. O. B.

☐ Prepaid   ☐ Collect

TERMS: NET

CUSTOMER'S ORDER NO.	SALES ORDER NO.	DATE
	13665	October 27, 1954

QUANTITY	DESCRIPTION	UNIT PRICE	AMOUNT
	WAYCROSS — Car 1 and Car 3		
10 - 9	Sheet Dates	@ $ .98 ea.	$ 9.80
30 - 8	" "	.87 "	26.10
10 - 6	" "	.66 "	6.60
30 - 4	" "	.44 "	13.20
30 - 3	" "	.33 "	9.90
100 - 2	" " (Spec.)	.22 "	22.00
200 - 1	" " (Flat)	.11 "	22.00
200 - 1	" " (Up)	.11 "	22.00
270 - 1/3	" "	@ 5.46 C	14.74
270 - 1/4	" "	3.97 "	10.72
270 - 1/2	" " (Flat)	7.94 "	21.44
270 - 1/2	" " (Up)	7.94 "	21.44
270 - 7x21	"	3.97 "	10.72
270 - Panel	"	7.94 "	21.44
20 - 9	Sheet Cloth Banners	@ 4.89 ea.	97.80
			329.90

WE HEREBY CERTIFY THAT THESE GOODS WERE PRODUCED IN COMPLIANCE WITH ALL APPLICABLE REQUIREMENTS OF SECTIONS 6, 7 AND 12 OF THE FAIR LABOR STANDARDS ACT, AS AMENDED, AND OF REGULATIONS AND ORDERS OF THE UNITED STATES DEPARTMENT OF LABOR ISSUED UNDER SECTION 14 THEREOF.

QUADRUPLICATE

In addition to the pictorials, dated material was ordered on a custom basis for each stand. This was the order for date sheets to bill Waycross, Ga., in 1954. Each such piece would read "Waycross, Thurs., Nov. 18." The order was delivered to the bill car about November 1 at Montgomery and posted in Waycross about November 4. While the order mentions Car 1 and Car 3, the show had a single advance railroad car. Car 3 and Car 2 each was a station wagon to which were assigned four and five men respectively. **Circus World Museum.**

budget a quarter of the daily expenses for that department alone. The budget for performers probably would be less.

In all, the circus reached every part of the population in the town's trade territory. It was flexible enough to amend plans as needed to accomplish the task at hand. And it put out such a campaign that a Dartnell publication noted that circuses once were the "leading national advertisers." A printers' journal once commented that the circus "taught America how to advertise."

As if the mounds of posters didn't get everyone's attention, circuses pioneered in the use of electric spectacular signs in the heart of New York. The O.J. Gude sign company built this animated display for Barnum & Bailey in 1910. **Fairleigh Dickinson University.**

When the bill car hit town, its crew of billposters swarmed over the city to post the startling circus paper. Every shed was fair game. This was the handiwork of the 1948 Cole Bros. billers. **Authors' Photo.**

CHAPTER 4

The Billposters

Morning—and starting time—came early on the car. Billposters, like farmers, laborers, and many others of the time, might well start their day before dawn. As the population of the advance car began to stir, a division of labor became apparent. The single paste maker started first. The largest group was the billposters, who, along with the lithographers and programmers, assembled for the instruction that they would receive from the car manager.

Advertising car managers were specialists who had grown up in the trade. Earlier, they had been billers on other cars and other shows. Billposters belonged to one of the oldest trade unions, but eight-hour days and forty-hour weeks were unheard of. The billers knew each other personally and by reputation because of the interchange of men among shows.

Sometimes the crew slept and ate breakfast on the car, a self-contained operation. But often they stayed in a hotel near the depot, or perhaps a railroad YMCA. In latter days, motorized advance crews stayed in a local Milner Hotel, a chain that catered to low budgets long before today's bargain motels existed. Around dawn, the entire crew would have breakfast in some white-tiled restaurant near the depot, where the car was side-tracked.

Going to work, the billposters gathered at the car. Their local transportation for the day might be buckboards from the local livery stable or show-owned panel trucks. The paste maker had stirred the flour and water, added blue vitriol, then blasted it all with steam to create a creamy white concoction that was parceled out to tubs for individual billers. By ones or twos, the billposters were assigned to their routes. Vehicles were loaded with paste tubs, brushes, and the day's supply of posters. The car manager made the assignments, sending some billposters to specific thoroughfares and neighborhoods in the town and others on detailed country routes. A third group assembled its paste, brushes, and paper at the depot platform to await local passenger trains that would take the men to the assigned villages.

Billposters were experts in geography. They knew railroad main lines, branches, and junctions. They felt at home in nearly any city, town, or hamlet, and they were familiar with the streets, principal buildings, and highways. They were truly walking gazetteers. Having made the same routes before for this or other circuses, they noted the changes—a shed was gone, a new owner denied them permission to post, or a new building presented opportunity.

Typically, the billposter made his way along a country lane, stopping to wrap a barn in pretty posters, peering around a bend to see if a familiar shed was still there—a six-sheet pictorial and two three-sheet dates will cover the side that faces the road. More stores and fences, barns, gins, cribs, silos, and elevators—and then the hod of paper was gone, the route was billed.

While the men on country routes were posting their wall work, their counterparts were making the town routes in a similar fashion, stopping at each place that had been posted in the prior year or by other shows. The billposters covered the walls of stores and factories. They decorated the sheds, barns, and fences. They posted paper in downtown alleyways, though car managers complained when such paper was too obscure for normal traffic to view.

It was the same for those who rode the locals, the mixed trains, and the cabooses—getting off at each station to post wayside walls. Often, they plastered excursion bills around the depot and yards, announcing that there would be extra trains on circus day to take villagers to town.

In the horse-drawn era, towns without railroads were billed as far out from the show town as would make a comfortable trip by carriage. Railroad towns were billed out to forty and fifty miles away. Billposters using trucks and station wagons could cover great distances, and, similarly, with improved highways, people could get into town easily. In 1929, when the Ringling circus was playing Minot, North Dakota, the billers posted Jamestown and Valley City, North Dakota, 165 miles away. Jake Rosenheim recalled that it was billed off of Number 3 car, under manager C. J. Snowhill.

The billposter's route was a far cry from the hubbub of his circus and its midway. Often, he had never seen the circus that he advertised. But billposters still were circus people, dedicated to their show and to their profession.

Their procedure at each daub was the same. First, they sought permission to post the paper—from an owner if possible, a real estate office if necessary, a janitor on occasion, or a neighborhood kid if all else failed. Not all else—there was always the possibility of strong-arming the hit—posting paper without permission. This often meant trouble, but trouble many billposters would risk. If it was a site frequently used by billers and bearing other posters, there might be no heat. If the worst happened, they could plead innocent and try to step to the side of the leveled shotgun. Or perhaps they would be two weeks along and twelve towns down the road when the fence owner voiced his beef to the circus manager. While playing in Philadelphia in 1930, the Ringling circus received the following letter:

Dear Sir:

This is to inform you that I have this day reported to the Police Department of Lower Merion Township at Ardmore, Pa., the fact that someone has plastered up the side wall of my property with advertising bills describing your circus.

The Superintendent of Police has advised me that if the aforesaid advertising bills are not removed immediately, I am to swear out a Warrant for your arrest, and they will come and get you. The adjoining building has recently been torn down and I was just getting ready to plaster up this wall.

Yours Respectfully,
Thomas Maguire

Whether Mr. Maguire got any more satisfaction than a few tickets could provide has escaped recorded history.

If the biller was working a familiar stand, that stand probably already exhibited other billing. The question then was whether the prior paper was dead or alive, whether it heralded another circus long gone or some rival still to come. Ethics said that one never covered live paper, but the rule often was broken.

Billposters boasted of the number of sheets they could post in a day and of those places where they posted the biggest displays. They bragged about getting posters into prime locations and wrapping up everything from outhouses to huge grain elevators. They had a keen eye for size, always able to estimate what combination of big posters would fill a given wall. Arriving at the site, Jim Crews said, "The billposters 'lay out the daub,' in other words, step it off. One long step equals a one-sheet flat, 42 inches." Crews, a Hagenbeck man, said that one could quickly determine what size paper and date sheets to use for the area to be posted. Billposters were consummate artists who loved their lithographs and often stood off to admire, even photograph, their handiwork. They spoke fondly of their pretty pictures—the circus pictorials.

One billposting crew was admiring a great hit. The building fronted the main drag in town and the entire side had been covered with circus posters and date sheets. "I hope she lives until show day," said one of the men. He was saying that he hoped the stand would still be there when the circus got to town. He knew that a driving rain could raise havoc with the paper, and he realized that a competitive show hitting this town six weeks later might cover the beautiful stand with its own paper.

Billposters, by nature, seemed to thrive on their yarns, on pride in their work, and on the lore of their business. There were tall tales from other seasons and other shows. There were tricks to play on rivals. This was a world of their own, far from the show of which they boasted, cast out among the towners, and sharing common interest only with other billposters. Who else could share the victory when a biller posted a choice spot or a crew completed a stand six sheets high and thirty sheets wide, all sixes and nines and date sheet threes?

An old showman, Starr DeBelle, worked with many a mud show, sometimes posting practically the same route through the South each season. Starr remembered one farmer's telling him, "You can post the barn if you put up pictures of lions and tigers. Last year you put up horses and I got sick of looking at them." Another said that DeBelle could post his chicken coop if he agreed to paste a picture of a pretty girl on a white horse on the wall on his living room. DeBelle told the usual tales—that some sheds and outhouses had so many layers of circus paper on them that this is what held the buildings together; or that the posters were the best siding and windbreak that some barns ever had.

Any stand of paper put up with paste was called a daub. Wild cat circus paper on isolated (and perhaps unauthorized) locations was called snipe—posting wherever you could get away with it, as opposed to using commercial billboards. Once, shows used paper called guttersnipe. It was only inches high and several feet wide, designed to go on eaves or rain gutters or lean-to canopies on store fronts. Larger horizontal paper of great length was called a streamer and generally carried the show's name. Billposters expected to put a streamer across the top of any big hit of paper. The day's quota of posters assigned to each man was called a hod, a mix of designs stemming from the varieties specified in the shipping lists of show printers.

In town or on a country route, the livery stable team nodded

while the billers slopped paste on a wall and dramatically unveiled the pretty nine-sheet with which they would honor the residents thereabouts. Even though he always was far from the excitement of the circus itself, a biller was something of an actor when he unfolded the paper and stunned the neighborhood kids with a full-color display of a daring lion trainer or human cannonball.

"As car manager for Ringling, Babe Boudinot, loved those country routes and wanted us to put up plenty of sheets," said Roy Long, boss billposter. "He was forever telling the men not to just frame the paper. 'Iron it, iron it, rub it in, rub it in.' He was telling them to paste the entire space, not just around the edge of a six-sheet with an X of paste in the middle; this was framing the poster. It was faster but the paper would not last as long as if you ironed it on.

"If we were having a good day and getting lots of good daubs we sometimes ran out of paste. There wasn't time to go back to the car so we bought flour, added water and stirred up our own mixture. We had to add lye, which would cook the mixture so it was usable. But we had to be very careful not to rub this paste too hard on the surface of the poster as it would make the inks run."

While his crews were out, the car manager experienced an equally demanding day. He claimed those bundles of posters at the express office and had them stowed on the car. The telegraph office was a regular stop, where the manager might find wires detailing new routing plans for the circus, clearing up problems about shipments of paper, or transmitting money with which to operate the car and pay the crew.

Sometimes the work of the circus crew was augmented by use of local billboards. The car manager would rent the local twenty-four-sheet boards—and often would find that the city billposting plant was operated by former circus billers.

The manager restocked his car with all supplies. The most active advance crew might use up to ten barrels of flour per day, so there was more to buy and store on the car.

Perhaps the most urgent duty was preparing assignments for his crews to use in tomorrow's town. The manager would write out instructions for each man or team, telling the billposters on country routes what roads to take, what familiar hits to look for. He would make similar instruction sheets for those on town routes, giving assignments on streets and structures as if he had lived in every town that they worked. He knew how many sheets a biller should be able to post on each route. He also could guess when a billposter might "charley" some paper, that is, ditch it into a garbage can or creek rather than post it.

There were great car managers, all revered by other specialists on the advance for their individual kinds of skills. John Brassil was the Ringling car manager in late years. Elmer Kaufman, formerly a biller on railroad shows, was car manager for King Bros. Bill and Jackie Wilcox made a husband and wife team that might handle all of the billing for a smaller truck show. Bill Oliver was another leading car manager for rail shows. Francis Kitzman was car manager for several truck shows.

George Gallo posted for Ringling-Barnum, King Bros. Circus, Clyde Beatty-Cole Bros. (where he was car manager in 1974), and other shows. Gallo was asked if there was a trick to insure that your paper did not peel off:

"We would daub the hell out of it. It meant we would rub our paste into the wall first. Then put up the paper, again rubbing it in hard. Finally we would take clear water and splash it over the paper, rubbing it in hard with our brushes. That damn stand won't peel or flag for sure. Trouble is we didn't always have the time to do this, or sometimes we couldn't spare the water.

"What kind of men did we want on the crew? Hard workers. We needed sheeters, guys that could really put up the paper, guys you could trust not to slough, or charley, their hods; and we wanted guys that had the ability to get Main Street locations. Some guys found and used doniker locations; you know—outhouses and chicken coops out back—just to use up their paper.

"We encouraged our men to use their imagination, and some of them came up with fantastic spots. One that comes to mind is a train wreck that occurred right on the edge of our show town along the main drag. Boxcars were piled up at all angles. At night our man covered five or six of these cars with paper. The best part of it was they didn't get the mess cleaned up until after the show left town. We have pasted water tanks, and even an old launch that was parked in front of a junkyard.

"Railroad shows carried steam boilers in the advertising cars to cook their paste. Truck show billposters would find a dairy, or a laundry where they could get steam. A few tickets always got the job done. But today most billposters use Bloety's Paste Flour made in England. It is great stuff only you have to let it sit for two hours before you use it. And it doesn't take steam to cook it. Just add the dry powder to water and stir.

"Let's say we found a building with a wall that faced a busy street. It was ideal for pasting but we could not find the owner. If I saw it had been pasted before, why I would just arm it; you know, strongarm the place. If the owner showed up to ask 'What's going on here?' I would tell him, 'Mr. Armstrong gave me permission.' We would keep on pasting—never indicate you're scared. 'Who is he? I own the building.' 'Why, Mr. Armstrong is on the Police Benevolent Society's committee. They are sponsoring the show,' I would answer. Then I would quickly add, 'Sir, we run a high-class show and surely we don't want any trouble. Now I would like to give you tickets for your whole family—how many do you want?' The minute he gave me a quantity I knew I had him, and I always gave him two or three extra for his friends. I went back to posting without any further conversation. While I worked, he would ask some simple questions about the show, and finally he would walk away. You always had to be polite and be a diplomat and have a pocket full of tickets. You could get want you wanted.

"I knew quite a few good billers. We called them 'Triple A billers.' You could depend on them to put up paper that was framed right, square with the building, and the daub looked good. Jim Crews was one of the best in the business. A 'Triple A biller' could paste an alligator wall—that's what we called a rough surface—or a velvet wall. It didn't make any difference—his daub looked good.

"A good billposter seemed to find many good spots in the groove—you know, the main drag of a town. The other guys seemed to find spots in the slough—skid row—where it was easier to get the paper up.

"We always had a variety of paper to fit any spot. However, a Chicago two-sheet seemed to really stand out on a hit. This was a flat with the date on it or a title on it, and sometimes both. It was a little larger than a regular two-sheet. It looked good.

"When a farmer, or a building owner in town didn't like the idea of pasting paper on his wall, we told him we used a new product called ten-day paste. We assured him the posters would easily peel off in one piece in about ten days. While I was telling the towner this, I was flipping through a bunch of tickets and offered him two or four or whatever I thought the hit was worth. They usually weakened."

Every billing crew member knew the value of an "agent's" or

"owner's showing" of so-called "office" paper. This was the posting of large quantities of paper where circus executives would see that the billers had been hard at work. There might be prominent stands of paper at the crossing where the circus train would be unloaded. It was helpful if there was paper around the hotel and depot for the general agent to see. And if a barn would be visible to a circus owner standing on the show grounds, it was best to have that barn wrapped in posters bearing his name.

By late afternoon, a billposter may have pasted from 300 to 600 sheets covering up to 7,000 square feet of space. A few bill-posters, over the years, became known as "thousand sheeters"—men who were adept and quick enough to post 1,000 sheets in one day.

On a good day, the hod was posted before time ran out, but always there was the dash to "make the car." After reaching into remote neighborhoods of a city or riding miles out into the country, there was the problem of getting back to the advance car at the distant depot. There they would meet again with the rest of the crew before their home on wheels was coupled to a regular passenger train for the trip to their next town.

Fences were especially enticing to the circus billposters. Hagenbeck-Wallace clowns share billing with a theater and Helen Hayes in this 1935 Chicago spread. **Circus World Museum.**

Big red dates and brilliant pictures declared the circus was coming. A show's hometown was just like any other to the billers. This stand of paper heralded the opening of Downie Bros. Circus at its Macon, Ga., quarters in 1938. **Ed Tracy Collection.**

While some billed the town routes, other billposters were assigned to the country routes, putting circus paper on every flat surface in the surrounding villages and countryside. This stand of paper spruced up a shed in Waunakee, some 20 miles from Madison, Wis. **Authors' Photo.**

Billers liked to "wrap up" a shed, as they did with this one in California. Sometimes they called it "the parcel post treatment." **Circus World Museum.**

On a country route out of Houston, Ringling billposters decorated this store in Dickinson, Texas, thirty-nine miles away. **Joe M. Heiser Jr.**

77

Bigger wall space was a biller's delight. Ringling men posted dates and title bills in Oconomowoc for a Milwaukee stand in 1945. **Authors' Photo.**

Buffalo Bill's advance showed the Europeans how to do it. This was a stand of Cody paper in Rimini, Italy in 1906. Having wrapped up the empty building, the billers moved on to the adjacent fence and kept going. **Buffalo Bill Memorial Museum.**

Schell Bros. billing demonstrated two economies in 1936. The date sheets carried no town name, thus saving on the custom printing costs, Showmen thought only minor "ragbags" would use "here" paper. The poster at left was printed for Zellmar Bros. Circus, and Schell merely posted its own new name over the old one. In this case, they represented the same show with a title change. Often shows bought bargain paper from defunct shows and crosslined their own name over the old. **Joe M. Heiser Jr.**

A vacant house serves billers as well as an old barn. Telltale tatters of earlier billing informed the circus men that the house was fair game. They might have strongarmed the stand. The bills even covered up many of the windows. **Al Conover.**

Opposite Page: Blacksmith shops were favorites of circus billposters. This one displays Buffalo Bill paper at South Boylston, Calif. Showmen sometimes joked about "Bill's billing" and "Bill's bills." **Henry E. Huntington Library. Above:** Neighborhood kids came out to stare at the new art in town. This 1945 Ringling paper was on a Hartland, Wis., shed that billposters covered for one show or another year after year. **Authors' Photo.**

Above: The wider or higher the better, so Gentry Bros. billposters posed proudly for a picture alongside this work of art in 1905. **Authors' Collection. Left:** Even a shed's roof could be attractive to billposters, and this shed seems to be in need of the help a layer of posters might give in holding those loose boards in place a while longer. **Authors' Collection.**

Circuses frequently rented local billboards to augment their own billposting. And hardly a stand of paper ever was photographed without a proud billposter posed in front. Long jumps between scattered towns of Western Canada sometimes left time for only a single performance in a day, as with this Wheeler Bros. afternoon-only stop 491 miles from Winnipeg in 1918. **Circus World Museum.**

The Floto Shows' billposters outdid themselves with this 1905 stand. The pictorials appear to include several twenty-four-sheets and even a thirty-two-sheet poster. Shows often used streamers across the top of a billing stand to tie it all together. **Circus World Museum.**

Lacking big posters, King Bros.' crew nevertheless made a good showing with this combination of thirteen one-sheet pictorials, then one-sheet dates and three two-sheet titles, all for Goshen, Indiana, in 1965. **George Gallo.**

The daubs that show billers got on fences and barns were augmented with the purchase of space on regular billboards in some towns. The short-lived Tim McCoy Wild West Show of 1938 bought local boards at Dayton. **Circus World Museum.**

A double-decked billboard at Bridgeton, N.J., made for a spectacular stand of Barnum & Bailey paper in 1906. **Everett Porch.**

These Sparks billposters had finished their work but posed dutifully at the town board for an Oil City, Pa., appearance in 1922, while another man waits in the REO Speedwagon. Circus billers often rented local transportation to take them on city and country routes. **Circus World Museum.**

In more than a few cases, local billboards were owned by a former circus billposter who had settled down in the town. These boards are identified as property of Cal. M. Gillette, who along with L.C. Gillette, was on the advance of several shows. His boards served the Forepaugh-Sells Circus for a stand in July 1905. **Authors' Collection.**

Little of the building was visible after the Cole Bros. bill crew finished with the structure in 1917. Billposters liked to arrange their posters in balanced combinations such as this. There are date sheets at each side, big posters at center, smaller ones in between, a huge date on top and streamers across the center and bottom. **Circus World Museum.**

Not only the spectacular circus features but also the billposting itself was new to the residents of Groningen, Holland in 1901. Barnum & Bailey billposters had erected the signboard and then decked it out with two forty-eight-sheet posters and appropriate date sheets. **Ringling Museum of the Circus.**

May 1 was the traditional opening of the new circus season, and this stand of paper was for Forepaugh-Sells Circus in its former hometown, Columbus, Ohio, in 1911. The billers carefully posted around the windows. Actually, the show had played several earlier towns before coming back to perform for the home folks. This was the show's final season. **Circus World Museum.**

The Kelly-Miller circus was one of the latter-day shows that believed in heavy use of billposting. This 1956 stand for Wagoner, Okla., brightened up a dingy brick wall and boasted of hippo, rhino, and giraffe. **Circus World Museum.**

Sometimes circus billposting added a little something to the neighborhood, as in the case of this John Robinson Circus daub in 1919 near Greensboro, N.C. **Jim McRoberts.**

At other times things got out of hand. The Old Fulton Market at Troy, N.Y., is somewhere behind all of that 1903 Ringling Bros. paper. This included 516 sheets of posting paper and 594 sheets of banners. **Gene Baxter Collection.**

For some billposters, no challenge was too great. Norris & Rowe scored this hit in downtown Seattle in 1906. **Circus World Museum.**

Billposters and their bill car managers liked to make a big splash near the show grounds so the circus owner would see how well they were doing their job. This was such an "office showing" at Concord, N.H., for the appearance of the John Robinson Circus in 1918. **Authors' Collection.**

Pages 93-103: Circus billers knew every shed in the country and came back to the same ones time after time to post paper for a steady procession of circuses. This unique series of pictures starts with Dailey Bros. Circus billing for Watertown, Wis., in 1950.

The little Kelly-Morris show came along in June, 1951, to advertise its appearance in Oconomowoc, where the shed stood near a busy feed mill frequented by many farmers.

Then Ringling-Barnum covered Kelly-Morris paper to tell the wonders of the Greatest Show on Earth later in June 1951.

Wallace & Clark decorated the same shed in August 1952. The coal shed was alongside the Milwaukee Railroad's main line.

Kelly-Miller did its part in September 1952. At far right, the Wallace & Clark tiger paper still was intact, so K-M billers merely applied their own date sheet to hide the old name and let the tiger work for Kelly-Miller. Older Ringling paper still is seen behind the tree.

Diano Bros.' billposters started the 1953 procession. By now the old coal sign had disappeared, but circuses kept coming. It is likely that some of the same billposters had been here for different circuses in different seasons.

Ringling-Barnum replaced the Diano stand in late July for its August 1953 engagement in Milwaukee. The show's information on country routes would describe the shed and steer billers to it.

Clyde Beatty Circus used the shed to bill both Waukesha and Watertown stands in 1953. But more significant, the Beatty show covered Ringling's paper before the Ringling date had been played. Covering "live" paper was frowned upon but frequently done. One date sheet was posted sideways to be sure all signs of the Ringling paper were obliterated; there must be no evidence of the covering.

Hagen Bros. was the feature for 1954. Tatters of the old Beatty paper remain as well.

Nothing but remnants are seen in 1955.

But Miller Bros. makes a modest showing in 1956. Its rearing horse poster is the same style of stock paper as Kelly-Morris had used here five years before.

Hagen Bros. keeps up the tradition in 1957. Shows were using less paper per stand than in earlier seasons. In 1958, Hagen Bros. posts some new paper for its latest Oconomowoc appearance. Remains of the 1957 paper still are to be seen. Since 1955 a tree has been growing at the lefthand corner of the shed. As long as the building would stand, circus billposters would return to it. **Authors' Photos.**

94

97

DAILY CAR REPORT

WEATHER COLD

TOWN SUMTER, SO. CAR.,   DATE BILLED Sept. 27/1940   SHOW DATE SAT. OCT. 5/ 1940

TOWN POSTING	SHEETS	TICKETS	COUNTRY ROUTE NO. 1	SHEETS	TICKETS
10 - locations (Gunnels)	263	43	POSTING: 9 - locations (Sadowski)	258	43
			LITHOS: 6 - locations (Sadowski)	14	13
Banners:Pruitt-Meaney 10 - locations	116	53			
Window Cards: 19 - locations (Frazier) 8 -(Seward)	38 16	38 x			

TOWN LITHOS	SHEETS	TICKETS	COUNTRY ROUTE NO. 2	SHEETS	TICKETS
17 - locations (Frazier)	84	57			
24 - locations (Seward)	107	79			

TOTAL SHEETS 896

TOTAL TICKETS 326

REMARKS _Harry Chipman_

Harry Chipman/ Car Mgr.,

Posting wasn't the only paper work that was required o[f] a billposter. He also had to report the location of all hi[s] hits of the day. Then the Car Manager summarized hi[s] crew's efforts in daily reports to the general agent. In thi[s] one, Harry Chipman reported that his various crewmen had posted 896 sheets and issued orders for 326 ticket[s] at Sumter, S.C. in 1940. **Authors' Collection.**

COLE BROS. CIRCUS

WEATHER Hot

At Salt Lake City, Utah   Show Date Aug. 5th   Car Date July 23rd

R. R.   D&RG   Arrive 7:40 AM   Depart 8:00 A.M.

	Sheets	Price	CHECKS ISSUED	Amount
Town Bill Poster 20 panels	Sheets	Price	The Packer Corp.	$106.00
Sniper	Route	Price		
Livery				

PAPER POSTED	Sheets	Tickets		Sheets	Tickets
Town Bill Boards	480	10	Town Lithographs	1579	843
Country Posting	433	49	Town Banners Murphy		
Country Lithos.	296	119	Cards		
Town Daubs none			Programs		
			Total	2788	1021

COUNTRY ROUTES	Sheets	Tkts.	COUNTRY ROUTES	Sheets	Tkts.
Malley Posting			Rhodes Lithographing		
Saltair	1	18	2		
Garfield	1	18	4	8	4
Magna	2	60	6	50	18
Granger	1	24	4		
Murray	1	28	3	65	26
West Jordan	2	76	5	17	4
Taylorsville				6	4
Midvale	2	60	4	26	10
Sandy	2	34	8	46	16
No. Salt Lake	1	28	2	2	2
Bountiful	1	36	4	39	15
Centerville	1	24	3		
Farmington	1	24	4	25	16
Woods Cross	1	3		4	2
	17	433	49	296	119

```
Could only do one route as needed rest of men in town to litho.
Did not use sniper as he had live paper on most of his daubs,
anything left was not worth paying for.
```

13 men on car

Car Manager V. A. Williams

For Cole Bros. at Salt Lake City in 1940, the car manager reported use of 20 local billboards, plus the work of two men who made a country route that took them to fourteen nearby small towns. One of them posted 433 sheets, the other put up 296 lithographs. Others placed 1579 sheets of window work. **Authors' Collection.**

SUN BROTHERS' WORLD'S PROGRESSIVE SHOWS, (INC.)

WALL CONTRACT

No. _1048_   *Elloree S.C.* _____ 191_

I hereby grant the exclusive privilege to the above-named Shows to post their Bills on

my _Restaurant_   Situated _on Main St_

Elloree S.C. (191)

from date until the day after above-named Shows have exhibited at _____ (191)

the bills not to be covered up or defaced until after the date named above. In consideration of said privilege I have

received an order for _2 two_ _____ Tickets, which

is in full of all demands for the privilege above named. No other Bills to be posted on said premises until after date

of exhibition as stipulated above. If there should be any disagreement or question about my right to grant the above permission, I agree

to assume all responsibility for damages arising under this contract.

_____ Agent. _____ Owner.

ERIE LITHO. & PTG. CO., ERIE, PA.

At each location, the billposter was expected to get permission to post his bills. In 1914 the Sun Bros. billposter was cleared to put bills on a restaurant wall in Elloree, S.C. in return for two circus tickets. **Authors' Collection.**

Many shows used a two-part billing contract. The building owner kept one for presentation at the circus pass gate. The billposter forwarded the other to the show. A checker-upper determined both that the paper had been posted and that the owner had not removed it prior to circus day. If all was well, the owner received his free admissions to the show. **Authors' Collection.**

Col. Tim McCoy's REAL WILD WEST and ROUGH RIDERS OF THE WORLD

1938

TOWN BILLING

CONTRACT FOR BILLING

NOTE: The order bearing duplicate number of this contract is of no value if coupons are detached. All advertising placed under this contract must remain on display as placed by Show, and is subject to inspector's check on day of show. Good only on day for which issued.

№ 4530

On presentation of order bearing duplicate number to this contract please admit number of persons as per coupon attached in consideration of the exclusive

privilege of displaying bills on his..................

from..........................1938 to.........................1938,

town of...in full payment of which the order bearing duplicate number is issued, with the distinct understanding that the party signing this contract has the legal right to grant said permission and agrees that no other bills are to be posted on said premises and that our bills shall not be destroyed or covered until after date specified above and also agrees to assume all responsibility for damages arising under this contract.

.........................Owner or Agent

BARNEY KERN, Mgr. Adv. Car No. 1

This Pass is good for one general admission upon payment of Federal Admission Tax, State Admission Tax, if any, and service charge.

GOOD FOR ONE GENERAL ADMISSION
Not Good For Reserved Seat—Not Good If Detached
Good For One Adult or One Child—Will Not Admit Both

GOOD FOR ONE GENERAL ADMISSION
Not Good For Reserved Seat—Not Good If Detached
Good For One Adult or One Child—Will Not Admit Both

Col. Tim McCoy's REAL WILD WEST and ROUGH RIDERS OF THE WORLD

1938

TOWN BILLING

ORDER FOR ADMISSION

NOTE: The order bearing duplicate number of this contract is of no value if coupons are detached. All advertising placed under this contract must remain on display as placed by Show, and is subject to inspector's check on day of show. Good only on day for which issued.

№ 4530

On presentation of this order please admit number of persons as indicated by coupon attached in consideration of the exclusive privilege of displaying bills

on his..................

from..........................1938 to.........................1938,

town of...in full payment of which this order is given, with the distinct understanding that the party signing duplicate contract has the legal right to grant said permission and hereby agrees that no other bills are to be posted on said premises and that our bills shall not be destroyed or covered until after the date specified above. He also agrees to assume all responsibility for damages arising under this contract.

G. AUDETTE

.........................Agent

BARNEY KERN, Mgr. Adv. Car No. 1

This Pass is good for one general admission upon payment of Federal Admission Tax, State Admission Tax, if any, and service charge.

MAY 5-19

GOOD ONLY

Number of Sheets	AL. G. BARNES
	BIG
Nº 11298	5-RING CIRCUS
A	ADV. CAR No. 1

———————————————————————————————, 192——

I have this day received an order on the above-named Shows

for one ticket for the EXCLUSIVE privilege of placing——————————

———————————————————————————————on my premises at

No.——————————————————————————————————

————————————————————————————————Street,

which is acknowledged as full payment for said privilege. Said display advertising to remain where placed until after the closing

date of the exhibition of above-named shows in——————————————

—————————————————————————————————————

————————————————————————————————Owner.

1929

I accept this ticket with the understanding that I am to pay a ten-cent service tax thereon payable only at the front door of the circus.	AL. G. BARNES
Nº 11298	BIG
A	5-RING CIRCUS
	ADV. CAR No. 1

BILL POSTING

AGENT: ——————————————————————————, 192——

You will please give Mr.——————————————

ONE TICKET for the EX——————VE privilege of placing——————————

——————————————————————on his premises a—

No.——————————————————————————————

It is understood that the di——— advertising is to remain up an— be taken care of by him unt—— closing date of the above-name— Shows in this city. THIS —————R IS NOT TRANSFERABLE and MUST NOT BE BOU————OR SOLD. GOOD FOR ONE ADMISSION ONLY. VOID —— ALTERED.

JACK GLINES, Adv. Mgr.

THE BLANCHARD PRESS ————— · 222 GOLDEN GATE AVE., S.F

ADMIT 1 PERSON ONLY

Paying for posting privileges with free tickets was advantageous to everyone. The building owner appreciated passes even more than cash. The circus could not have paid any meaningful amount of money but could hand out many orders for tickets. Moreover, only sixty percent of the orders ever were actually presented at the circus for admission. **Authors' Collection.**

Charley Smith checks supplies as he and Bob Deckman work a country route for the Ringling advance in 1949. The large vat contains paste; the milk can has water for thinning the paste if necessary. Smaller quantities of paste are poured into the black buckets for carrying to the job. **Authors' Photo.**

Smith and Deckman already have posted the three-sheet date and six-sheet clown poster. Deckman squares up a section of the twenty-sheet elephant paper before he rubs it into place with his brush. Smith is covering the wall—and old carnival paper—with more paste. **Authors' Photo.**

Deckman places the second half of the giraffe six-sheet, while Smith works the three-sheet date into place. They are working at Sturtevant, Wisconsin. **Authors' Photo.**

This location completed, Deckman sits in the show's station wagon to make out his report on the location, while Smith loads their gear. **Authors' Photo.**

Any self-respecting circus billposter would have barked at that kid to keep his distance. So it is safe to assume that all three people have been posed for the picture after completion of work on the stand of paper for Kelly-Miller in 1959. Despite such growling, billposters reveled in the excitement they created by unveiling circus posters. **Jim McRoberts.**

In the service of Cristiani Bros. Circus in 1960, a billposter works the paste into proper consistency and then places his date sheet for a July appearance over the "dead" King Bros. paper for May. **Authors' Photo.**

On behalf of Birnam Bros. Circus, Jimmy Ray deftly brushes the paper against the block wall he has coated with paste. Long before this 1964 tour, Ray was a circus wrestler and concessionaire. **Authors' Photo.**

Norris & Rowe placed a neat display on a fence-style billboard at Ukiah, Calif., in 1908. **Circus World Museum.**

Burr Robbins Circus was great for putting up its own "fences," or billboards, after the billers had covered everything else in town. This was about 1885. Later Robbins founded the General Outdoor Advertising Co. **Authors' Collection.**

Cloth banners tacked to the walls of high-rise buildings gave circuses outstanding advertising exposure. In the heart of Manhattan's theater district, Cole Bros. scored this great hit in 1937. The show challenged Ringling-Barnum's claim to sole ownership of New York by playing the Hippodrome prior to the R-B run at Madison Square Garden. **Circus World Museum.**

CHAPTER 5

The Bannermen

No single hit of other circus bills was as effective as a stand of banners. All kinds of circus art caught the eye because of newness and color where drab bricks and boards once stood. But banners seemed even brighter, appeared in surprising places, and proved simply impossible to overlook.

Their prime downtown locations had less distraction and enjoyed greater traffic—more people, more exposure, more advertising impressions. It is a wonder that other advertisers were not successful in copying this circus scheme.

Banners were circus posters placed high on the sides of tall buildings, reached by long ladders from the ground up or the roof down. The banner man's "human fly" characteristics sometimes were as daring as those of aerialists pictured on the posters. Printed on cloth instead of paper, banners were put up with tacks rather than paste. Some landlords would allow tacking but refused permission for pasting paper—mostly because the tacked banners would be removed.

The business district of an American city counted buildings of varying heights—two stories, five stories, or maybe eight. If the three-story dime store was next door to a seven-story office building, there was a four-story difference of solid brick. Unnoticed by the public, that was just what aroused the professional passions of a circus banner man. That was where the banner bloomed.

The wall, blank and ignored for untold years, suddenly popped out with brilliant reds, blues, and yellows. The colors screamed a message that Downie Bros. Circus was bringing lions—or that the Sparks Circus elephants were to be seen in two weeks—or that Cole Bros. would appear on May 24.

For all their value, banners were hard to handle. Not all circuses used them. They required different manpower and special printing. Yet they proved to be worth the effort. Nothing in advertising carried quite the jolt of banners; nothing so surprised the beholder.

To get this job done, the banner squarer was first on the scene. This specialist contacted the owner of the building and convinced him that it was a good idea for someone to tack advertising on the wall. The squarer sometimes traveled ahead of the bill car. He roamed the town to find the ideal walls and their owners. Having made the arrangements, he forwarded details to the advance car manager.

The building owner might agree or not; the banner squarer had to be a diplomat and salesman to succeed in squaring the deal. His weapons were passes; complimentary tickets could buy things beyond the reach of money, something known by circuses a century before rock shows discovered the trade-out for radio time.

He could assure the owner that these posters, unlike others, actually would be taken down, not left for the winter winds. The banner squarer used the same type of combined ticket order and contract as his earthbound cohorts. The owner would sign the contract portion for the biller and would take the other portion to

Banners gave unique downtown attention that circuses could not have gotten any other way. This Cole Bros. paper dominates the very center of Columbus, Ohio—Broad and High Streets—in 1937. **Circus World Museum.**

the circus later to receive a specific number of tickets in return.

As posters go, banners were expensive. In 1937, the Central Printing and Illinois Lithographing Company charged $1.71 for a nine-sheet banner and $.96 for a six-sheet banner. In 1954, the Chicago Showprint Company charged Ringling-Barnum $5.18 for a nine-sheet and $3.45 for a six-sheet. An eighteen-sheet cost $11.55 per copy.

And then there were the passes. When Bobby Paul tacked banners for Ringling Bros.' World's Greatest Show of 1916 in St. Louis, he put up 205 sheets of banners and gave out orders for 240 tickets. A Chestnut Street saloon was festooned with fourteen sheets, another on Washington was decorated with twelve sheets. An empty down the street took sixteen sheets on the wall, while a hotel on Olive Street displayed twenty-three sheets of bright banners. The day's work took him on to more stores, cafes, liveries, and barns.

Bob Burns, a lithographer for a decade, spent one season in the 1940s as Ringling's banner squarer. It was little problem to square a "solid" building—one squared properly in seasons past. But some buildings were "hot," meaning they had been posted before without the owner's permission. This called for diplomacy.

If a potential location was controlled by a real estate company, Burns had to square his way up to the owner. Or he had to square his way down through the office secretary, the renter, the renter's wife, the janitor, and perhaps the neighbor on whose roof he would have to trepass. Either way, it took a fistful of ducats to get the spot squared.

Burns checked the main streets, looking especially for any big building correctly placed at a jog or curve. He called this a head-on hit, where oncoming traffic could see his banners from a couple of blocks away. In big cities, buildings along elevated railroad tracks were choice sites.

Sid Foote was a banner squarer for Ringling-Barnum in 1955 and 1956. "I would square my spots and then wait at the hotel for the crew," he said. "In each city we knew what hotel to use so everyone could be found in case of any change in plans. When the banner crew turned up, I went over the locations with them, advising of any particular problem on the buildings or with the

Big cities or small, banners were attention-grabbers. This was Hastings, Neb., in 1911. Gene Staats was banner squarer. Harry Raines, Walter Boan, and Harry Gensemer tacked the banners. There are 17 Ringling portrait banners; the show title appears forty-six times. In addition to banners on the walls, there are lithographs in the windows. **Mrs. Harry Gensemer.**

people involved. The crew knew I had squared the locations and given the necessary reserved seat ducats. I would then take off for the next town on the route. The crew would be up and on the job by 4 or 5 A.M. They always worked early so there was less confusion and fewer parked cars to get in their way.

"I was always well-dressed and presented my pitch in a business-like way to the building owners. I explained we wanted to put up cloth banners with a few tacks, that these banners were like a cloth American flag, that on circus day these banners would be removed. If I sensed any opposition, I pulled out a book of tickets and idly riffled through them as we talked. This usually weakened his negative attitude. We usually offered two to four tickets, depending upon how important the hit was to the circus. We never asked how many in the family, because the answer always was nine. It never failed.

"Many a time we could not locate the building owner. He might live in some other city. We would settle for the manager or someone from the realty office or even a janitor, but we had to have a signature on the posting contract."

Foote took on the task of squaring banners as Ringling prepared to open the 1955 season in New York. "Being eager to impress my boss, I checked over the area well and decided on Eighth Avenue. I went up the street block after block and squared some fine hits. The next day the crew tacked the banners, and when I looked it over I felt the street was really lit up.

"When I got back to the hotel, feeling good about what I had accomplished, I was met by the bill car manager, who promptly gave me a first-class 'reaming.' 'Those are great hits for the walking people,' he conceded, 'but that's a one-way street and every hit is behind the guy in the auto!' Lesson 1 was learned fast.

"I was only supposed to get the spots, but I also estimated how many sheets would be tacked at each one. It was helpful to the

Ringling banner men—tack spitters—placed this stand in a prominent spot in downtown Boston in 1934. The "terrific innovation" it promised was the Zacchini dual human cannonball act. **Circus World Museum.**

Cole Bros. banner men kindly left the man's parking lot sign but blanketed the rest of this wall with their huge display. There are nine-, sixteen-, and twenty-sheet posters along with numerous title bills and the ever-present date sheets. This 1935 stand in Chicago was the premier appearance of the new Cole circus. **Fred D. Pfening Jr.**

Tacks are visible in this banner display for Ringling at Milwaukee in 1945. Unlike other circus billing, banners usually were removed by the show after the date. Banner men and banner pullers both preferred to work with brick walls. Tacks were driven into the mortar. **Authors' Photo.**

banner men to know what to anticipate. I had no authority over the men. They could swing the building or use ladders from the ground. They knew their business well and went about it with dispatch."

Among such able banner men was Jim Crews, many years in the trade and working off of the advance cars of Hagenbeck-Wallace, Sells-Floto, Walter L. Main, Ringling-Barnum, and Sparks circuses. He always used an eight-ounce Robertson magnetic ham-

mer, as did most banner men. The tacks were heavily coated so that they would not pull out so easily.

Crews said that a good banner man was always in demand. If a rival show offered to raise a man's thirty-five-dollars wage by five dollars a week, he often would switch shows. One season he tacked banners for three different circuses. Each morning when Crews left the car to bill another stand in the 1930s, he carried two sixteen-foot ladders, his magnetic hammer, fifty pounds of

Parking lots were the bane of banner men's life. Space next to a blank wall often became a parking lot. To place banners, it was necessary to arrive early enough to beat the morning traffic and place ladders where cars would soon be left for the day. Moreover, a quantity of tacks often was dropped and that frequently meant damage claims for cars that developed flat tires. But this hit is square on the wall, any passing population is sure to see it, and the business for Ringling in Houston, 1941, was surely better because of it. **Joe M. Heiser Jr.**

Banner men were veritable circus aerialists. For this 1943 Chicago location, one ladder has been placed flat on the roof and an unseen man sits on it as a counter-balance. The banner man has lashed his ladder to the first one, then climbed down to work on his posters. His partner works from a third ladder based on the ground or adjacent roof. He tacked the left side of his banners first, then moved the ladder and now tacks the right sides, minimizing the number of times his ladder must be relocated. **Authors' Collection.**

tacks, and a small coil of rope. The tacks were divided between two canvas apron bags, twenty-five pounds in front, twenty-five pounds in back. He also carried the hod of pictorial and date sheet banners that he would tack that day. A cardinal rule proclaimed that one never returned at night with a date sheet. Pictorials could be used elsewhere, but dates were good only at one town and on one day.

On his ladder and hard at work, Crews would pop a handful of tacks into his mouth. With his tongue, he would position one so that the head would emerge from between his lips. At that instant, the magnetic hammer would pick up the tack, turn, and— whammo—strike the banner on the wall. Quickly, he would bring the hammer back for the next tack. The process was unbelievably fast, although a nine-sheet banner required about four pounds of tacks. Understandably, the banner men were called tack spitters. There was also the danger of breaking front teeth with the hammer or driving a tack through a fingertip as it moved along the mortar groove. And occasionally a banner man would swallow a tack.

Tacks were driven into the mortar, not the bricks. The forefinger of one hand would slide along the mortar joint to show where to spot the next tack. Crews hated Louisville because many of the brick buildings were so old that the mortar was soft, causing tacks to pull out too easily.

121

Veteran banner man Jim Crews demonstrates how he held his heavy, magnetized tack hammer. Some banner men shortened the handle of the hammer. **Authors' Photo.**

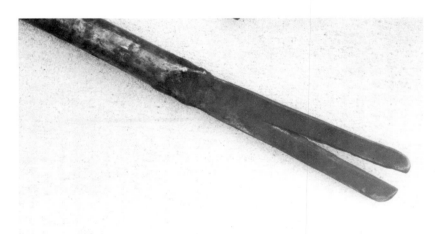

This forked tool was on a sixteen-foot handle and was used to remove tacks, roll up part of the banner, and then yank the whole thing off the wall. **Authors' Photo.**

Their banners in place, Carl Goehman and Delber Ulsted lower their ladders and prepare to move on to another site on behalf of Ringling-Barnum in 1933. **Circus World Museum.**

Development of cheap poster printing came first to those using wood blocks, among them the firm of James Reilley, which manufactured this poster for the Howes show of 1873. Use of pine blocks rather than mahogany and the advent of steam power for presses cleared the way for the use of posters in nearly unlimited quantities. **Circus World Museum.**

This creation for the Raymond menagerie in 1847 was the first in the proud and prolific stream of many-colored circus posters that have adorned so many walls and fences since. It was produced by Jared W. Bell, one of the pioneer show printers. **Circus World Museum.**

COLOR PLATE 2

Townsfolk of the 1850s were likely to be bug-eyed upon seeing any color printing at all, to say nothing of a huge eight-sheet poster depicting circus wonders. So this spectacular example drew wide attention when it heralded an appearance of the A. Turner & Co. Circus at Reading, Pa., on May 15, 1851. It was printed on wood blocks by the veteran showprint house of S. Booth, New York. Donated to the Circus World Museum in 1984 by Jim Dunwoody, the poster remained a display of brilliant colors after more than 134 years. **Circus World Museum.**

Another of the new era show printers was the great Courier Company, of Buffalo, New York, which handled many substantial orders from Ringling Bros. Circus. This poster for the show's 1903 spectacle was a Courier product. **Authors' Collection.**

COLOR PLATE 4

Poster work began with minatures of the proposed final product. This page from a printer's book carries the original art for a Sells Floto six-sheet. The Floto art demonstrates that occasionally circuses and their printers departed from the later norm in circus poster art. **Authors' Collection.**

Roadside country sheds were a billposter's happy hunting grounds. Veteran billers knew every such shed in state after state and pasted annual layers of bright circus paper on each side that was visible to traffic and some that weren't. **Authors' Photo.**

Long-handled brushes and paste buckets were tools of the billposters' trade. Circus billers might paste up a three-sheet on an established location like this. Or they might post hundreds of sheets of huge posters where no one expected to see them. **Authors' Photo.**

Above: One of the biggest posters ever created, this Buffalo Bill 100-sheet marvel is more than 87 feet long and nine feet high. It was used with two four-sheet end-pieces that brought the size to 108 sheets. From the left, there is a 20-sheet Indian battle scene, then a 24-sheet section of cowboy sports and a stagecoach in trouble. The 12-sheet center is a noble equestrian portrait of Cody himself. Then comes a 24-sheet combination of Rough Riders and acrobats. At the right end was a 20-sheet view of the Charge at San Juan Hill, which is missing now. This photograph was made from the 3.5x5-inch panels of original art from which the poster was first made in 1899. They and an original copy of the marvelous lithograph itself were hidden away in the basement of the Enquirer Printing Company for more than half a century, then discovered and acquired by the Circus World Museum. One of the end pieces describes the Cody show as something of a national treasure and the other tells about eh poster itself. **Circus World Museum.**

Left: This standard one-sheet, reproduced in scale, demonstrates the great contrast between the usual poster and the giant Sells Bros. and Buffalo Bill lithographs. **Authors' Collection.**

Left: Give the Sells Bros. billers a big enough fence and they were likely to startle the townsfolk with this 36-by-9-foot pictorial of the menagerie. The giant 48-sheet was produced by Strobridge in 1893. Typically, the same artwork was used in smaller sizes and sections to create standard sized posters and even pages in little couriers. Posters this large probably were rationed one per town. The original of the spectacular lithograph is as the Circus World Museum, Baraboo, Wisconsin.

Far Left: Color in newspapers of more than 100 years ago! Sells Bros. Circus accomplished this with two versions of its advertising in newspapers of Janesville, Wisconsin, and other cities on its 1881 route. The show supplied quantities of small colored pictures to the newspaper, and one by one these were "tipped in"—pasted into each copy of the edition. **Circus World Museum.**

Left: The Forepaugh circus gained color for its newspaper ads of 1891 by inking rollers on the press in a fashion that gave the paper a multi-colored background onto which the usual black type and artwork were imprinted. It startled readers in Keokuk, Iowa, and elsewhere, who were accustomed to monotonous grey make-up in their newspapers. **Circus World Museum.**

COLOR PLATE 10

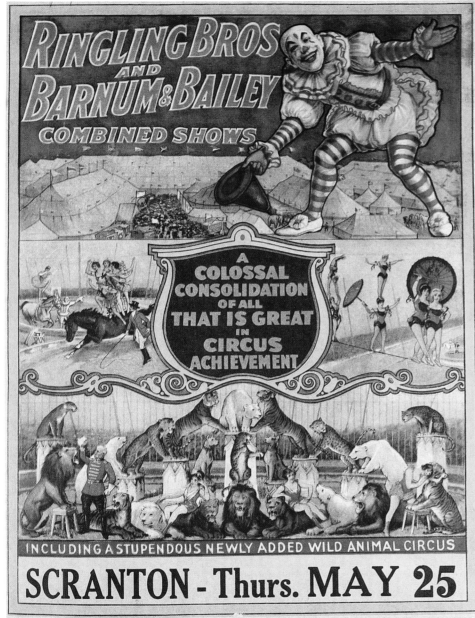

Attractive color printing marked circus couriers, which were among the earliest and most numerous examples of direct mail advertising. Shows sometimes used the post office services, sometimes hired boys to deliver them door-to-door or to take one to each place of business in town. This was the cover of a 1922 Ringling-Barnum courier, typical of many 16- and 24-page booklets crammed with extravagant circus verbiage. **Authors' Collection.**

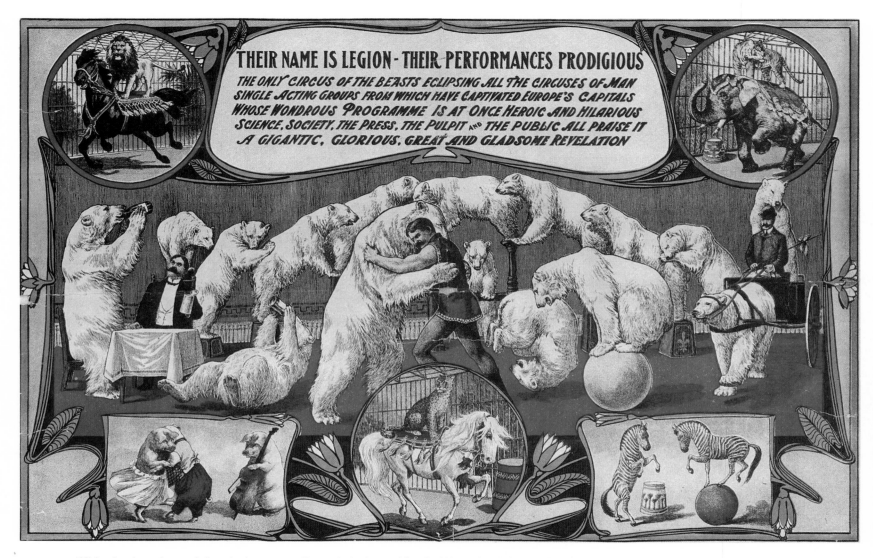

Wild animals and especially polar bears were the main features of the Carl Hagenbeck show, so it was to be expected that the centerfold of its 1906 courier would be a beautiful color spread of such performing beasts. Printers who produced posters often were the suppliers of color couriers as well. **Authors' Collection.**

COLOR PLATE 12

Circus heralds were everywhere. Advance crews stacked them in stores and stables, tossed them off the back of trains at each crossing, and passed them to pedestrians on the streets. They were used in seemingly endless quantities. In 1895 Ringling Bros. Circus displayed unusual color in its attractive herald. **Authors' Collection.**

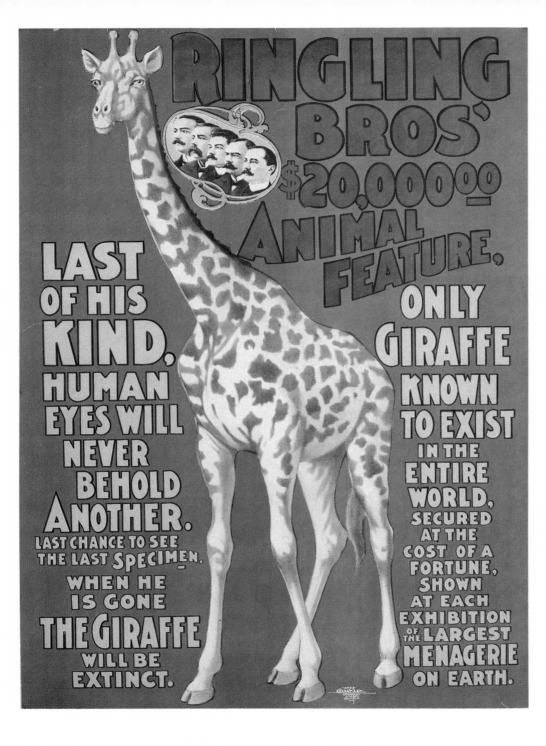

Bill writers were especially prone to the most imaginative copy, but this was beyond the usual limits even for that craft. Ringling Bros. Circus and others had giraffes both before and after this 1902 specimen. Only a year later the same circus advertised two giraffes, but the bill writers played it straight and did not claim a miracle. **Authors' Collection.**

Glorious golden bandwagons and dramatic tableau wagons were features in the great free street parades put forth by most circuses. Lithographs advertised the parade, which itself was an advertisement of the circus. Thousands of people lined the streets in town after town to see the parade — and likely as not decided then to buy tickets for the big show. **Circus World Museum.**

Special parade wagons transported the musical devices unique to circus parades. The Cooper & Bailey show boasted of a steam calliope and a chime of bells in this 1879 poster. **Ray Dirgo.**

·WORLD'S GREATEST SHOWS·

OFFICES AND QUARTERS (NOV. 1 TO APR 1) BARABOO, WIS.

CHICAGO OFFICES—140 MONROE ST. CHICAGO, ILL.

Baraboo, Wis., Jan. 18th, 1909.

Cleveland-Akron Bag Co.

Prices for cloth banners sumbitted and accepted.

1000---9 sheet Tiger,	84 x 122 inch.	$.75 each.	R.B.
1000---9 sheet Lion,	84 x 122 inch.	.75 each.	B.B.
1000---Streamers,	42 x 122 inch.	.27½ each.	R.B.
1000---Streamers,	42 x 122 inch.	.27½ each.	B.B.
1000---Portraits,	42 x 122 inch.4 col.Litho.	$.45 each.	R.B.
1000---Portraits,	42 x 122 inch.4 col.Litho.	$.45 each.	B.B.
500---Streamers,	42 x 244 inch.	$.60 each.	R.B.
500---Streamers	42 x 244 inch.	.60 each.	B.B.

Chas Ringling
for Ringling Bros & Barnum & Bailey

E. J. Warner
Cleveland-Akron Sign Co

By this memo, Charles Ringling agreed to the prices quoted for cloth banners in 1909. Most styles were ordered in lots of 1,000 each. The agreement covers both the Barnum and the Ringling show—"R.B." and "B.B." Mister Charles has written "Ringling Bros. & Barnum & Bailey" ten years before that combined title would become a single reality. **Hallie Olstadt Collection.**

COLE BROS. CIRCUS
(INCORPORATED)

N° 1387 .... 194......

I hereby grant the EXCLUSIVE PRIVILEGE to the above-named Shows to tack their cloth signs

on my .... at .... St.,

.... (city) from this date until the day after the Cole Bros.

Circus, have exhibited at .... 194 ...... Said signs not to be covered up or defaced, and no other advertising to be posted on said premise until after the date named above. In consideration of said privilege I have received an order for .... (......) Tickets, which is in full of all demands for the privilege above named. If there should be any disagreement or question about my right to grant the above permission, I agree to assume all responsibility for damages arising under this contract. It is further understood that no person, firm or corporation, other than Cole Bros. Circus, has any right, privilege or permission for the use of the above mentioned premises for advertising purposes.

This Order Good
$\frac{1}{9}$
Only On MAY 1 8 1945 ^{4}

I have not previously leased the above mentioned space to any circus.

JACK S. SMITH
.... Agent. .... Owner.

Form 18—1500—12-41   Exchange This Order for Tickets and Pay Federal Tax at Main Entrance if Required.

COLE BROS. CIRCUS
(INCORPORATED)

N° 1387 .... 194......

TREASURER: Pay to ....

.... Tickets for full and exclusive permission to tack Cole Bros. Circus'

Cloth Banners on my building .... at .... St., ... (city)

according to conditions set forth in a contract bearing even date and number herewith, any of the conditions of which if violated renders this check null and void. Said advertising is not to be covered up and no other Show's advertising to be posted on said premises until after the exhibition of Cole Bros. Circus at city here advertised.

This Order Good
$\frac{1}{9}$
Only On MAY 1 8 1945 $\quad4$

I have not previously leased the above mentioned space to any circus.

JACK S. SMITH
.... Agent.

Form 18—1500—12-41   Exchange This Order for Tickets and Pay Federal Tax at Main Entrance if Required.

Banner men used contract forms similar to those of the billposters and lithographers. Landlords agreed not only to allow the tacking but also to keep other show advertising away. Again, the show paid off in tickets. **Authors' Collection.**

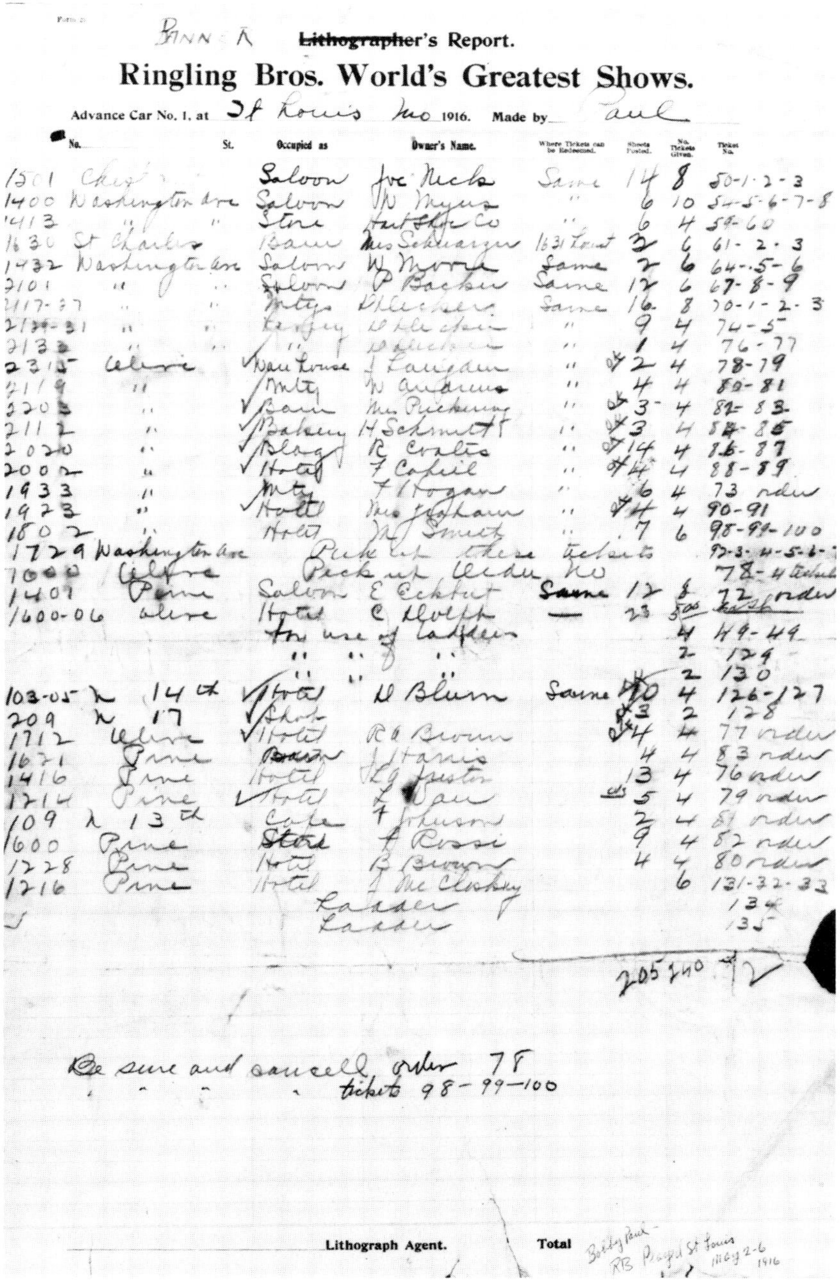

Banner ~~Lithographer~~'s Report.

Ringling Bros. World's Greatest Shows.

Advance Car No. 1, at St Louis Mo 1916. Made by Paul

No.	St.	Occupied as	Owner's Name.	Where Tickets can be Redeemed.	Sheets Posted.	No. Tickets Given.	Ticket No.
1501	Chest	Saloon	Joe Nick	Same	14	8	50-1-2-3
1400	Washington Ave	Saloon	W Myers	"	6	10	54-5-6-7-8
1413	"	Store	Hat Shop Co	"	6	4	59-60

Be sure and cancell order 78 tickets 98-99-100

Lithograph Agent. Total

A hard-working banner man on the Ringling Bros. advance of 1916 turned in this account of his work in advance of the show's St. Louis engagement. He tacked 205 sheets and gave up 240 tickets. **Authors' Collection.**

Two weeks before the show date in 1955, crews from the Ringling Advertising Car tacked these cloth banners on the brick wall. Pedestrians or motorists passing by were quick to see the huge red and black date sheets. **Ed Tracy Collection.**

Sizing up a situation, a banner man would decide whether to make a swing from the rooftop or tackle the job from the ground. To swing from the roof, he would lash the two ladders together to form a right angle. One sixteen-foot length would be laid on the roof, the other ladder would be hung down from the roof. One man would sit on the roof ladder, while the another would go over the side to tack. For high walls from the ground, they could lash two ladders together to reach twenty-eight or thirty feet. Guy ropes were tied to each side of the ladder; while one man tacked, two others would steady the ladder with the guy lines.

Swinging from ladders and fighting wind did not make the job particularly easy. Another hazard of the profession was being arrested for dropping tacks, many were dropped into the alleys, parking lots, or rooftops below. On one occasion, Crews was threatened with a fine of one dollar per dropped tack, but he squared that by agreeing to sweep the entire alley. Sometimes he eliminated this risk by unfolding a nine-sheet on the ground to catch the dropped tacks.

A cloth banner never was more than three sheets high. Anything larger would be too unwieldy and require more ladder changes, but several of the three-highs could be used together when desired. Title streamers were used across the top of pictorial and date combinations.

Jim Crews once took part in a banner man's kind of olympics. Headquarters for the American Circus Corporation was in Peru, Indiana, and three of its shows—John Robinson, Sells Floto, and Hagenbeck-Wallace—soon would open their 1929 season. They called in some 150 banner men and billposters to work a large brick building facing an empty lot. While all of the bill car bosses watched, waves of men posted their allocated sheets of paper. First, the billposters worked low, then the banner men went to work from their ladders. The bosses rated the men for speed, dexterity, and deftness, and the best were hired. Those who did not make the grade were accorded the usual circus courtesy— enough railroad script to take them wherever they wanted to go.

Crews quit tacking banners when the shows halted that kind of advertising in the 1950s. Oddly, when he quit swinging from ladders on high buildings, he developed acrophobia for the first time. The fear struck him in later years as he crossed high bridges or peered out of tall buildings. In another age, the circus press agents would have relished that story possibility.

In a sense, Joe Brown was the closing act of the circus and its advance crew. He was Ringling's lone banner puller. He tried to be in each town on show day so that if any problem arose, the show's legal adjuster could take care of it. This happened if the banner squarer had gotten his signature from the wrong man or if the banner man tacked up a hit that had not been squared at all. More routinely, Brown got a list of banner locations from the advance car manager. He, too, worked in early morning hours to avoid traffic in alleys and cars in parking lots. He had a truck with two eighteen-foot ladders and a supply of sixteen-foot poles equipped with special tools for removing tacks and banners.

To remove a banner, Brown started at the left side with his special forked tool fastened to the end of a pole. He pulled the edge loose, poking the fork through the banner. He proceeded to roll the banner on a pole, prying tacks out or jerking the muslin loose. When about half of a nine-sheet was rolled on the pole, there was enough weight so that one big yank would pull the rest of the banner free. On wood siding, the tacks often remained imbedded, while on brick walls, the tacks usually came free and were rolled up in the banner. If a building owner insisted, Brown produced another tool of his one-man trade—a spadelike device attached to another pole with which he could snap tacks out of the wall. Brown had still another device of his own design. He perfected a magnetized steel bar that accumulated most of the loose tacks that were missed by sweeping.

Whether to reuse banners was a question debated on circus advance cars. Removing them caused many rips, so banner men did not like to put the banner up a second time. But when economy was in order, various shows reclaimed banners, even to the point of salvaging the big red digits and reassembling them to comprise the date for a new town.

For Joe Brown, his job of banner puller was a sad one. "I'd like to see all that pretty artwork stay up forever," he said. But for the rest of the banner crew, it was a happy task, this decorating old bricks with new blue and red, all to herald the coming of the circus.

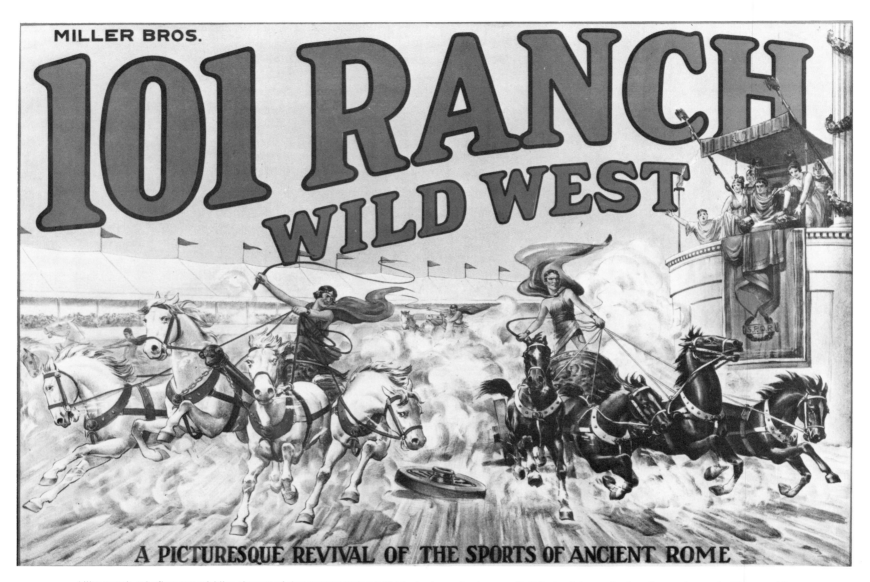

Lithograph art often caught the drama of dangerous acts and historical spectacles, as with this chariot race that performs at once for Caesar at the right and 101 Ranch Real Wild West at the left. **Authors' Collection.**

CHAPTER 6

The Lithographers

Senefelder, Courier, and Morgan—these were the lith-*ahhh*-graphers—artists indeed. Coming off the car each dawn in a new town were the *litho*-graphers—artists as well. They were the Eddie Jacksons, the Ed Cauperts, and the Sam Clausens—not the men who created the posters, but those who placed one-sheet lithographs in store windows.

After the billposters, lithographers made up the biggest portion of the advance crew. They started the day in the same way, making up their hods. Sometimes the half-sheets and one-sheets for lithographers arrived from the printers with the varieties already mixed together at random. More often, the lithographers had to "circus" their paper. In this, each variety was stacked in a pile, and the lithographer took from one and then another pile to create his collated hod. During the day, as he pulled each poster from the rolled supply, it would be different from the last, thus assuring variety in any hit that he made. The mix was in proportion to quantities on the shipping list.

There were posters in half- and one-sheet versions of the same art seen in the billposters' multiple-sheet paper. Lithographs might depict the menagerie or individual animals, the whole arena filled with aerialists, or maybe elephants, clowns, or performing horses. A popular variety made sure that everyone knew that this circus traveled by rail and therefore was to be considered gigantic. The assortment included a heavy share of parade lithographs. Often the most numerous were those that featured the title of the circus and portraits of its owners.

The large shows could afford special paper; that is, paper designed exclusively for them and, in many cases, illustrating features found only on their circus. A flat one-sheet was wider than deep—forty-two by twenty-eight inches. An upright one-sheet lithograph was longer than it was wide—twenty-eight by forty-two inches. There was also a one-sheet panel—twenty-one inches wide by fifty-four inches long, designed for narrow locations in store windows, or a one-half sheet panel, fourteen by forty-two inches.

An additional chore was attaching date strips, or date tails, to each lithograph. In addition to the separate date sheets already prepared, lithographers pasted smaller pieces of paper to each pictorial to provide the town and date information. Each man learned to riffle or stagger the sheets in his hod so that the edge of each poster was exposed. He spread paste on the series of edges and attached a date strip to each.

By the time the first shops opened, the lithographers were ready. Each man was given a route to follow for the day, and it was his job to post his hod of approximately 120 one-sheet and half-sheet pictorials and date sheets in store windows. This was good for about thirty locations. Typical was the route that Manager John Brassil gave to his lithographers for putting up paper in Richmond, Virigina, in the 1930s:

2 Men—Work West Broad Street from 3rd Street to 4400 block
—work all side streets one-half block.

1 Man—Work East Broad Street from 3rd Street to 34th Street—work all side streets after passing 18th Street.

2 Men—Work Main Street from Mulberry Street to Lester Street.

2 Men—Work Hull Street from Southern Depot to 42nd Street.

1 Man—Cary Street from 14th Street to Mulberry Street.

2 Men—Work 1st, 2nd, and 3rd streets from Cary to end of stores.

2 Men—Work following streets from Cary to end of stores: 4, 5, 6, 7, 8, 9, 10, 11, 12, 13, 14, 15, 16, 17, 18th streets.

1 Man—Work Clay Street from College to end of stores.

1 Man—Work Louisiana Street from Lester Street to Williamsburg Street; then Williamsburg from Fulton to Michelson.

1 Man—Marshall Street from 2nd Avenue to Meadow Bridge.

1 Man—Work Franklin Street and Grace Street—from Hamilton to College—than take streetcar to Meadow Bridge and 2nd Avenue. Work this section.

The routes chosen were usually on bus or streetcar lines. They were in commercial districts that had a great deal of local pedestrian and auto traffic. On his assigned routes through the city, each lithographer stepped into cafes, barbershops, garages, barrooms, and stores to convince the managers that circus posters should grace their front windows. A lithographer usually gave a shop owner free tickets for the privilege of posting the owner's windows. In the simple contract, the owner agreed to leave the paper up until the show date. If the lithographs were not in the store window when the inspector from the circus called, the store owner relinquished his right to the free tickets. Again, there had to be a signature. In occupied stores, this was less of a problem; if the man gave approval, he likely would sign the agreement. The trick was to be sure he had authority to sign.

But empty stores were a lithographer's special territory. Empties nearly disappeared in boom times but existed in quantity during depressions. A lithographer might find the owner and get the signature. Failing in that, he might find his own way into the vacant store and fill the entire window space with tidings of circus joy. The back of the shop might be filled with old paper pulled out of the window by earlier billers. If there was a lock on the door, any veteran lithographer's collection of skelton keys probably would eliminate that problem. On the way out, it might be well to jam the lock full of sand so that no landlord or rival billposter could get in too easily and tear out the paper.

The boss lithographer, if not the car manager himself, would inspect the day's work and know whether the lithographer was posting his hod in easy places or the better, more difficult, downtown locations. The ace performers were called "Main Street Lithographers," and there were tales of their convincing high-line fashion shops and banks to accept the circus posters.

Having gained permission, or at least access, the lithographer would attach small glued strips to each sheet. With his pair of six-foot sticks, the lithographer could place the poster high in the show window, level it, and rub the sticky tape so that the paper was in for good. Some men in some eras preferred to post lithographs at the top of show windows. Other men in other times preferred the lower portion. Each was careful to leave enough room for the storekeeper to see out; otherwise, he might tear out the posters before circus day. Each location was carefully recorded as to address, owner, and how many posters were hung, and this was turned in at the end of the day to the car manager.

The lithographers, like their billposter brethren, spoke familiarly to each other about specific locations remembered in each town. They recalled "that big empty on the hill beyond the stone bridge," or a particular auto supply store that would accept a great number of posters. If the lithographer later told the car manager that the owner of a good hit was still troublesome, the information would be filed away for the route list that next year's lithographers would receive.

Sid Foote joined out in 1953 as a lithographer on Ringling's bill car Number 1 under Manager John Brassil. In an interview, he had this to say:

"The first thing we had to do was circus the posters. You see, when we received a shipment from the printer they were bundled; for example, 500 clowns, 500 tiger acts, 500 hippos, and so on. Now it would not do to grab your hod from one bundle because your entire route would be all hippo posters. So we opened all the bundles and laid the posters on the work bench. Then the gang lined up and went down the line taking one poster of each design and stacking them at the end of the line. Then we would start through the line again. Very quickly the posters were well mixed — we circused the posters.

"The second step was to date up the posters. Each man had to date up his own hod, which varied in size but was generally 120 to 150 posters. He would brush the edges with paste and lay on the date strips. It was a quick and easy operation once a man got the knack. We also had to put the Billposters' Union stamp on each poster.

"The car manager gave the orders. It was never guesswork. First of all, he knew his crew. Some guys always got the skid row routes where any dummy could get his paper up. Others worked 'in the shine' — the downtown area where a little finesse helped get the paper up. When the manager gave you a route, he let you know he wanted locations — the more the better. Filling one or two empty stores with paper made a flashy hit and the lithographer liked them, as they would quickly lighten his load. But the car manager always told his men to spread out the paper to cover the route. And no 'pencilling;' if the checker-up found evidence of phoney names and addresses on a daily report, it was tough on the lithographer and sometimes cost him his job.

"At the end of the day, occasionally a lithographer would complain that he was given a 'field and stream' route. He was upset because there were great gaps of empty fields or block after block of homes with no place to post his paper. The car manager, knowing the routes from previous seasons, would tell a man to 'bend the corners,' go down the side streets for two or three stores and post his paper, then return to the main street.

"An old-timer named Eddie Jackson taught me the ropes. He explained the importance of getting grime, oil film, or dust off glass where you will rub in your stickers; otherwise they just won't hold. Get the stickers on the posters square. Two for a half-sheet, and three for a one-sheet. Hang the posters square with the window frame so from the outside they look neat. Eddie said he never put the stickers on the posters until the store owner said it was okay to hang. If you had stickers on posters ahead of time and got caught in the rain, you would have a mess.

"When we found an empty and could not find the store owner, we tried the front or back doors. Frequently, one or the other was unlocked, or perhaps a rear window was open. We went in, did our posting, and got out quick. Sometimes we would leave three or four ducats taped to the door. This would cool off the owner."

Once, almost all work was billposting, but later, lithographers came into their own. Then storekeepers began using window space for their own posters, and architecture changed, making fewer places for lithographers to work. Chain stores did not like lithographs.

Circuses cut back on the number of men in each billing category. In the most recent decade or two, many sizable circuses limited their wall and window work to that accomplished by few, perhaps even one man. They might use a few lithographs and fewer multiple sheets per day, but mostly they had date sheets on card stock that they stapled to telephone poles. Little there for a proud biller to stand off and admire! But usually there were many lithographers, much paper, and good reason to be proud of work well done. They often were unabashed in their sentiment for a big stand of paper.

Veteran lithographer Eddie Jackson found a huge empty store on his route in Milwaukee in 1951. Locating the owner, he got permission to hang his Ringling paper — twenty-three date sheets and thirty-two lithographs. After the job was done, the soft-spoken lithographer went across the street to better see and admire his artistic work. "My, that's beautiful," he said to himself. And to an observer he added, "It's right on an important bus line, too!"

After many windows, many shops, many steps, the day's work would be done. The route would be billed. His hod gone, the lithographer would turn to go back. All over the town and county, other lithographers and billposters also were retreading the long blocks and miles back to the bill car. They were ready to leave a town that was newly brilliant with circus posters, a town that could not help but know that the great show was coming.

Circus under glass—posters were placed in store windows by the show's lithographers. This was part of a windowful of Hagenbeck-Wallace one-sheets at Natchez, Miss., in 1934. It was done much the same way for a hundred years before and half a century since. **Joe M. Heiser Jr.**

Empty store fronts were a lithographer's goal. Here he could place a good number of his day's hod and get a strong showing. Typically, Cristiani Bros. Circus used a variety of one-sheet pictorials and date sheets in 1958. **Authors' Photo.**

Left: "Window work" brought circus billing downtown. For whatever reason the photo was taken, it preserves a view of Great Wallace Circus paper in a Springfield, Ill., store in 1903. **Illinois State Historical Society. Right:** The flags and crowd suggest the Fourth of July—or circus day—at Boonville, N.Y., in 1909. Mr. Ryder's store displays paper for the Sparks Circus. **Ron Ryder.**

Ringling paper fills the windows of a Madison, N.Y., storefront, advertising the Utica stand in 1947. **Circus World Museum**.

Kelly-Miller lithographers filled this empty store on the main street of Fort Atkinson, Wis., in 1962. **Author's Photo**.

And Beatty-Cole lithographers showed their wares at a Winter Haven, Florida, store in 1975. **Author's Photo**.

Circus veteran George Gallo recreates the lithographer's procedures. Two sticks are tools of the trade for placing the poster and rubbing the stickers into place. **Authors' Photo.**

His efforts on display, the lithographer glances at the newly placed posters as he moves down the street to square another location. **Authors' Photo.**

Sometimes the lithograph printers supplied the show with free supplies of stickers for use in windows. A half-sheet required two stickers, a one-sheet, three. **Authors' Collection**.

Like his co-workers with billposting and banners, the lithographer used a two-part contract and ticket order. The shop owner agreed to keep the posters in place until circus day. The circus reimbursed him with free passes. The procedure was the same for Wm. P. Hall in 1905 or a circus today. **Authors' Collection**.

THE GREAT WM. P. HALL SHOWS

Lithograph Order, Car 2   No. 5325

--------------------------------------1905.

I have this day leased to the above-named Shows, full and exclusive permission to display_____Lithographs

at No._____street, and to remain undisturbed until after the date of the

above-named Shows at_____
In consideration of the above, I have this day received an order, bearing duplicate number and date

to this contract, which will pass_____persons.

This Order is Not Transferable, and no other Lithographs will be allowed in my windows until after date above named.

Owner or Agent.

The highest single figure or numeral in this column indicates the number of persons this order will admit **AT ONE TIME ONLY**

1/2

No. 5325

NOTE–This order is of no money value and is also null and void when used for purposes other than designated, and in no case will it be recognized unless the contract for which it was given has been strictly carried out.

THE GREAT WM. P. HALL SHOWS

Order for Admission, Lithograph Order, Car 2

On presentation of this order you will please grant_____admissions **only** to your Exhibition in consideration of the EXCLUSIVE privilege of displaying_____Lithographs in his windows at_____street city of_____

until date of Show.

----------------------------------- **Manager**

This order for admission must always be ready for presentation when called for. **No Half-Tickets Allowed.**

Adv. Agt.

To display a one-sheet on the side of the bill car, a 1923 World Bros. lithographer manipulates the sticks of his trade in the same way he would to place the paper in a store window. **Circus World Museum.**

Early posters utilized detailed scenes and extensive type; the public then would stop long enough to read it all. The Doris show in 1883 conducted a history lesson with this Strobridge product. **Authors' Collection.**

A MONSTER HERD OF AMERICAN WHITE ANTELOPE AND DEER.

The John Robinson Circus bought Russell-Morgan paper to advertise its animals; it rarely passed up a chance to mention its big spectacle as well. **Library of Congress.**

Flag etiquette was different when Strobridge artists made up this lithograph for W.W. Cole's lady principal riders of 1882. The trio of ringmaster, clown and rider was typical of most riding acts. **Cincinnati Art Museum.**

139

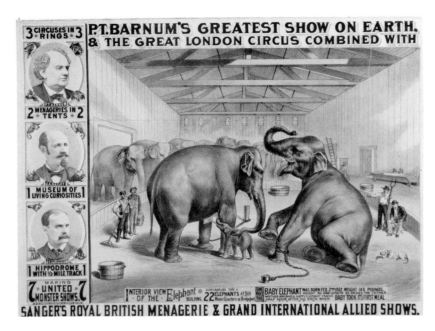

Shows often produced lithographs in a series. The Barnum & London show had many posters that included the three portraits alongside varying main art. This one depicts a newly born baby elephant. **Cincinnati Art Museum.**

Left: In a later series, the portraits of Bailey and Barnum, along with the show title, appeared on an extensive number of posters, while the main picture varied from poster to poster. This series was in use in the 1890s. **Circus World Museum. Above:** Finely detailed art marked the animal posters for Sig Sautelle's show in 1900, printed by Erie Lithographing. **Circus World Museum.**

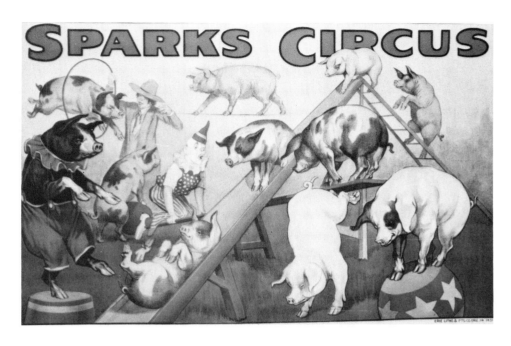

Pigs on the Sparks show or elephants with Cole Bros., the posters of Erie artists took on an identifiable style, as did those of other printers. **Circus World Museum.**

Opposite Page, Left: In addition to the standard half- and one-sheet posters, each in both flat and upright configurations, circus lithographers sometimes had half- or one-sheet panels—intended for tall, narrow window spaces. Robbins Bros. used this 14 x 42 panel in 1938. **Authors' Collection. Opposite Page, Right:** Sometimes circuses departed from their standard poster art form and experimented with other art styles, but never successfully or for very long. Courier did this 1896 half-sheet for Ringling Bros. **Circus World Museum. Above:** Similarly, the Ringling-Barnum show experimented in 1928. Fragmentation of "the Greatest Show on Earth" slogan hardly seemed promising, however. **Authors' Collection.**

Left: Closing of several shows in the 1930s left the Ringling organization with great supplies of posters for inactive show titles. As an economy move, someone spent the winter scissoring the titles away and pasting the assorted half-sheets into single posters for the 1934 Al G. Barnes outfit. The top portion was a Barnes half-sheet; the middle scene had been a Sells Floto poster and the lower third was once a Sparks half-sheet. Other combinations used up old John Robinson paper and some became new varieties for Hagenbeck-Wallace. **Circus World Museum. Below:** Separate date strips with special information on time and place had evolved well before John B. Doris Circus billed Providence, R.I., in 1883. The localized strips were pasted to the bottom of the lithographed pictorial one-sheet. **Authors' Collection.**

The same style of date strip was used throughout most of the heyday of circus billing. This was the Tom Mix Circus example in 1935. Lithographers pasted the strips to the lithos before starting on their routes each day. **Circus World Museum.**

While some circuses continued the use of date strips, the Ringling circus designed posters in the 1970s and 1980s which called for imprinting local information directly on the one-sheet. By this time, the show was using very little window work and had no billers or lithographers of its own. **Ringling Bros. and Barnum & Bailey Circus.**

Billing practices changed for some other circuses as well. The Beatty-Cole show cut back on pictorial lithographs and used mostly window cards. The cards were taped to the exterior of store windows. **Authors'-Photos.**

Other billing often was restricted to more cards stapled to utility poles. Here George Gallo staples two cards back to back, higher on the pole. **Authors' Photos.**

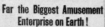

Far the Biggest Amusement
Enterprise on Earth !

THE BIGGEST MARVEL

TWENTY TIMES THE

SMALLEST LIVING ELEPHANT!

LIVING HIPOPOTAMUSES!

The Biggest Natural History Sensation,

The Only Pair of Living

Woolly Elephants

THE BIGGEST AND ONLY

Towering, Living Giraffe.

$22,000 TWO-HORNED WHITE RHINOCEROS.

6 PERFORMING COLORADO CATTLE.

THE BIGGEST AND ONLY

$50,000 ARCTIC AQUARIUM

OF AMPHIBIOUS MONSTERS.

MIGHTY MANDRILL

ODDLY TINTED OF ALL ANIMALS.

ON TUESDAY JUNE 28.
And Not One Hour Sooner or Later,
IS THE TRANSCENDENT WONDER DAY OF THE
BIGGEST IN THE WORLD.

SELLS BROTHERS'
BIG MILLIONAIRE CONFEDERATION
OF

BIG RAILROAD SHOWS,   **BIG FREE ROMAN HIPPODROME!**

Will positively pitch its big tents, and make the biggest day on record, at

Wooster, Tuesday, June 28th

One Ticket Admits to all the Advertised Big Shows.
CHILDREN UNDER NINE YEARS, HALF PRICE.
ONE THOUSAND EXTRA FOLDING OPERA CHAIRS.

Two Exhibitions Daily. Afternoon and Evening.

Low Excursion Rates on all Railroads.   Remember the Date, Absolute, Fixed and Unalterable.

TUESDAY, JUNE 28.

THE BIGGEST and ONLY

Pair of Full Crown

Polar Bears !

The Biggest $200,000 Herd of

Elephants & Camels

The Biggest Bareback Equestrian,

JAMES ROBINSON !

THE GREAT,

The Biggest Creedmoor Champions

Baughman and Butler

The Biggest Asiatic Marvels,

KING SARBROS'

ROYAL JAPANESE CIRCUS

The Biggest Arena of Performing Animals

FULLY SIXTY TONS
OF
Educated Beasts !

The Biggest Fun for the Little Folks

WILLIS COBB'S $25,000 MINIATURE CIRCUS !
OF TRAINED DOGS, GOATS AND MONKEYS.

Circuses pioneered in the use of full-page ads. This one was placed by Sells Bros. Circus at Wooster, Ohio, in 1881. **Authors' Collection.**

CHAPTER 7

Newspaper Advertising

As a circus launched its advertising campaign, the pages of local newspapers blossomed with distinctive display ads that grabbed attention and declared that the show was on its way. Circuses were expert in designing unusual ads; they had been since the beginning of both advertising and circuses. Show ads were new and different from those that one was accustomed to seeing in the paper. In part, that was because of the artwork—clowns and animals were not seen every day. In part, it was because of the type faces—unusual lettering, sometimes large, sometimes compact and busy. And it was because the show's title signature or logo was unfamiliar; it stood out amid the other advertisers' names that were well-known locally.

A circus newspaper advertising campaign began with the arrival of the advance car. The contracting press agent usually was aboard, although he sometimes traveled apart from the car. While the billers were at work elsewhere, he called on the local newspapers and placed orders for ads to appear. With the car two weeks ahead, his ads might run from ten to fourteen days in front of the show date. The agent provided the newspaper with advertising material. He determined the size and the dates on which the ad was to appear. He filled in the local information about show-grounds and street parades. He also left an assortment of publicity stories and pictures for the editorial side to use.

In the earliest decades, general newspaper advertising approximated today's classified format. There was no national advertising.

Local ads were merely directory listings in most cases, and always they were quite plain. Circuses broke out of that boundary with their first ads and continued to make trail-blazing improvements in technique thereafter.

Even before the first American circus, distinctive newspaper advertisements heralded bareback riders, lions, and rope dancers in their separate appearances. The first show, Ricketts, used newspaper advertising in April 1793, and by September it had included a woodcut illustration in the ads. The Lailson show of 1794 attracted attention with unusual display type in its ads. And West's Amphitheater at Charleston, South Carolina, in 1817 had a particularly good mix of display and body type in its newspaper advertising.

Some of the earliest shows, especially those of the Zoological Institute, made use of special layout techniques right at the outset. There were eye-catching logos to announce the name of the show in special art. Shows made use of white space, reverse cuts, startling drawings, and uniquely shaped blocks of body type. All of this was new to advertising, to newspapers, and to readers. Other shows followed. Usually, the public, represented by local advertisers, was years behind.

As early in 1835, shows were using bigger, wider ads than anyone else. In a five-column, twelve-inch display ad, the New England Zoological Exhibition told readers that it would bring wild animals, a hot air balloon, and such a famous rider as Richard

Monday Evening.

Genteel and furprifing *Feats* of *Activity*, At the Affembly Room, PORTSMOUTH.

Don Pedro Cloris,

The principal Performer in *Donegani's* Company, who exhibited fome years fince, with great applaufe in this town— has the honor to inform the Ladies and Gentlemen that on MONDAY next, Aug. 8, he will perform curious feats of activity on the

WIRE,

AND

Extraordinary balancing. Likewife,

Tumbling Feats,

In a furprifing manner.

Dances the Spanifh Fandango, blindfolded, over thirteen EGGS, placed in different fituations, and, imitating the drunkard, ftaggers amongft them, without breaking. *To which will be added, a great variety of entertaining Performances on the*

SLACK ROPE.

Merryman, the *Clown,*

will perform a number of tricks and feats.

☞ Tickets of admiffion may be had at the place of performance—price 2/3. Children 1/6.

Doors opened at 7, and performance to begin at 8 o'clock.

N. B. The particulars are expreffed in the hand bill of the day.

Sands to Concord, New Hampshire, on May 12. Twelve inches on five columns—when local ads ran an inch or two on a single column!

Another special logotype replaced ordinary type in proclaiming the coming of Purdy, Welch & McComber's show in 1837. A few years later, Spalding & Rogers had not only such a logo, but also a long illustration along one edge of its single-column ad, and Howes European Circus used a logo plus a tall edge drawing of its street parade. There was nothing else like it in the papers.

By this time, cuts, or drawings, were routine in all circus ads, but not in others. Shows often used one-column-by-five-inch space, usually the largest in the paper. Herr Driesbach's Menagerie ad benefitted from a fancy art border that set off the ad from the rest of the page. L. B. Lent ads in the 1850s featured many cuts with only a small amount of type. The familiar names of Purcell and Morse appeared as makers of the engravings. While most circus advertising was becoming more sophisticated, there was at least one misstep: the Franconi Hippodrome in 1853 used some ads in an odd editorial type of layout. It filled one column and then jumped to a few inches in the next column as if it were a news story.

By the 1850s, other ads had started to follow the circus lead. Among the first were stagecoach, railroad, and steamship schedules with small drawings of appropriate vehicles to head up the arrive-and-depart columns. Circuses, however, consistently stayed ahead of others in development of advertising techniques.

These circus advances appeared almost every place but one. Last to change were the newspapers of New York City—and those in a few villages. Apparently, those printers did not have or

C I R C U S,

GREENWICH-STREET;

TO MORROW Evening, 13th September,
Will be added, to a great variety of
SURPRISING FEATS OF
H O R S E M A N S H I P,
Mr. RICKETTS will
LEAP FROM ONE HORSE, in full speed,
THROUGH A HOOP, suspended 12 feet
high, and recover his situation on the other
side——This Feat never performed by any but
himself.

He will likewise, by PARTICULAR DESIRE,
perform the MANUEL EXERCISE on Horseback.

The TWO FLYING MERCURIES.

DOORS open at 4 o'clock—to begin precisely at a
quarter after five o'clock.   Sept. 12.

B L O W N   S A L T.

TWO Thousand Bushels fine Liverpool SALT, for
sale, on board the Ship Active, lying at Jackson's
Wharf apply to William Dodge, or
                            JOHN DUFFIE & Co.
Sept. 12, dtf   Old Slip.

did not want to use adequate display type. But showmen managed. Where the eighteen- or twenty-four-point type was ruled out, circus agents had the same material set in eight- or ten-point type, had it set three or four times, then stacked the duplicate lines on top of each other. This approximated the eye-catching appeal of large type and came off as the largest material on the page. Barnum used this device to announce Lavinia Warren, the tiny lady who eventually became the bride of Tom Thumb. The ad had no art and no large type, just the repetition of each main line several times before going on to the next.

In regional newspapers, circus ads not only spoke to the local engagement but sometimes announced the show's plan to tour the surrounding area. Thus, in the *Chicago Tribune*, L. B. Lent's Circus announced that it would play Chicago three days in June 1864 and that it would "exhibit in all the principal cities and towns throughout Illinois and Wisconsin" during that summer. Then it listed a month's route (in Illinois and Iowa, not Wisconsin). The idea was that through the exchange of papers among editors, others would see that the show was coming their way. Some such ads told local editors that a circus agent would arrive so many days ahead of the circus.

Continuing to develop advertising methods, such circuses as the Howes and Robinson shows made use of thumbnail cuts—small drawings about one-third of a column wide—with assorted ornate type in the other portions. In contrast, the brash Mike Lipman Circus of 1866 stacked big cuts and big type in its full two-column ads. The Yankee Robinson Circus continually utilized great selections of unusual type faces.

Use of white space was prominent in the Maginley & Carroll

From the outset, circus advertising dominated everything else in local newspapers. When June, Titus, & Angevine placed this ad in Albion, N.Y., in 1834, no other ads were more than a single column wide. None was so large. None had any illustrations to equal the circus. The show's title logo was quite unusual in the newspaper filled with hand-set type. **Authors' Collection.**

JUNE & TURNER, Proprietors.

THE Proprietors would most respectfully announce to the citizens of URBANA and vicinity, that their Equestrian Troupe will open in this place for exhibition, on

Wednesday, the 1st day of Oct., 1845.

The scenes in the circle will be introduced with the utmost order and regularity, and will combine Horsemanship, Vaulting, Tumbling, Dancing, Singing, Posturing, Pyramidical Devices or Animated Architecture, Air Diving, Juggling, Living Pictures and Classic Statuary, Comic Songs, and Fancy Dances, together with the Congo Screnaders. The whole to be enlivened by a first rate BAND OF MUSIC.

The managers pledge themselves that the whole shall be conducted with a strict regard to chastity, morality and virtue.

Doors open at 1½ o'clock. Performance to commence at 2 o'clock, P. M.

☞ ADMISSION: Box 30 cents—Pit 20 cents—Children to Box 20 cents.

Sept. 16, 1845.

☞ The above will be exhibited at *West Liberty*, on *Tuesday*, the 30th inst.

Far Left: Extensive use of illustrations and reverse printing set Van Amburgh's advertising apart from everything else in the newspapers of 1836. **Lebanon (Pa.) Historical Society. Left:** By the time this 1845 example appeared, nearly every circus ad included an illustration and nearly no other cuts appeared in most newspapers. The June & Turner ad was typical of many. **Authors' Collection.**

MISS CASTELLA'S GRAND ÆRIAL ASCENSION!

She will walk and wheel a Wheelbarrow on a Single Wire, 300 feet in length, to the topmost height of the towering Pavillion of NORTH'S NA
TIONAL CIRCUS, every day previous to the opening of the Afternoon Performance. She *being the only person in the world* that can accomplish thi
Wonderful, Daring, ann Beautiful Act of the WALK IN MID AIR! which is given outside the Canvas, as represented in the Cut above, and is
FREE FOR ALL TO WITNESS WITHOUT COST!

LEVI J. NORTH'S

NATIONAL CIRCUS OF THREE COMBINED COMPANIES!

North's Great National Circus, (from the National Amphitheater, Chicago,) being the only Legitimate Circus in the West

Levi North's Circus displayed numerous drawings and a variety of type faces in 1857. The wood cut had been made by the well-known Morse shop. **Circus World Museum.**

154

Lacking type of sufficient size to get the desired effect, shows hit upon the device of repeating each line several times. By this move, Nixon & Co's Mammoth Circus drew extra attention to its 1859 newspaper ad. **Circus World Museum**.

Circus ads for Clinton, Iowa, in 1867. That circus also experimented with display type placed in a spokelike configuration and set small body type in an hourglass shape rather than plain rectangular blocks—all to gain greater attention.

The John Robinson Circus realized the merits of the reverse— of white type on a black background for its logo of 1871. Van Amburgh bought a full page in each of its 1870 towns, filling part of it with a big advertisement and the rest with news-type articles about the circus, all under its own newspaper-style masthead. Circuses were finding more ways to make newspaper advertising effective.

In the 1870s, full-page circus ads, splashed with big type and many illustrations, were commonplace. This was a period of peak newspaper usage. More advertisers were following the circus lead. Now local space buyers were using larger ads and distinctive type faces. National advertising expanded beyond the circus ads to include eye-stopping displays from plow manufacturers and circuslike patent medicine ads.

For nearly a century, circus advertising had stayed ahead of others, usually with progressively bigger ads, innovative layout, and more illustrations. But at the full-page level, shows struck a ceiling, and local advertisers began to catch up. So, circuses took a new tack. They dropped ad size and devised new typography. In the 1880s, many circus ads ran two full columns or more; in the 1890s, the typical show space was about half of that. But the art and layout were unique, and the compact use of varied type transmitted a busy and exciting element.

In that period, circuses provided their own art in the form of loose engravings or woodblocks for each newspaper. (On show day, they retrieved the cuts for use again elsewhere). Shows also supplied the text, or copy, but often it was set into type locally by each newspaper. The procedure left much of the style and creativity to local printers, not the show, and the final product dependent upon the local paper's fonts of type. That began to change in 1896, when a frisky young show, Ringling Bros., provided each paper with an engraving or plate of the entire ad, type and all, in one piece prepared in advance. Nothing was left to chance. The circus bill writers and artists developed the entire ad,

making maximum use of typographic features, using all of the space well, and allowing local printers to add only the date and name of the town. This, too, had been done before, notably by the Spalding & Rogers show in the 1850s, but there was a lapse and now it was revived. In the second season, Ringling devised a scheme for fitting several preset plates together so that the ad could be expanded or contracted as desired in each town. In the third year, the John Robinson Circus used the same plan. Then Norris & Rowe and the Great Wallace Circus followed in 1904 and 1906. Between then and 1912, nearly every other show adopted the fully produced ad, often with much reverse and some with circular logos. Hagenbeck, Sells Floto, Barnum & Bailey, and Forepaugh joined in. Often, their ads were made by the same show printers and artists who did their posters.

The 101 Ranch Real Wild West Show introduced the next departure; from 1908 to 1913 it used several different styles of ads in each city. There had been isolated cases of this before, Forepaugh among them. But the Ranch now set a trend. A contracting press agent had six or eight different styles of ads and instructed the newspaper to use different ones on different days during the campaign.

The Walter L. Main Circus began using a different ad each day of a local campaign in 1921, and the American Circus Corporation's outfits—Hagenbeck, Floto, and Robinson—started the practice in 1923. By 1926, the only significant holdout was Ringling Bros. and Barnum & Bailey Combined Shows. It held to an old pattern of using either one large design or a small alternative, depending upon how high the local ad rates might be. Ringling-

Barnum changed during the 1930s. The newly prominent motorized shows—Barnett, Downie, Tom Mix, and Seils-Sterling—also began changing ads daily in each town then.

At the outset, circus ads often buried the name of the town and the date in a mass of tiny body type. It was sufficient to say that the show was coming; readers apparently knew when and where, probably because of billing. But over the years this changed, too, and press agents gave greater attention to date and town. By the 1920s, they had decided that the only place to put this information was at the top, not the bottom, of the ad, with the date set in the largest possible numerals and a clean, boldface type to blare out the name of the town. Some latter-day press agents ridiculed any newcomer who did not follow this rule.

In the 1940s, the Ringling-Barnum show developed a striking format for announcing the start of a new season in Madison Square Garden. In New York papers they ran a full-length, single-column ad that led off with remarkable logo art by Roland Butler. Then they sprinkled small drawings of new acts in with the varied and unique type for the rest of the space. It was a throwback to Spalding, Lent, and Howes, but it was most effective in getting attention in the grim, gray *New York Times*, where rates and rules prohibited much innovation. Each spring that kind of ad appeared on a Sunday or two. Most other New York circus ads were small.

In this era, the Clyde Beatty, Cole Bros., Dailey Bros., and Russell Bros. circuses were making good use of newspaper ads. And after them came the King show, displaying the special skills of Floyd King. But the Al G. Kelly & Miller Bros. Circus in particular had an elaborate campaign for its route of county seats. It began with a big daily ad for the show itself, perhaps two- or three-columns by ten or fifteen inches. This was augmented by even larger tie-in ads that featured both the circus and the local dealers for national ad connections—Chevrolet, Philco, and others. A separate ad announced that the circus wanted to buy large quantities of horse meat, hay, and feed. The show actually needed the supplies, but this ad had the extra benefit of telling the populace again that this was a big show with many wild animals, horses, and elephants. Kelly-Miller also made masterful use of coupons. Its most successful campaign provided that the lady of

When the Dan Castello Circus played Denver on its way to California in 1869, its advertising overpowered everything else on the pages of the Rocky Mountain News. **Denver Public Library.**

RICE LAKE ONE DAY ONLY THURSDAY JULY 24

"AU REVOIR" RECEPTION

Another European Tour Arranged for This 1902

SUPERLATIVELY POPULAR HISTORICAL ENTERTAINMENT.

BUFFALO BILL'S WILD WEST

AND ROUGH RIDERS OF THE WORLD.

An Educational Exhibition | LIVING OBJECT LESSONS

That really means something.

A Veritable Kindergarten of History

Teaching facts and not on fiction founded.

FEATURE PILED ON FEATURE

This season surpasses its own stupendous self.

MORE Peerless Riders, Warlike Pageants, Chivalrous Characters, Strange People,

Than ever before presented.

NEW Nations and Nomads, Pictures of Border Life, Equestrian Feats and Skill, Scouts, Soldiers and Horses,

Fresh from field and foray.

FEATURES U. S. LIFE-SAVERS. ATLANTIC COAST GUARDS. Thrilling Rescues by the Breeches Buoy.

All under the personal command of "The King of Them All",

COL. W. F. CODY, "BUFFALO BILL"

And NATE SALSBURY, Director-General.

Taken from the pages of realism, and illustrated by the very men who have assisted in making the fame of the

World's Mounted Warriors

Together with those true born Pioneers of the Plains who have told the story of progress in the Great Drama of Civilization. New and interesting arrangement of well-known Wild West Incidents, such as

The Stage Coach "Hold Up", Cowboy "Round Up", and Attack on the Emigrant Train.

GRAND FREE STREET REVIEW

On the morning of Exhibition, exact hour and route of parade to be announced.

The piece de resistance being the vivid and

THRILLING MILITARY SPECTACLE OF THE BATTLE OF SAN JUAN HILL

TWO PERFORMANCES DAILY, 2 AND 8 P. M., RAIN OR SHINE

One Ticket Admits to All   Children Half Price

Reserved Seats on Sale day of Exhibition at Heintz's Drug Store.

Buffalo Bill's Wild West enlisted the assistance of artists at the Courier Co., poster printers, for illustrating its newspaper ads. Type and art were interwoven for unusual effect. **Greg Parkinson.**

The Great Wallace Show's newspaper art was picked up directly from its poster and courier art by Erie Lithographing Co. Such ads left less to local printers and assured the same results in each city. **Authors' Collection.**

CIRCUS, GALESBURG, FRIDAY, AUGUST 21.

Admission Tickets and numbered reserved seats will be on sale show day in the drug store of **JUDSON W. HOOVER AND CO., 251 MAIN ST.**, at exactly the same price charged in the regular ticket wagons on the show grounds.

Left Page and This Page: Ringling Bros. experimented with ad styles at the turn of the century. Fortunately, the 1897 jumble of irregular reverse lines set no lasting trend. The picture frame drew reader attention in 1896 newspapers. The 1908 circle surrounding the title and flanked by drawings gave the desired results. Others, including Hagenbeck-Wallace, imitated the style thereafter. From this era onward, shows supplied plates of pre-set ads, leaving local printers little to add or change. **Authors' Collection.**

Tickets on Sale Show Day at McIntyre's Drug Store, 25th and Washington, at same prices charged on Show Grounds.

161

STANLEY, THURSDAY, **JULY 30**

Grand Street Parade at 10:30 a. m.

MORAL, ENTERTAINING AND INSTRUCTIVE.

SPARKS

WORLD-FAMOUS

SHOWS

THE SHOW THAT NEVER BROKE A PROMISE.

25 YEARS OF HONEST DEALING WITH THE PUBLIC.

A TREMENDOUS EXHIBITION OF WEALTH AND SPLENDOR

PERFECT SPECIMENS OF THE EARTH'S MOST CURIOUS CREATURES GATHERED TOGETHER INTO ONE IMMENSE MENAGERIE.

THE CHAMPIONS OF ALL COUNTRIES COMPETE IN FEATS OF DARING AND GRACE.

THE PRINCELY SALARIES PAID BY THIS MAMMOTH ENTERPRISE HAVE ROBBED ALL EUROPE OF THEIR MOST VALUABLE ARTISTS.

MALE AND FEMALE RIDERS, AERIAL ARTISTS, LEAPERS, TUMBLERS, GYMNASTS AND SENSATIONAL DEATH-DEFYING FEATS OF SKILL AND DARING BY BOTH MALE AND FEMALE PERFORMERS.

A BIG TROUPE OF HIGH-SCHOOL HORSES, AN IMMENSE HERD OF WONDERFULLY TRAINED ELEPHANTS. TWO GROUPS OF FOREST-BRED, MAN-KILLING LIONS PERFORMING IN GREAT STEEL INCLOSURES.

5000 SEATS THAT WILL COMFORTABLY SEAT 5000 PEOPLE.

TENTS THAT ARE POSITIVELY WATERPROOF.

TWO TRAINS OF MONSTER RAILWAY CARS.

A GRAND, FREE, STREET PARADE EACH DAY AT NOON

"MARY"

THE LARGEST, LIVING, LAND ANIMAL ON EARTH.

3 INCHES TALLER THAN JUMBO AND WEIGHING OVER 5 TONS.

A POSITIVE FEATURE AT EACH EXHIBITION

TWO PERFORMANCES DAILY-RAIN OR SHINE 2 AND 8 O'CLOCK DOORS TO MENAGERIE OPEN 1 HOUR EARLIER

20 FUNNY CLOWNS

1914

162

Sparks Circus of 1914 was among the many that developed plates that could be delivered to the newspaper much as with "camera-ready" ads of seventy years later. This ad made great use of reverse printing—white on black—to get greater attention on the page. **Greg Parkinson.**

the house be admitted free—that might gain her approval of the project, and the whole family would come to the circus. Women who redeemed those coupons are now grandmothers whose daughters save coupons from local papers for weekly grocery bargains.

Color advertising in newspapers never has taken hold with circuses. No doubt price is the major reason. For a period in the 1970s, Ringling-Barnum liked to buy half-page ads in the Sunday comics sections. This brought color, but the main purpose was to reach children. So it is amazing that far back in 1881, the Sells Bros. Circus achieved color in daily newspaper advertising by supplying full-color pictures to be tipped in—glued in by hand— at the right spot in its otherwise black-and-white newspaper ads. Only low rates and small circulation could permit this. Apart from such special circumstances, circuses have not been buyers of color space.

With the perfection of the stereotype process, circuses made much use of matrices, or mats. In this, a paper product is pressed against the original type and art to create a mold or matrix. These were produced in great number at little cost. A press agent no longer had to carry the heavy blocks or engravings. Instead, he could give each paper an assortment of mats, and the paper

The 101 Ranch Wild West Show pioneered several steps in newspaper advertising. This 1914 example is appropriate Western art. Press agents agree the town and date should appear at the top of such ads. **Greg Parkinson**.

could "roll" each as a mold to create a type block reproducing the original ad ready for printing.

Mats were the rule for decades. But in the 1970s, offset printing—recalling Senefelder's lithography—transformed newspaper printing throughout the country. No longer did newspapers use cast type or mats. Circuses switched from mats to so-called slicks—proofs of the advertisements—which the papers photographed to include in their pages. Some shows in the 1980s supplied not only the completed ad, but also the various elements—logos, borders, reverses, and illustrations—as a press agent's Erector Set with which circus ads could be assembled locally for special needs.

The entire purpose of newspaper ads changed for circuses. At the outset, posters comprised the main effort; newspaper ads supplemented the poster campaigns. Typical of many others, the 1835 New England Zoological ad said, "See bills posted up at the principal hotels." Later, newspapers were more on their own as a powerful advertising medium, and circuses used them in a primary role to build interest in seeing the show. The reader had only one decision to make at the time—whether to go to the circus. All other questions were postponed until circus day and the reader's arrival on the midway.

For several years Ringling Bros. and Barnum & Bailey Circus placed uncommonly large ads in New York City newspapers to launch the new season. Roland Butler was a master at drawing the title logos. Bev Kelley mixed varieties of type with thumbnail cuts to achieve a special effect throughout the 1947 ad. **Authors' Collection.**

More recent seasons have brought two changes. Newspaper ads are again supportive—this time backing up the television spot announcements, just as they once supported the billposting. And now a circus seeks advance sales, causing the buyer to make several decisions early in the process. With many circuses now coming to a city for several days or a week instead of one day, the reader must decide not only if he wants to see the circus, but also which day and performance are best for him. He is offered different prices for different seats depending upon location. He must consider special terms for children, senior citizens, large groups and industrial discounts. Having jumped those hurdles, the buyer needs information on how to buy a ticket. It is not just a ticket wagon on circus day. Now he buys early to get a better seat, and he has a choice of paying by cash, check, or credit card. He can place his order in person at the box office or by phone, mail, or computer service.

The newspaper ad has much business to transact and many details and numbers to transmit—material that cannot be accommodated in broadcast advertising. Color television fills the role formerly held by colored posters—it sells people on the idea of going to the show. Then newspaper ads provide the details that each show-goer needs. This requires that ad space be filled with prosaic information. There is a little art and a logo but not much else of a selling nature. It does not try to tell about the show's great features. It does not say why, but only how, to go to the circus. Once the ads said, "See the bills for details of the program." Now television says, "See the newspaper ad for the details." The ad is burdened with unexciting but necessary data.

This affects the campaign. Traditional contracting press agents placed newspaper ads for the ten days or two weeks before circus day. The budget might call for buying 200 or 250 column inches. Today's aim is to gain advance sales, and the typical campaign runs thirty days or more. Extended time is needed to motivate a customer; buying twice the ads in half the time will not accomplish the same goal. But thirty ads would be too costly, so space is used only on weekends in most cases. The data-packed ads appeared in the Sunday amusement sections.

Even with today's earlier deadlines, newspapers remain one of

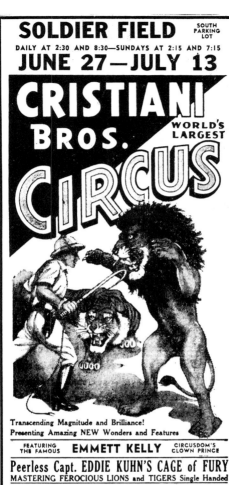

Variety was a key to the ad campaign for Cristiani Bros. Circus for 1958 in Chicago. Styles were rotated so that the same ad did not appear two days running. The idea of changing ads every day during a campaign began with 101 Ranch in 1909, and most shows followed suit thereafter. **Authors' Collection.**

165

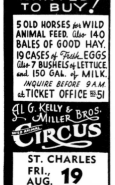

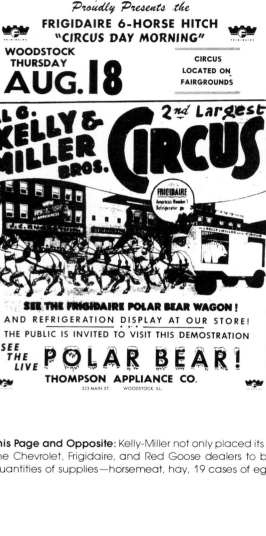

This Page and Opposite: Kelly-Miller not only placed its own sizeable newspaper ad in each town, but it also persuaded the Chevrolet, Frigidaire, and Red Goose dealers to buy larger tie-in ads. The circus capped it all by offering to buy quantities of supplies—horsemeat, hay, 19 cases of eggs—all indicating a huge operation. **Authors' Collection.**

the most responsive media. Ads can be changed easily to read "June 19," then "Tomorrow," and finally "Today." Even television spots or outdoor posters can become old-hat in two weeks, but changing newspaper ads daily can help keep a campaign renewed and fresh. Along with radio, newspapers can handle urgency. Perhaps most important, newspapers are tangible items to be held in one's hand and kept in reach until the information that they contain can be utilized.

Circus ads still pep up any newspaper page. They augment what might be accomplished with broadcasting, posters, or promotion by members of a sponsoring club. The Ringling-Barnum circus prepares most of its newspaper advertising in the show's central offices. Its two units play about ninety cities and use space in about 400 publications. Where once circus ads provided the only illustrations in a paper, today they compete with color photography and are grouped in concentrations of theater ads and television schedules. Now, as always, they usually are charged the highest advertising rate. But newspapers are still a vital part of circus advertising.

On the front page of the June 10, 1870, **Milwaukee Sentinel** appeared this ad of Castello's & Coup's Great Circus. The next year these two showmen had talked Barnum into joining them for a venture that became known as The Greatest Show On Earth. **Milwaukee Public Library, Milwaukee, Wisconsin.**

Circuses distributed heralds in unbelievably huge quantities. The tall, narrow handbills were in reach everywhere the public gathered—general store, gas station, blacksmith shop, feed store, and in recent times the shopping center. In extravagant language, they told the wonders of the great show. L.B. Lent circulated this style at Springfield, Mass., in 1870. **Springfield (Mass.) Public Library.**

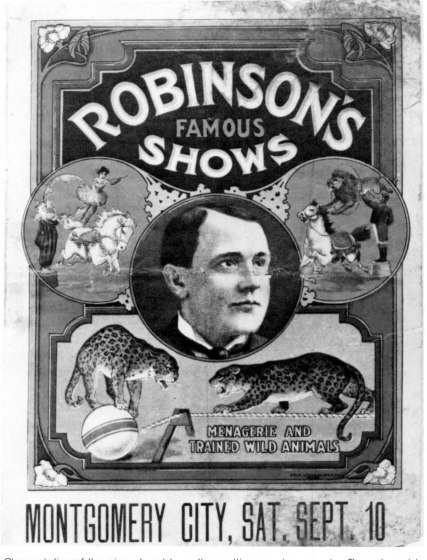

Close relative of the circus herald was the multi-page circus courier. Shows bought these by the hundreds of thousands. Typically couriers ranged from four to forty-eight pages, all crammed and jammed with ballyhoo for the big shows. Danny Robinson's show had a four-color lithographed cover for its 1911 courier. **Circus World Museum.**

CHAPTER 8

Heralds and Couriers

ircus advertising is categorized in the public's mind for its extravagance, its bombastic superlatives. There is a vision of the top-hatted ringmaster declaiming about the greatest, the biggest, the smallest, the only, and the most. The same language is anticipated in the advertising. Actually, very little such verbiage turns up in newspaper ads or posters. There are some superlatives—a modest sprinkling to make it clear that one is dealing with a truly gigantic amusement enterprise.

But examine the heralds and couriers. That is where the circus runs true to form, where it earned and retains its reputation for uninhibited claims and ornate language. Heralds and couriers are the epitome of hyperbole, the very starting place for sesquipedalianism, the amazing amalgamations of alliteration awing all the ages and antedating antediluvian arrangers of alphabetized attractions.

Heralds and couriers earned some superlatives of their own. They were the most numerous of all the circus promotion pieces, second only to ads in newspapers of great circulation. A herald might proclaim the "biggest circus in the world" when the show is only sizable. A courier might hail the advent of "train after train of palace cars" that turn out to be twelve railroad cars barely able to pass the interchange inspections. Advertising might announce the coming of "three ponderous herds of pachyderms," which exist in real life as three elephants. But when circus agents spoke about millions of heralds and couriers, the numbers were there to back them up. These advertising pieces were used in fantastic quantities.

They have come in all shapes and sizes, but today two formats describe them best. A herald is a long, narrow advertising piece printed on both sides. Usually it is ten by twenty-eight inches with black ink on colored newsprint. A courier is a folder or booklet. It might have from four pages to forty-eight. It might be in newspaper style or magazine size. It is likely to have generous swatches of color illustrations.

Earlier, the show printers and circuses used different definitions, sometimes varying from one printer to the next. Often such definitions hinged on how a one-sheet size of paper was folded and cut into smaller sheets or booklets. This procedure survives today in that a herald is still called a quarter-sheet.

The earliest form of such handbills was the broadside, a show advertisement usually printed on one side of the paper and distributed hand to hand. These dated to early times in Europe and to the first circuses in America. Soon they utilized both sides and then more pages. Jonas Booth, the pioneer show printer, produced couriers for the June, Titus & Angevine Circus in the 1830s and thereafter; the 1841 edition was a twenty-four-page booklet telling of the wonders to come and urging readers to "see the large bills in the principal hotels" for time and place of exhibition. Wesley Barmore's Grand Adriatic Circus had a broadside printed by the *Cincinnati Enquirer* in 1854. Spalding & Rogers for a broadside in 1865 used a large number of cuts that also appeared in the newspaper ads. There were many more. Printing presses were spewing circus advertising in great quantities at nearly any step in the history of show business. Whiting Allen, an early Ringling press agent, said that this show used twelve styles of heralds and couriers in a typical year, totaling 5,400,000 copies.

The Courier Company quoted prices to Ringling Bros. for a full line of heralds and couriers in 1897, including an eight-page newspaper at $5.00 per thousand and a quarter-sheet program at $1.30 per thousand, both in lots of 450,000 copies each. Ringling ordered 450,000 sixteen-page newspaper couriers and another 450,000 sixteen-page booklets. It also ordered a million quarter-sheet heralds. Another season, Ringling ordered 500,000 couriers "the size of *Harper's Weekly*" and a second 500,000 sixteen-page couriers in two colors. But there was a squabble about price, not the last that Ringling would originate. Courier had quoted $12.50 for the Harper's model, but the show understood that it would be $12.05. The printers blamed a telegrapher for transposing the digits. In that same preparation for the 1901 season, Ringling was negotiating with Erie Lithograph for a million copies of a booklet with four-color lithographed covers and sixteen pages of one-color print and art.

For the 1911 season, the Central Printing and Engraving Company of Chicago quoted fifteen dollars per thousand for 750,000 sixteen-page books for Ringling Bros. and the same for another 750,000 copies to Barnum & Bailey. These were printed in four colors on one side and a single color on the other—all folded, pasted, and dated, ready for distribution. The printers pointed out that each piece would go through a press six times.

Not surprisingly, the circuses went to newspaper printers for newspaper work. Courier did its Ringling newspapers on presses that printed the Buffalo daily. And in 1917, the Barnum show used a sixteen-page tabloid and a four-page newspaper courier from the McClure Newspaper Syndicate, producer of features and "boilerplate" for regular daily and weekly newspapers.

McClure shipped 30,000 of these for use in Philadelphia, 5,000 for Chester, Pennsylvania, 6,000 to Pottsville, 8,000 to Reading, 3,000 to Plainfield, 8,000 to Allentown, and 8,000 to Easton. These were the first towns to be played after the New York opening. Later in the tour, McClure shipped 10,000 to Peoria, Illinois, 11,000 to Davenport, Iowa, and 12,000 to Cedar Rapids. The difference in numbers reflects the size of towns and surrounding territory.

Typical of many shows in the years before World War I, Lamont Bros. had four-color lithographed covers and centerfolds for its courier. In 1912, the Mighty Haag Shows had another loaded with photos, line drawings, and exciting headlines. Both were the work of Erie Lithograph, which also did the poster work for Haag and Lamont.

In the 1930s, rotogravure was popular with Sunday newspaper supplements—and with the circuses. Hagenbeck-Wallace claimed a million circulation for *The Amusement World*, an eight-page newspaper courier that carried many commercial ads for national corporations, along with a heavy dose of circus coverage. Barnes–Sells Floto, Downie Bros. Circus, and 101 Ranch Wild West all had rotogravure couriers that were printed in Louisville. Shows like Sells Floto–Tom Mix, Sparks Circus, and Al G. Barnes used two-color, four-page pieces from Central Printing & Engraving in the 1930s. Russell Bros., in 1938, produced a courier that looked a little like the then-popular *Life Magazine* but which also included newspaper-style pages and a colorful back cover. Cole Bros., in 1935, 1936, and 1937, distributed great quantities of a twenty-four-page courier with lots of color, gold ink, and rotogravure, all printed by a branch of the Cuneo Press. In 1938, that company proposed an eight-page courier at $5.53 per thousand in lots of one million or more. Imprinting dates and towns cost another $1.10 per thousand.

Given these hundreds of thousands of advertising pieces, it fell to the advance department of each circus to distribute the day's allocation in each town. Squeezed on board the car among the more numerous billposters and lithographers were the programmers. Their title stemmed from the old name for some quarter-sheet heralds, not from the souvenir program booklets sold at the circus. With little help, these few fellows planted the plethora of heralds and couriers that would clutter the town and surrounding territory. Working neighborhoods as assigned by the car manager, they delivered some pieces by hand. When F. A. Boudinot joined Hagenbeck-Wallace in 1912, he was young enough to be nicknamed "Babe" and as a rookie programmer was instructed to place three copies of the show's courier at every place of business in town.

Often, a string was threaded through a stack of perhaps fifty or more heralds. Such packs were hung in grocery stores, blacksmith shops, saloons, hotels, barbershops, hardware stores, livery stables—in fact, just any place where the programmer could find a hook and a willing proprietor. In the same way, stacks of couriers could be left in well-trafficked places for customers to pick up and read. Sometimes townspeople complained about the litter, because heralds were left nearly everywhere. Readers circulated some, and breezes scattered more.

The Ringling billers boasted in 1894 that, as their advance car moved through the countryside, they tossed off bundles of heralds in each village, more at each crossroads, and even some at individual farms. If the circus had its way (and it usually did), heralds were placed everywhere to declare that the great show was coming. Sometimes the programmers hired local kids to help in delivering printed matter to every house in town. Special heralds told not only about the show, but also about excursion trains that would bring people to the show town on circus day. Bundles of these were stacked up in the express office, at the freight dock, and in the passenger depot so that everyone could take a copy. The excursion herald usually listed the arrival and departure times for each of the towns in which the special trains would stop for circus passengers.

To circulate heralds and couriers, circuses utilized another major helper—the United States Post Office Department. Special low postal rates were intended primarily to encourage circulation of books, magazines, and newspapers as a public service in the spread of knowledge. But somehow a lot of that knowledge began to involve menagerie animals, amazing museum features, great performers, and circuses in general. It began in 1852 with the book rate. Circulars and advertisements of all kinds were dumped into the mails, and circuses were well represented. Many pieces were printed to look like periodicals so as to get the cheapest rate. Something called *The New York Herald Extra* turned out to advertise the Seth B. Howes Menagerie & Circus of 1855, a ten-by-twenty-eight-inch piece much like the heralds of today. In 1863, second and third classes of mail were created to allow lower rates and prepayment of postage. By 1874, postal rules allowed second-class privileges to any publication that claimed a subscription list and some literary merit. Circuses moved in. L. B. Lent's New York Circus published *The Plebiscite* with a masthead and format typical of many periodicals of the time.

P. T. Barnum's *Advance Courier* came out in 1871 as a sixteen-page magazine claiming 800,000 circulation and containing advertising of several other businesses but stressing both advertising and editorial matter about the big circus. Other editions of the *Advance Courier* all looked like magazines to get the favorable bulk rates. In 1876, it was called P. T. Barnum's *Centennial Advance Daily* and appeared with a three-color cover. Fifteen of its pages trumpeted circus superlatives; the sixteenth depicted the signing of the Declaration of Independence. The show claimed a circulation of 2 million.

Nearly every sizable circus was doing much the same. The Great London & Sanger Show published a newspaper-style courier in 1880 and so did another twenty-five or thirty circuses. All of this launched the heyday of circus heralds and couriers. It also was a time of public outcry. By 1881, the deluge of cheap-rate postal material caused loud complaint against what later would be known as "junk mail."

John Wanamaker, the famous Philadelphia merchant turned postmaster general, launched Rural Free Delivery with tests in 1891. There were 44 routes in 1897 and 43,445 routes by 1920. This set up a new wave of advertising mail by the turn of the century. Low rates combined with delivery direct to each farm house meant that rural families began to see a lot of patent medicine ads, local circulars, and the marvelous new catalogs from Sears, Roebuck and Montgomery Ward. Right in there with the best of them were the nation's circuses, with couriers by the millions.

From 1904 onward, bulk mail could include printed postal wording instead of a stamp and "U.S. Postage Paid" began to appear on all sorts of printing. Under one procedure, the circus could address couriers to "R.F.D. Boxholder, Local" and for the low fee, a copy would be placed in each rural mailbox. Under another system, the circus could have a copy delivered to each post office box at post offices where villagers picked up their own mail. Another plan called for the pre-printing to address mail to "Occupant," and every household received a copy. The local postmaster would tell the circus agent how many post office boxes or R.F.D. boxes his office served. It was a system still unchanged in the 1980s, when growing tonnage of mail-order catalogs was circulated along with a continuing rivulet of circus heralds and couriers. Typical was a four-page rotogravure piece printed in 1930 by Erie for the Barnett Bros. Circus and mailed from the show's winter quarters at York, South Carolina. Postmasters welcomed the extra volume, which might put their office in a higher category. More often, the mailing was handled by the printing company, with lists of towns and numbers of mailboxes supplied by the circus agents.

In 1938, Robbins Bros. Circus bought heralds and newspaper-size couriers for distribution both from the car and by the mails. Most towns received 3,000 heralds, but Akron and Youngstown were big enough to warrant 5,000 each, and Minster, Ohio, could use only 2,000. The show's newspaper couriers were mailed by a printer at Oak Park, Illinois, to box holders—3,010 at Kokomo, Indiana; 4,982 at Minster; 4,705 at Lima, Ohio; 2,420 at Marion; 5,573 at Wooster; 4,903 at Akron; and 4,259 at Youngstown. Those 29,552 couriers cost $11.05 per thousand, or $329.86 for printing, packaging, and delivery to the post office. Postage was another $462.50, or twelve cents per pound. A ticket to Robbins Bros. Circus was one dollar—considered very high at the time. This meant that the show had to sell 796 tickets to pay for this part of its weekly advertising material.

R. M. Harvey was associated with the newspaper and job shop of the Chief Printing Company at Perry, Iowa. Harvey was also general agent of Dailey Bros. Circus, so the Chief shop was mailing 6,000 heralds a day for the show. Harvey said then that he thought the effectiveness of newspaper-style heralds had been diminished because so many smaller shows were using them. But his print shop continued to turn them out for all comers in the 1940s and 1950s. One customer was Obert Miller, the shrewd operator of the successful Al G. Kelly & Miller Bros. Circus. The Kelly-Miller bill crew distributed from 1,000 to 4,000 heralds in each town. In addition, the Chief Printing Company mailed from 6,000 to 8,000 Kelly-Miller newspaper couriers per stand. Simul-

taneously, Cole & Walters Circus was using from 2,000 to 4,000 a day, and the Wallace & Clark Circus ordered 1,500 to 3,000, depending upon the size of the town and its R.F.D. routes. Thus, more than 2 million pieces of circus advertising per year were mailed from Perry, Iowa.

Nor was the Chief clientele the only users. Floyd King was partial to red-and-black printing on pink paper and to the Central Show Printing Company of Mason City, Iowa. It mailed his newspaper-sized couriers to R.F.D. routes for King Bros. in 1951, King-Cristiani in the next two seasons, and Clyde Beatty Circus in 1956, all on the same format and changing little but the show title from year to year. Bailey-Cristiani picked up the King material for mailing to Alaska in 1954. Clyde Beatty Circus in 1953 had a newspaper courier printed by Neal Walters Poster Corporation, Eureka Springs, Arkansas, for distribution on R.F.D. and Star postal routes. Even Ringling Bros. and Barnum & Bailey mailed thousands of sixteen-page couriers to rural route box holders in 1952 and 1953, with heavy emphasis on soliciting mail orders for tickets—an unusual move for a circus playing one-day stands under canvas.

After it switched to arenas, Ringling continued with direct mail, but the old R.F.D. and occupant plans were used less often. In their stead was a new format of six-by-nine-inch leaflets, still called heralds, sent to all the names on the mailing lists maintained by arenas in which the circus appeared. Anyone who had ordered tickets by mail in prior years for circuses, ice shows, sports events, or other attractions in the auditoriums now was on the list to receive full-color heralds advertising the show and including local information about dates, performance times, and ticket prices. Additional copies of this herald often were distributed from counters at hotels, banks, stores, and restaurants, just as in any of a hundred circus seasons before. By the late 1970s, however, most shows found that direct mail was not producing sufficient orders to warrant the cost. So circuses found another way. They used smaller pieces designed to fit into billing envelopes. Often, local promoters could induce department stores, banks, or public utilities to include the circus herald in their cyclical billings.

The old ways so effective with the Kelly-Miller circus were modified for use on the family's later Carson & Barnes Circus. In

1981, for example, the show printed more than 500,000 copies of a tabloid-size newspaper about the show. In some cases, 2,500 copies were delivered to the sponsoring organization in each town. In a more unique system, the show arranged to insert one in each copy of the local newspaper. Pre-printed inserts of this nature were being utilized by national advertisers; Sears, Ace Hardware, K-Mart, and others printed their own special sections to be circulated as part of many local newspapers. Carson & Barnes adapted the age-old courier system to the newly popular newspaper insert plan.

Circus season after circus season, the flow of words was nearly endless. The Burr Robbins Circus shouted, "Make ready for the jubilee! Suspend operations for a day!" and spoke of "Panoramic feast of gorgeous splendor, golden conquests of regal brilliancy, a rival to famed Eastern romance." The Forepaugh circus bellowed about "King of all mastodons, the leviathan monster elephant, Bolivar, the largest and heaviest ever captured." Sells Bros. whispered cautiously, "Make no mistake, our massive, mighty, mammoth, and plentudinous 50-cage menagerie 50 has just that number. Never since the days of Noah has the world witnessed such a rare, ponderous and ploygenous collection." Glance at a Sells Bros. herald and it seemed to say, "White elephant," but look carefully to include the smallest type, and it read, "The nearest approach to a white elephant."

Again, Sells Bros. advertised "The only living albatross ever exhibited in a gorgeous crystal tank filled with genuine South Sea water . . . kept in nearly the same condition with us as when the boundless sea and the empyrean blue were his limitless home." It was just a circus conversational tone when Ringling Bros. of 1901 announced its "tremendous free spectacular street carnival, 30 big parades in one massive phalanx, a mighty moving panorama of the opulent splendors of old earth's rarest glories, a cosmopolitan array of grand, new and bewildering sights without a parallel in processional amazements." Charles Lee's Great London Show was "honestly presented, honestly conducted, truthful, moral, instructive. The date is fixed and no change will be made. Rain or shine the Great London Shows always appear as advertised."

And the Holland-McLaughlin Monster United Shows said in its courier, "Everywhere wearing the purple of superiority; moral, mighty, magnificient, truthful, towering, triumphant. We never change dates, we never divide, we never disappoint, we will be with you to the hour advertised."

Sells Bros. heralds told about "our wondrous ophiological and reptilian department in which is collected in conglomerated masses and sinuous folds all of the sub-vertebra, species, oviparous, amphibious, or batrachean, in short all crawling, creeping venomous things of the horrible repitle world."

Such phraseology could not be spent in wastelands of gray paragraphs. To startle the mind, one first had to please the eye. So heralds and courier not only used illustrations of all kinds, but they also pioneered in color printing and demonstrated what marvels could be accomplished with type.

Color was a specialty of circus couriers. Covers, center spreads, and sometimes whole booklets were splashed with excellent color printing well before it was in signficant use much of any place else for advertising. Some was on enameled stock and some on newsprint. The latter in particular resulted in warm and pleasing tones. In early circus color printing, the register—or alignment of various colors—was outstanding, better than much of that seen elsewhere in later years. Often, the multi-colored pictorial lithographs for billposting were reduced and duplicated as beautiful color pages in couriers. Barnum & Bailey booklets in the 1890s were typical. After the turn of the century, even small circuses used great quantities of color printing in couriers. The lithographing houses offered stock couriers in full color at low prices.

Both heralds and couriers often were masterpieces of the typesetter's art. The most ornate type-faces in great variety pepped up the readability of every such circus publication. Even ordinary type faces took on special characteristics when type-setters arranged them in geometric figures, stars, spokes and circles. With circus heralds and couriers, display type enjoyed its finest hour.

Hardly any citizen could sidestep or overlook this summer snowstorm of advertising. There were heralds and couriers in every public place. Distributors proffered more. There were colorful circus ads in every mailbox, on every doorsill. There was no escape.

Mr. POOL,

The First *AMERICAN* that ever exhibited
the following

EQUESTRIAN FEATS
OF

HORSEMANSHIP

On the Continent, intends PERFORMING on *Saturday* Afternoon next, near the POWDER-HOUSE. The Performance to begin at Half past Four o'Clock in the Afternoon (if the Weather will permit, if not, the First fair Day after *Sunday*). Tickets to be had at Mr. *Gordon*'s Tavern, Price *Two Shillings* each. There will be Seats provided for the Ladies and Gentlemen.

A *CLOWN* will entertain the LADIES and GENTLEMEN between the Feats.

1. MOUNTS a single Horse in full Speed, standing on the Top of the Saddle, and in that Position carries a Glass of Wine in his Hand, drinks it off, and falls to his Seat on the Saddle.

2. MOUNTS a single Horse in Half Speed, standing on the Saddle, throws up an Orange; and catches it on the Point of a Fork.

3. MOUNTS a single Horse in full Speed, with his right Foot in the near Stirrup, and his left Leg extended at a very considerable Distance from the Horse, and in that Position leaps a Bar.

4. MOUNTS two Horses in full Speed, with a Foot in the Stirrup of each Saddle, and in that Position leaps a Bar, and from thence to the Tops of the Saddles at the same Speed.

5. MOUNTS two Horses in full Speed, standing on the Saddles; and in that Position leaps a Bar.

6. MOUNTS a single Horse in full Speed, fires a Pistol, and falls backward with his Head to the Ground, hanging by his right Leg; and while hanging, fires another Pistol under the Horse's Belly, and rises again to his Seat on the Saddle, without the Use of his Hands.

7. MOUNTS three Horses in full Speed, standing on the Saddles, vaulting from one to the other.

AFTER which Mr. POOL will introduce two Horses, who will lay themselves down, as if dead; One will groan, apparently through extreme Sickness and Pain; afterwards rise and make his Manners to the Ladies and Gentlemen; Another having laid down for a considerable Time, will rise, and sit up like a Lady's Lap-Dog.

THE Entertainment will conclude with the noted droll Scene, *The* TAYLOR *riding to* Brentford.

Mr. POOL informs the Ladies and Gentlemen, that he can only stay to perform once in this Place.

☞ He beseeches the Ladies and Gentlemen, who honour him with their Presence, to bring no Dogs with them to the Place of Performance.

Providence, August 23, 1786.

PROVIDENCE: Printed by *JOHN CARTER.*

Heralds picked up where posters left off—and captivated their readers. Youngsters and their seniors found the words as awesome as the illustrations. These boys were reading Campbell Bros. Circus heralds in about 1912. **Ed Bardy.**

Heralds were outgrowths of the earliest handbills. Mr. Poole was a trick rider well before full circuses existed in this country. He distributed this handbill in 1786 to tell the populace what he would do in the show—and to ask them not to bring dogs. **Rhode Island Historical Society.**

WELCH'S NATIONAL CIRCUS

Dress Boxes and Parquette, ... 25 CENTS.
Seats in Private Boxes, ... 50 CENTS.
Second Tier, ... 12 1-2 CENTS.
Commodious Boxes for Persons of Color. 25 CENTS.
GALLERY . . . . 12 1-2 CENTS.

DOORS OPEN AT HALF-PAST 6. TO COMMENCE AT 7 O'CLOCK.

THE BRIGHTEST STARS!!

CHEERING APPROBATION,
ADMIRING SPECTATORS.
HUZZA FOR NATIVE TALENT!

ON EVERY SATURDAY AFTERNOON

A DAY PERFORMANCE

SEE AND BELIEVE.

ON FRIDAY, NOV. 29th, 1844,

KNIGHTS OF PALESTINE!

And their Ladye Loves.

A NEW COMIC SONG. BY MR. DICKENSON.

THE SON OF OSCEOLA.

MISS LOUISA WELLS

HORNPIPE!! GRECIAN GAMES.

Observe that, on Friday Evening Only,

MR. JAMES McAULEY,

THE BROAD SWORD & SABRE EXERCISE,

THE GREEK CHIEFTAIN'S

Defence of the Banner of Liberty.

MR. J. J. NATHANS

POSTURE AND GYMNASTICS!

A CARD.
On Every Saturday, a Grand Day Performance at 3 o'clock.

LOVE IN A VILLAGE!

Or—The Shepherd and the Milkmaid.

A VERY QUEER SONG. BY Mr. DICKENSON.

A BOLD AND BRILLIANT ACT!!!

Scene of Personal Gymnastics.

MIRACULOUS RIDING

OF T. V. TURNER,

THE SHOEMAKER OF BAGDAT!

EXTRAORDINARY NOVELTY is in Industrious and Continual Preparation.

Heralds soon took a form they would retain to this day, although the spelling of Bagdad might have changed. Once heralds were called programs because they itemized the running order of the show, as this one did for the Welch circus in 1844. **John Van Matre.**

It was with heralds and couriers that circuses engaged in the superlatives and exaggerations for which they became known—or blamed. W.W. Cole's 1886 herald demonstrates the knack. **Authors' Collection.**

Circus bill writers thrived on numbers. This 1880 example claims 500 wild animals, 200 ring stars, and endorsement of the entire national population. More down to earth, it admits to two elephants. **Authors' Collection.**

Superlatives ranked high in circus values. In this 1891 herald, Sells Bros. announced thirty-one "greatest" items, including satisfaction. There were thirty-two "biggest" listings and thirty-four "mosts," as well as two "onlys" and one "rarest." **Authors' Collection.**

⋆ A GRAND GALAXY OF EQUESTRIAN CHIEFS! ⋆
In Spirited and Earnest Rivalry for Disputed Titled Supremacy.

A SCORE OF MALE AND FEMALE CHAMPIONS
Producing every style of Equestrianism known to Ancient or Modern Arenas. This long-contemplated meet between

EUROPE'S AND AMERICA'S LEADING BAREBACK HEROES
Was finally consummated, and America agreed upon for the trial, in consideration of extremely liberal propositions made through my foreign agents, which, besides being the only occurrence of the kind ever in this country, is the

FIRST GENUINE CONTEST in 20 YEARS
By which is to be forever settled the sundry questionable claims of supremacy, and to the winners, each,

A DIPLOMA OF "CHAMPIONSHIP"
Awarded by a Board of Judges as a universal title to the following :

CHAMPION Male Somersault Rider of the World.
CHAMPION Lady Somersault Rider of the World.
CHAMPION Male Jockey Rider of the World.
CHAMPION Lady Jockey Rider of the World.
CHAMPION Male Four and Six Horse Rider of the World.
CHAMPION Lady Four and Five Horse Rider of the World.

CHAMPION Male Trick and Hurdle Rider of the World.
CHAMPION Male Principal Rider of the World.
CHAMPION Lady Principal Rider of the World.
CHAMPION Blindfolded Rider of the World.
CHAMPION Lady Manege Rider of the World.
CHAMPION Lady Entree Rider of the World.

The enthusiastic efforts of these most formidable rivals

TO WIN A LASTING LAUREL CROWN
And to hold the proud achievement in bosom embrace, is fitting assurance of the

HIGH-CLASS DEEDS of DARING HORSEMANSHIP

A GALA DAY UPON THE ARENIC COURSE
Equestrian Victories and Surprising Horsemanship that parallel the glorious successes of Rome's Colisseum days, eclipsing by twenty-fold the feeble attempts of modern times.

AN ARENIC ILLUMINATION THAT WILL SHINE FOREVER
These matchless triumphs of Esquestrian Skill are daily repeated in the handsomely appointed Circus department of

THE GREAT BURR ROBBINS SHOWS
THE GRANDEST TENTED EXHIBITIONS IN AMERICA.

Champions were almost as good as numbers. Burr Robbins Circus of 1887 announced the coming performances of twenty in one place and twelve in another with this courier. **Authors' Collection.**

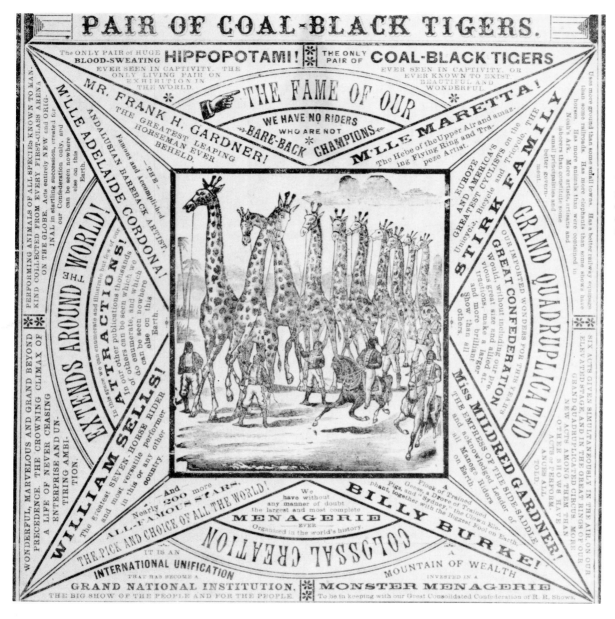

The printers performed wonders as well. This portion of a Sells Bros. herald demonstrates the ends to which type-setters went to make the copy readable and attractive. **Authors' Collection.**

180

Layout added much to the excitement and appeal of circus printing. The artist for this 1896 herald even coped well with the cumbersome title of Adam Forepaugh & Sells Brothers. **Authors' Collection.**

When there was a circus herald to print, the type department broke out every font in the house. **Authors' Collection.**

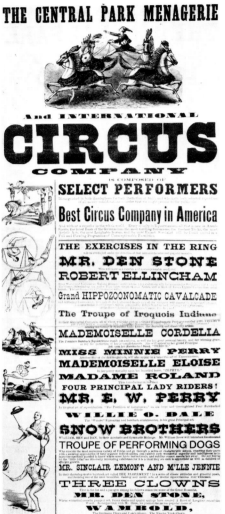

P.T. Barnum promised "the best of all things" but didn't name any of them except himself, and he rarely actually traveled with the show. Illinoisians would swarm to Ottawa in 1879 because of interest aroused by this and other circus advertising. **John Van Matre.**

Typical of heralds at their best, this example from Wallace & Co's Circus utilized many line drawings along with other illustrations and the great variety of type faces. **Authors' Collection.**

Heralds frequently featured the show's parade, a case of advertising the ads. John O'Brien promised a "kaleidoscopic cortege." **Circus World Museum.**

The herald for Ringling Bros. and Barnum & Bailey of 1924 did indeed describe the Greatest Show on Earth. Lillian Leitzel and May Wirth were among the greatest names in circus talent, and the show actually included many more. Line drawings and interesting type mark the herald. **Authors' Collection.**

183

Cole Bros. Circus made wide use of heralds in the 1930s. Floyd King produced the show's advertising matter, using drawings and photos that had appeared in many other similar pieces for numerous circuses. **Authors' Collection.**

No show made better use of heralds than the Kelly-Miller Circus. This 1949 edition was circulated by the thousands in each town the show played. **Authors' Collection.**

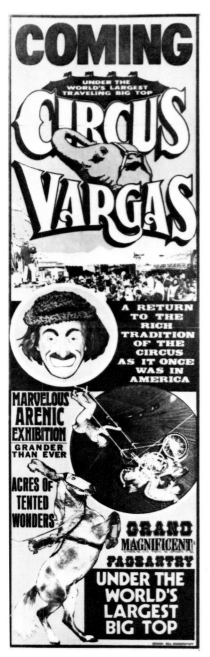

Bringing heralds up to modern times, the Circus Vargas used this layout in the 1976 season. **Authors' Collection.**

THE GREATEST COMBINATION OF

OLYMPIC EXERCISES,

AND

THE MOST MAGNIFICENT COLLECTION

OF

LIVING WILD ANIMALS

Ever presented together in one Caravan in the United States.

THE MENAGERIE OF LIVING WILD ANIMALS,

AND

THE CIRCUS PERFORMANCES

Given by the Company of JUNE, TITUS, ANGEVINE, & Co., of the Bowery Amphitheatre, New-York have been the wonder and admiration of the million wherever they have been exhibited. At no time, nor in any other country, has there ever been collected together so general, so beautiful, or so healthful a Menagerie of Living Animals, or an entertainment in the arena comprising such an array of talent, as the one now offered by the above named proprietors, for the patronage of the public.

FOR TIME AND PLACE OF EXHIBITION

See Large Bills in the Principal Hotels.

USUAL HOURS OF EXHIBITION FROM 1 TO 4 o'CLOCK, P. M.

NEW-YORK:
PRINTED BY JONAS BOOTH, SEN'R.
1841.

Couriers were a fixture of circus advertising almost from the outset. This is the back cover of a twenty-four-page courier printed by Jonas Booth for the June, Titus & Angevine show to distribute in quantity in the towns it would play in 1841. **Circus World Museum.**

Couriers were booklets of several pages, all filled with vivid descriptions of the coming circus. This cover on Holland-McLaughlin's 1890 courier followed the same style as many heralds. **Authors' Collection.**

Many couriers featured full-color lithographed covers. The Courier Company, named for a newspaper rather than this form of advertising, printed several hundred thousand of these for the Ringling show in 1904. **Circus World Museum.**

Pawnee Bill's four-color courier cover pictured many of the leading performers in his show, including Geronimo. Couriers often were delivered to each business place in the show town. **Circus World Museum.**

Woodcuts preceded lithography in couriers as with posters. The United States Circus distributed a courier with this cover from the Jonathon Jeffery printing house, Chicago. **Circus World Museum.**

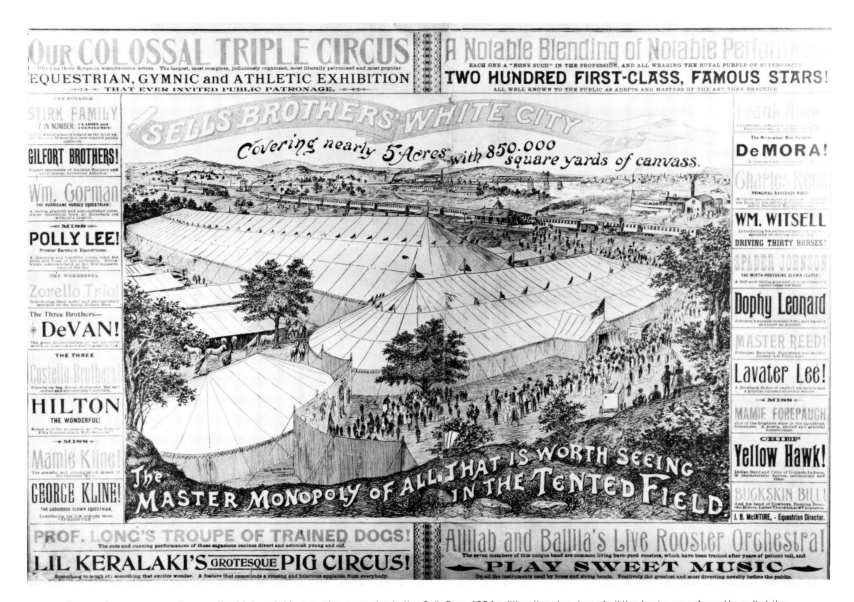

The center pages usually were the high point in any circus courier. In the Sells Bros. 1894 edition the drawing of all the tents was referred to as "white city," recalling a similar reference to the Chicago World's Fair of the prior year. **Authors' Collection.**

Ringling-Barnum featured its wild animal acts in the center spread of its 1922 courier. Circuses often dispatched couriers to "box holder" and "occupant" and "rural route" addressees via the U.S. Post Office. **Authors' Collection.**

The center pages of the Norris & Rowe Circus courier used many illustrations and assorted type to build excitement about the show. **Authors' Collection.**

A marvelous display of the typesetter's art made up the center spread of the Ringling Bros. courier of 1890. This was the show's first season on rails, and it was going first class with its courier as well. **Authors' Collection.**

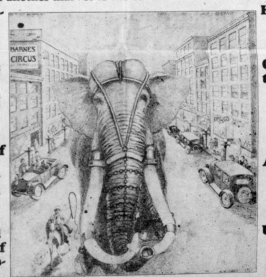

Al G. Barnes Circus issued a four-page courier about its biggest and best attraction, Tusko. The cover shows a street scene with a Barnes circus banner on a building wall.

While the back pages depicted the Mighty Tusko at ten times the height of other elephants and scattering natives in his path. **Circus World Museum.**

In the flesh, Tusko was big and mean but something short of the monster shown in the courier. **Gene Baxter.**

Back pages of couriers were intended to wrap up the sales pitch. Sells Bros. went for class—with dignified portraits and quality art work to frame a restrained "Word to the Public." **Authors' Collection.**

Featured color pages in couriers frequently were miniature posters. This back page of a Buffalo Bill courier in 1902 may also have been printed as a one-sheet lithograph. **Circus World Museum.**

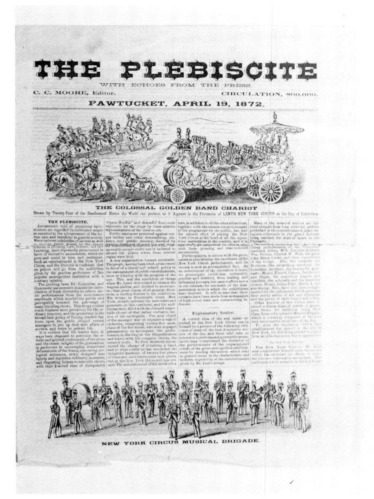

It wasn't the bent of circuses—this grim, grey make-up that looked like the cultural magazines of the day. But shows produced couriers in this format so as to look like all the other periodicals that enjoyed low postage rates. The disguise was only cover-deep. Inside they reverted to the usual intense hyperbole. Clarence Chester Moore was "editor" of The Plebiscite for Lent's New York Circus. **Authors' Collection.**

ONE DAY ONLY!

SELLS-FLOTO
FEATURING
BROTHERS

3 RING CIRCUS

THE LAST of the Old Time Circuses!
See it NOW...or Miss it FOREVER

From the earliest days of bargain postage rates for bulk mail and periodicals, circuses were major users of mailing pieces. In the 1950s much of such mailing was imprinted by "Permit 1, Perry, Iowa," home of the Chief Printing Co., which specialized in producing and mailing circus heralds and couriers. **Authors' Collection.**

Lemen Bros. Circus produced several pages of tightly packed type and amazing pictures in a newspaper courier of 1896. As with many shows, the Lemen courier was produced by a lithograph printer, Russell & Morgan. **Authors' Collection.**

To produce heralds and couriers, a circus press agent could choose from the printer's supply of stock cuts or ask the artist to create new pen and ink drawings. These are a stock cut of bareback riders from the Courier Company's shelves and an original drawing by artists of the Erie Lithographing and Printing Co. **Authors' Collection.**

COMING

LUCKY BILLS=AMERICA'S BEST SHOW

Consisting of 100 head of horses, 60 people, wild beasts from all parts of the world, elephants, lions, tigers, camels, leopards, buffalo, elk, gorilla, zebras, monkeys, baboons and many others. These trained wild beasts alone are worth many times the price of admission. Sensational and spectacular performances of all kinds, traps, rings, jugglers, acrobats, lots of trained ponies, dogs and funny clowns, Our MOTTO—THE BEST ARE NONE TOO GOOD.

LUCKY BILL SHOWS

A $50,000 collection of animals with this show. A reproduction of the days of the GOLDEN WEST. Real COWBOYS and COWGIRLS. Will pay $100 for any horse, mule or steer we can't ride. Bring UM in. COME EARLY. BIG FREE ATTRACTION ON SHOW GROUNDS AT 2 AND 7:30 P. M.

Remember Day, Date and Place

My Dear Friends:—

It affords me great pleasure to extend to you, once more, a most hearty and cordial invitation to visit our mammoth aggregations. Come early, combine pleasure with business, it is coming to you. Lets renew our most esteemed fellowship.

With best wishes for a good old handshake I await you

LUCKY BILL

A simpler mailing piece than most couriers was this card which the Lucky Bill Shows mailed to rural route boxholders. Lucky Bill Newton sent the cards to fellow Westerners who would warm to that "good old handshake." **Authors' Collection.**

Ringling Bros. and Barnum & Bailey still makes use of heralds by the millions. The 6 b 8 inch flyers are imprinted with local information for each engagement and distributed via ticket counters, hotel lobbies, utility mailings and arena promotion address lists. The art work is changed for each edition of the circus. **Ringling Bros. and Barnum & Bailey Circus.**

The billing game could get rowdy. Cole Bros. Circus was to play Washington, Ia., on August 26, 1909 and hung date sheets in windows of these shops. It also posted the billboard to the far left edge of the photo. Then the Buffalo Bill-Pawnee Bill opposition crew came to town and overwhelmed Cole with bills for the Two Bills show, playing August 13. They even draped a streamer over the Buick dealer's sign, and then posed for a picture in front of it all. **Buffalo Bill Museum.**

CHAPTER 9

Billing Wars

"All other shows are simply as though they were not." Thus Buffalo Bill's press agent dismissed the competition. It was part of an opposition battle, a fight between opposing shows. The ultimate in circus advertising came when the routes of two shows crossed. Then the volume of posters ballooned, newspaper ads grew, and all advance personnel went on the offensive. The result was battling what townspeople on the sidelines liked to call a "circus war." Show people called it "opposition."

Most of the resulting fireworks came from the advertising department, although others might be involved, too. One phase of the battle was to post more paper and place more ads. Another was to damage the other show's advertising and reputation. Based on uniqueness, circus advertising stressed that only occasionally did such a marvelous enterprise come to town. So when a second show came over the horizon, novelty was lessened, and bigness usually became the issue, although early shows liked to argue relative morality as well. Everything came to a high pitch. It was circus advertising at its most, not its best.

The basic move was to cover the opposition's paper, to place your posters on top of his. In the simplest form, a biller on a country route came across posters for a rival show and pasted his own on top. At issue was whether paper was live. If a show's appearance still was in the future, its paper was said to be live, and ethics dictated that it was not to be covered. In exemplary cases, the crew of the second show would find other places to put its posters. There could be opposition without covering.

But ethics often were not so persuasive. Then one show covered the other's paper, and the second retaliated in kind. Having posted its paper, a show stationed men to protect it. And if the other force returned, the two sets of billers might exchange blows, throw paste buckets, and swing brushes at each other. In its sterner form, each circus knew of the other and instructed its billers to cover or not. There might be opposition over a single town, or circuses might fight over a territory. Sometimes one show simply had a burning desire to put another out of business.

The instances were legion. With about thirty significant circuses roaming the country, their routes were sure to cross. Cole Bros. and Parker & Watts fought for dates in Michigan in 1939. Russell Bros. Pan-Pacific and Arthur Bros. Circus went to the mat in the Pacific Northwest in 1945. The 101 Ranch gave major circuses a merry chase in 1925, due at least in part to Agent Clint Finney's relishing a good fight. Cole Bros. and Hagenbeck-Wallace played much the same Ohio route in 1935. Perhaps the last billposting fight came in 1959, when Adams Bros. & Sells Bros. did battle with Cristiani Bros. Circus at Green Bay and Appleton, Wisconsin. Adams used ten times its usual order of paper. Its ads quoted prices and asked, "Why pay more?" Cristiani said that it was the "Only Big Show Coming."

When routes of rival circuses crossed, as they often did, the advance crews sometimes posted their competitive paper side by side. That's how it was when the Frank A. Robbins Circus was billed for Glassboro, N.J. in 1914, and the bigger Barnum & Bailey was playing Camden north and Bridgeton south of Glassboro a few days later. Their bills appeared simultaneously and peacefully. **Everett J. Porch.**

In anticipation of such shenanigans, each circus designated an opposition force. This might be a brigade—a handful of men detached from the regular billing crew and sent off to the point of conflict. Or it might be billers assigned regularly to such work. Occasionally, a show had an extra advance car for opposition. Its crew might operate first against another circus in the East and then jump vast mileage to take on another show in the South or West.

Once a battleground was identified, the car manager took on an extra supply of paper. He would need even more if it came to covering the opponent's posters and then "taking back" his own locations that the enemy covered. First, there would be more date sheets. It was necessary to stress which date the public should remember. Second, he ordered more pictorials, but not just any design. In opposition, one wanted more title bills, those that played up the name of the circus. And he ordered more portrait bills, those with pictures of the show owners. General circus scenes were okay for ordinary posting, but for opposition, the advertising aim was different. Title and portrait bills were important in selling one show over another.

With the shipments of poster supplies so important, opposition tactics sometimes centered on the express office. One who called for his own bundles of paper might see other packages awaiting a rival. Billposters often spoofed unsuspecting express agents into

The Kelly-Miller and Clyde Beatty-Cole Bros. shows were scheduled ten days apart at Madison, Wis., in 1962, so one took the top half of these windows and the other posted the lower half. But their advertising didn't quite come off as expected. Kelly-Miller claimed to be the second largest circus, meaning second only to Ringling. Beatty-Cole called itself the world's largest, ignoring Ringling or any other. With bills of both in one window it appeared that K-M was second to B-C, a status it would dispute loudly. **Authors' Photo.**

When the Sells & Downs Circus billers posted the lower left portion of this wall, they didn't anticipate that the Campbell Bros. Circus crew would overwhelm them with this huge stand of paper all around theirs. **Ed Bardy.**

giving them both shipments, leaving the enemy with none to post. Show agents also liked to tell the express company that there had been a mistake, that the paper was supposed to be in Danville, Virginia, not Indiana, or in Greenville, not Greensboro. Hence, the opposition's paper would be far away when the rightful owner called for it. Towners, even express agents, were easily confused about circus titles and ownerships, so these dodges were readily accomplished.

Out on the town and country routes, the billers would post extra paper and cover the rival daubs. There were extra niceties, such as "canceling" the other show or making its paper serve one's own show. On one such occasion, the Frank A. Robbins Circus was to appear on August 25 and Ringling Bros. on August 15. The Robbins people pasted a streamer over Ringling paper saying, 'Circus Day Changed to 25th." Similarly, there might be a fine six-sheet stand showing the Christy Bros. menagerie until a Mighty Haag biller pasted that name over the Christy part. The

same menagerie scene, still visible, was then doing service for the Haag show. Likely as not, the Christy crew would return and take back its daub.

Instructions from the agent to billers were explicit. Ringling's W. H. Horton wrote to F. A. (Babe) Boudinot in 1925 about opposition moves against the Sparks Circus. "Now the dirty work," he wrote. "One man is to stay in Columbus, [Mississippi] until the day of our show to prevent the covering of any of our daubs. Other two are to keep on the routes and keep knocking out Sparks paper with our dates and streamers, or anything that you have, just so that we knock them out. For the blowoff Thursday night, try your damnest to kill every Sparks daub in West Point, [Mississippi]. I don't think they will expect this, and the cost will be very little to the Big Show and there will be a world of satisfaction in it."

After taking care of Sparks in Mississippi, Boudinot's brigade of three men was to jump to Greenville, South Carolina, to help bill against the 101 Ranch. There, a Ringling crew was waiting, uncharacteristically, until the other show played that town. Then it would cover remaining Ranch paper. Meanwhile, other Ringling crews were combating the Ranch billers at Winston-Salem and Durham, North Carolina, where both shows would play in several days. Ringling's Number 3 Car completed its regular route, then doubled back to rebill Durham. The Ranch was in first, so Ringling covered Wild West paper. One woman said that she could not believe her eyes—billers covered her shed with pictures of cowboys and Indians, but the next time she looked, it was clowns and riders, then Indians again.

The Barnum and Ringling shows, separate or combined, often took out after Hagenbeck-Wallace. Hagenbeck complained of "the circus trust," and Ringling said, "wait for the big one." The Hagenbeck billers turned up in western cities that Barnum ex-

pected to play later in 1910. A Barnum bill car in Illinois was told to dash for Butte, Montana, and challenge the opposition. The crew badgered Hagenbeck-Wallace all through the Northwest. At North Yakima, Washington, Barnum paper appeared on the wires that spanned the main street. Hagenbeck induced a local church group to complain that the wires were only for Christmas decorations. The instigators said that they were paid to put posters up, not take them down. But by the light of the moon, the paper soon disappeared, thanks to Hagenbeck's opposition crew.

When Hagenbeck-Wallace played Topeka in 1923, Ringling-Barnum distributed "coming soon" heralds along the Hagenbeck parade route—an old dodge called "programming the parade." Within thirty minutes, Hagenbeck-Wallace employees swept through the downtown area, destroying the Ringling heralds. The story was much the same in several cities, and there were some

The courthouse at Shelbyville, Ky., was vacant in 1911, having been damaged by a fire, so the billposters of Sun Bros. Circus thought the tower's appearance would be improved by the addition of Sun circus paper for September 1. The Famous Robinson Circus was coming September 5. Its billposters slapped their date sheets directly on the courthouse clock face. Owner Pete Sun took the picture. Apparently, the county took it all quite calmly. **Al Conover.**

Cole Bros. was playing South Bend In., June 21-22. So the Ringling opposition brigade rolled into town and tacked these banners. 'Wait' is the first thing that catches the eye. **John Van Metre.**

sluggings and knocked heads. The Ringling opposition brigade had an answer for that; they hired uniformed Girl Scouts to distribute the next heralds. Naive scout leaders probably were completely unaware that their little charges were closely observed—but of course never challenged—by a thwarted crew of Hagenbeck huskies.

Any show that dared to play a town that Ringling wanted later was sure to see a lot of wait paper—big red posters that screamed "Wait" and "Wait for the Big One." This happened so often that the Ringling show was nicknamed Wait Bros. It also liked to swamp another show's billing with more Ringling paper that said "Coming Soon." Sometimes it did play that town later, but sometimes it was just being contrary—Wait Bros. did not necessarily intend to play all of the towns it billed this way.

In one case, Barnum & Bailey papered Beloit, Wisconsin, with "coming soon" bills against that frequent foe, Hagenbeck-Wallace. The latter retaliated with a herald that promised "A Few Secrets About the 'Coming Soon' Show." The herald explained that "the circus trust" was trying to put Hagenbeck-Wallace out of business. "It boldly attempts to deceive the public by pretending to be coming soon and practically begs the people to 'wait for us' . . . If they were coming soon, they would name the date," said Hagenbeck, the "mammoth anti-monopoly circus."

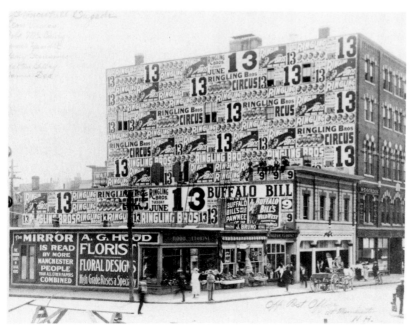

Ringling 13s far outnumber the Buffalo Bill 9s in this display of dates and pictorial banners in the opposition between the two shows at Manchester, N.H., in 1911. Ringling tack-spitters refrained from covering the paper of their rival; to overwhelm it was nearly as effective. **Circus World Museum.**

Ringling Bros. grabbed off all of the wall space for its 1901 Cleveland appearance, so the Buffalo Bill billposters had to improvise. They strung cloth banners on the front of the building. **Authors' Collection.**

ADVERTISING DEPARTMENT

Ringling Brothers' Shows

Daily Statement of Printing and Lithographs

Used at _Syracuse_

on _May 8th_ , 190 by Brigade _No. 1_

NAME OF PRINTING.	QUANTITY.
Wall Work posted in City,	None
" " Country,	3.2.9.6
" " on Railway,	
Total sheets posted,	3.2.9.6
Window Lithographs used,	1.8.7
Pamphlets or Books,	
One-fourth Sheet Programmes,	5.0.0.0
Lithograph boards covered,	
" " "	
Cloth Banners,	2.6.8
" "	
Special Bills,	

Number of Men in Brigade, _2_

" " Days at this City, _10_

In charge of _A J Snowhill_

Having covered paper, an opposition crew was open to retaliation by the other show. Not only was there more covering of paper, but also the likelihood of fisticuffs. Lumps and bumps were common. Again, Boudinot was in the fore. In later years, he recalled more of being on the receiving end. Once, his crew had covered John Robinson paper and in response, owner Jerry Mugivan and his roughnecks worked Boudinot over. Another time, Cole Bros., the first real challenge to rise up against Ringling in years, was to play Great Bend on July 29, Ringling on September 12. On a downtown street, Cole partner Jess Adkins and Agent Floyd King pointed out Boudinot to the Cole enforcers, who then beat him up. Boudinot made his presence known but finally came off second best and adjourned to a Kansas hospital for repairs.

Settling their own scores appealed to most showmen, but on occasion, someone called in the law. Once, an owner of Sells Floto had four Forepaugh-Sells billers arrested, but he was new in the business at the time and might not have done that again. Another time, the 101 Ranch sued Barnum & Bailey for covering its paper. However, the Barnum billers reached back for their cache of Ranch paper, then purposely posted it over a stand of their own posters, taking care that both layers were exposed enough for identification. A photograph of that trumped-up scene convinced an unsuspecting judge to throw the case out of court on grounds that both were guilty.

For several years before 1919, the Barnum and Ringling shows, separate but under one ownership, badgered the Hagenbeck-Wallace Circus. An opposition crew would jump halfway across the continent to post paper against Hagenbeck-Wallace. That's what happened at Davenport, Ia., in 1909. The Wallace show would play there May 29. This crew came in ahead of that to post "Coming Soon" paper for Barnum & Bailey. They have posted all of the adjacent building and part of the four-story structure. They will cover the rest of it to say "Coming Soon." Yet Barnum & Bailey wasn't due in Davenport until July 24, some fifty-six days after the Wallace date. This is the Barnum opposition crew. The regular crews will work Davenport about six weeks later. **John Van Matre.**

212

Barnum and Wallace shows were two days apart at Marion, Ohio, in 1915. Barnum people falsely announced Hagenbeck-Wallace had cancelled its date. So H-W placed this newspaper ad to say it would honor its lithograph contracts with free tickets even though building owners had allowed Barnum billers to cover H-W paper. It was all part of a massive opposition fight between the two shows. **Authors' Collection.**

Hagenbeck-Wallace retaliated for that and like skirmishes. In 1916 the Wallace show issued this herald to counter the "Coming Soon" Shows and what it belabored as the Circus Trust. "If they were coming, they would name the date," said Wallace. Barnum and Ringling did, in fact, bill some towns they never expected to play. But Barnum played this one. **Authors' Collection.**

RINGLING BROTHERS

Invite the Public to Compare the Size and Magnificence of the Great Ringling Circus with any other Show on Earth

No Other Show can bear Comparison
No Other Show has 89 Railroad Cars
No Other Show carries 1370 People
No Other Show Offers a Great Spectacle
No Other Show Presents 470 Arenic Acts

THE PUBLIC IS WARNED

Against the False Statements now being Circulated by the CARL HAGENBECK CIRCUS. It is not as Large, or even Half as Large as the RINGLING BROS. CIRCUS. The CARL HAGENBECK CIRCUS is a Show without Features. It has no Spectacle, no Street Parade that can be compared with the RINGLING PARADE, and no host of Great Arenic Acts.

THE PUBLIC IS FURTHER WARNED

To Beware of Pickpockets, House Breakers, Gamblers and Thugs and Thieves of all kinds are likely to be in Fort Collins today.

RINGLING BROS.

Carry a Police Department to Protect their Patrons.

RINGLING BROS.

Is an American Owned Show, for Americans

IT **NEVER** CARRIED THE GERMAN COAT OF ARMS on any of its Wagon, Cars or Equipment

The Carl Hagenbeck Circus

CLAIMS IT IS OWNED BY AMERICANS

BUT — On Every Wagon and Railroad Car and Even on the Private Automobile of the Owner, the Coat-of-Arms of Germany was Painted and Brazenly Flaunted in the Faces of all True Americans, up until the Time the United States entered the War.

WAIT FOR THE REAL AMERICAN SHOW

The most vicious opposition included rat sheets—special heralds that engaged in wild charges and name-calling. In this one, Ringling Bros. fired low blows against Hagenbeck-Wallace. It was 1917, wartime, when Ringling said its equipment "never carried the German coat of arms" but that every Hagenbeck wagon had "displayed the Imperial mark until the war started." Hagenbeck "claims it is owned by Americans," said Ringling, ignoring the Wallace part of the title. In fact, the Ringlings, German themselves, had once tried to buy the Hagenbeck show. Now that German family had been out of it a dozen years and the circus was owned by Indiana men. Circus agents considered such insinuations just part of the game. **Circus World Museum.**

The more frequent recourse for lesser cases came in the form of letters between show owners. Charles Sparks in 1927 wrote Jerry Mugivan that his Sells Floto billers "covered everything in the country out of Columbus, Georgia," two days before Sparks was to play there. "I have a fine chance to cover Floto at Birmingham and Pensacola but I will not do it. We have had opposition all fall with Robinson, and so far as I know neither they nor we touched a sheet. . . I hope you and Mrs. Mugivan are in the best of health. Please write me regarding Floto covering at Columbus. Your friend, Charles Sparks."

Invariably, the second showman in such an exchange responded that his billers were under the strictest orders not to cover any paper, especially that of their old friend on the aggrieved show. When the Hagenbeck-Wallace agent complained about a problem in Michigan to Gentry Bros. in 1927, Floyd King responded: "I am very sorry. . . I have notice posted in both our advertising cars, warning the men from touching other live paper. I have instructed the Car Managers particularly about not covering any Hagenbeck-Wallace paper. . . I am enclosing a check for $50 and trust it will at least show my attitude in the matter. . . ."

There was a sharp exchange in South Texas in 1941. Again, Babe Boudinot represented Ringling's interests; Vern Williams had the Cole Bros. car. Cole discovered that all of its paper in Port Arthur, Goose Creek, and nearby towns had been covered. The same was true at Lake Charles and Ruston, Louisiana. A Cole biller began to take back the daubs but soon realized that a Ringling crew was right behind him to cover them again. He gave them the slip at Ruston and covered Ringling paper there with the Cole town-name and date.

Ringling had a different version. Its men sought to protect their billing in six towns between Houston and Natchez. At Beaumont, they caught Cole Bros. men covering Ringling paper. It happened again at Goose Creek. Ringling found that its Monroe paper had been town-slipped to read Ruston, October 15, the Cole town and date, so they "took it back." The Ringling car manager sent three men back from Eldorado, Arkansas, to Ruston to protect paper and found the Cole car manager taking the Ringling lithographs out of store windows.

TIME AND TIDE WAITS FOR NO MAN

$10,000 GROUP OF TRAINED ANIMALS.

Come Now, We are the Biggest	Wait Not for the Puny
Come Now, We are Renowned	Wait Not for the Renownless
Come Now, we are Mightiest	Wait Not for the Small
COME NOW WE ARE A FEATURE SHOW	WAIT NOT FOR THE FEATURELESS
COME NOW, WE ARE SUPERIOR	WAIT NOT FOR THE INFERIOR
Come Now, we are Near You	Wait Not for the Uncertain
COME NOW, WHERE GLORY WAITS YOU	WAIT NOT FOR THE INGLORIOUS
Come Now, see the Bovalapus	WAIT NOT, THE LORD ONLY KNOWS WHAT YOU MAY SEE
Come Now, see the Riding Lion	Wait Not for the Mangy Lions
COME NOW, SEE OUR RACING STEERS!	Wait Not for the Wrong Steer
Come Now, See the Giant Camel	WAIT NOT UPON THE DESERT
COME NOW, SEE THE HIGH DIVE	Wait Not for a Low Dive
COME NOW, SEE EVERYTHING	WAIT NOT ON NOTHING
Come Now, the Big Feature	WAIT NOT FOR THE UGLY FEATURES
MIGHTY, MAGNIFICENT SHOW	Of the Little, Weakling Fellow

Sure as the Sun will Mount the Hill Tops
Sure as the Time is Speeding Bye, To-day
is Certain, To-morrow a Riddle, Wait Not

Left: With this herald the Walter L. Main Circus expected to counter "wait" paper it faced in 1898 at Middlebury, Conn. "Put not back until the morrow what ye can do today (So sayeth the Good Book)" and Walter L. Main. **Authors' Collection.**

WAIT FOR ME I AM COMING. BARNUM. And I AM WITH HIM. JUMBO.

AT GALESBURG, FRIDAY, OCT. 12.

AFTER THE MINNOWS COMES THE WHALE!

After the Puny Weaklings Comes the Giant that Holds the Keys of Wonderland.

The Great Barnum and London
8 UNITED MONSTER SHOWS. 8
—AND—
World's Exposition of Strange, Savage Men.

All exhibited for but one and the same price of admission charged by little shows, UNDER EIGHT FULL ACRES OF STUPENDOUS TENTS, large enough to swallow up all the other menageries and circuses in America combined.

GIANT-DWARFING JUMBO!

LAST OF THE MAMMOTHS—LORD OF ALL THE BEASTS.

From his immeasurable size the very show of shows alone, and yet EXHIBITED WITHOUT EXTRA CHARGE. Positively his first and only appearance here, as he must return to England in October.

1,500 Tons of Superlative Entertainment
MASSED IN A SOLID MILE OF CARS.

3 Biggest Circuses in 3 Separate Rings—2 Most Enormous Menageries — 1 Prodigious Museum—1 Huge Elevated Olympian Stage, and the

Grandly Great and only Roman Hippodrome,
With Nearly Half Mile Track.

For the first time exhibited anywhere in Christendom

A TRIBE OF NOBLE NUBIANS

Ebony Appollos, in Flowing, Snow-white Robes from the far-distant, mysterious Nile Land of the Pyramids and Catacombs. A rare assemblage none should fail to see.

29 EDUCATED ELEPHANTS 29
With the Crowning Zoological and Scientific Wonder,
THE ONLY
AMERICAN-BORN NURSING BABY ELEPHANT

A Grand Menagerie of Performing Beasts!

The first and only obtained Colony of
MALE AND FEMALE AUSTRALIAN CANNIBALS

The very Lowest Order of Mankind, and beyond all imagination most marvelous to look upon.

Whole Free Caravans of Mammoths on the Street.

JUMBO.

THE ONLY HERD OF
TOWERING LIVING GIRAFFES.

A TRIBE OF WILD SIOUX INDIANS.
The Royal rulers and fiercest warriors in the world

15 Open Dens of Wild Beasts in Parade. 15

THE ONLY CAMP OF GENUINE
Zulu Warriors and their Wives
GIGANTIC LIVING OSTRICHES.
HERDS OF RARE ANIMALS
Led and Driven upon the Highway.

The Wondrous Wild Men of Borneo.
GOSHEN, THE BROBDIGNAG OF GIANTS.
12 DIFFERENT KINDS OF MUSIC. 12

The Most Moral as well as the Mightiest and Cheapest of Shows.

PATRONIZED BY THOUSANDS NEVER SEEN AT ANY OTHER TRAVELING EXHIBITION.

Attracting the Greatest Crowds Ever Known—Securing the Cheapest Excursion Rates Ever Given.

Doing all it Advertises and a Great Deal More!

IN WHOSE HONOR CONGRESS, STATE LEGISLATURES AND COURTS ADJOURN.

The Only One that is Fair, Honest, and Liberal to the Public.

IF YOU HAVE NO MONEY TO SQUANDER
And can afford to take the Good Wife and Dear Children to but one Show this year, DO NOT BE DECEIVED INTO SORELY DISAPPOINTING BOTH YOURSELF AND THEM, but

Be Patient Yet a Little Longer,
AND THE GREAT
BARNUM AND LONDON SHOWS
WILL SURELY RETURN YOU MORE THAN
Ten Times Your Money's Worth

Who would pay 50 Cents for One Small Potato in May, when he could buy a whole bushel of Big Ones for just the same price on October 12?

BETTER WAIT, THEN, FOR BARNUM AND JUMBO!

"Wait," said Barnum. "After the minnow comes the whale!" The opposition shows found this kind of advertising difficult to overcome. **Robert Parkinson.**

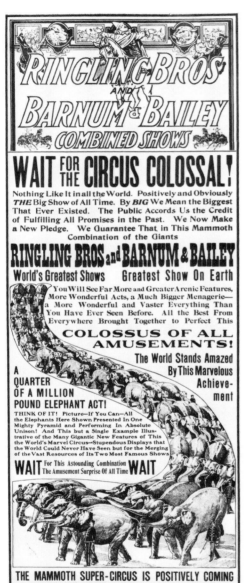

"Wait," said Ringling-Barnum, so often that it was known as Wait Bros. Circus. This herald was for Mansfield, Ohio, in 1919. **Circus World Museum.**

Zack Terrell of Cole Bros. complained to John Ringling North, saying, "I am surprised that Mr. Hopper [Ringling agent] would allow this fellow Boudinot to destroy our advertising." And with a likely reference to the time that Adkins and King had fingered Boudinot in Kansas, "Possibly there is a little score to be settled between Mr. Boudinot and the Cole Bros. Circus." Terrell was not far off the mark.

In earlier seasons, press agents cut loose with heralds so vitriolic that the ads were know as "rat sheets." Two shows were only two days apart at Chippewa Falls, Wisconsin. Sells Bros. Six Shows United, a "veritable giant among dwarfs, the Vulcan that forges thunderbolts for feeble imitators," urged the public to help "stamp out the miserable catch-penny humbugs by waiting for the only big show that will be here this season." W. C. Coup's New United Monster Show said that the first was best. "Beware of blatant boasts." It said, "Beware of shows claiming they have six shows united who never had or ever will have one show that will compare with W. C. Coup's . . . Wait for nothing. Wait for Nobody."

Often, rat sheets were tirades against another showman who perhaps had earned the distinction by his own vituperations. Adam Forepaugh got attention from many opponents. John B. Doris used two-inch letters to say, "Shame on you, Forepaugh! So you are still at your old outrageous tricks and continuing your method of deceiving the people. Alas! Once more you have dug a pit that will swallow you . . . You know that without reason you have most vilely attacked my reputation. I pity you. What a crowing old sinner you are!"

Of the same showman, the Great Eastern Show said, "He lives in enmity with nearly every relative. Reports say he turned his gray-haired father, unfed, unclothed and homeless, from his door of plenty. In 1868 he was arrested in Detroit for making fraudulent Internal Revenue returns. This is the man that talks of fraud, humbugs, etc., telling intelligent people to patronize only his show. Shame, where is thy blush?"

Some shows took the high road. Hyatt Frost in about 1870 announced, "We acknowledge no opposition and treat with silent contempt the slanders of minor and inferior and irresponsible shows." And when the Cole show and Tom Mix Circus played

CAUTION!

A base imposition is about to be practiced upon the citizens of Wisconsin by the so-called

INTERNATIONAL

and self styled

10 ALLIED SHOWS!

which, since its original organization in Missouri in April, has decreased its attractions by the withdrawal of

19 Principal Performers,

50 SUBORDINATES,

and a LARGER PORTION of ANIMALS who are NOW TRAVELLING IN SOUTHERN ILLINOIS, as a separate and distinct combination. These now attached to the OTHER SHOW gave

More than One-half of the

PROGRAMME

as presented in Missouri. The remaining remnant of the show—about

One-Third of the Original

are billed to appear in IOWA, NEBRASKA & DACOTAH. How can this ONE-THIRD of a show, advertised to exhibit in Iowa, Nebraska and Dacotah, late in June and July, exhibit even a

WHOLE OF ITS ONE-THIRD

in Wisconsin at one and the same time unless, as is undoubtedly the case, it AGAIN RE-DIVIDES to

ONE-SIXTH OF THE

ORIGINAL SHOW

a shrewd and heretofore unheard-of proceeding, only precedented by its own division in Missouri in April, inaugurating the new, or COOPER, BAILEY & CO. era of

CIRCUS on the Half-Shell!

whereby the cunning managers profit, and the public are victimized.

The rapscallion Pogey O'Brien tore into the Cooper & Bailey show with charges that it had divided, with part in Illinois, part in Missouri and part scheduled for Iowa and Nebraska. That would leave only about one-sixth for Wisconsin, he declared. False allegations like this convinced the public that circuses could and would split up to play smaller towns, an impossibility that still plagues shows. **Authors' Collection.**

Forepaugh asked the citizens of St. Joseph, Mo., if they had seen all the things the Great European show had claimed to have. The herald was circulated after the European's parade and urged everyone to skip the performance that day in favor of Forepaugh's a few days hence. It was "wait" paper at the very last minute. **Authors' Collection.**

Forepaugh-Sells circulated thousands of these heralds at Memphis on October 26, 1896, to discredit Ringling Bros. The 4-Paw show would be there six days later and consequently screamed "Wait!" **Authors' Collection.**

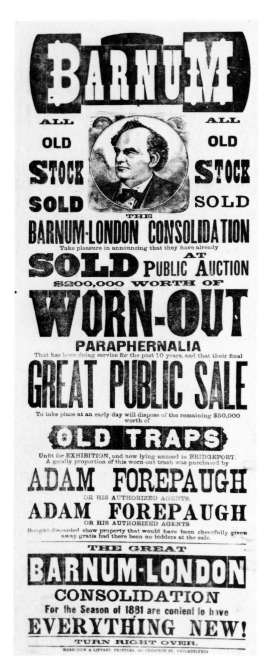

The Barnum organization conducted a big sale to dispose of surplus equipment prior to the 1881 season. When its old rival, the Forepaugh show, proved to be one of the buyers, Barnum's press agents rushed to the print shop and turned out this rat sheet. **Circus World Museum.**

218

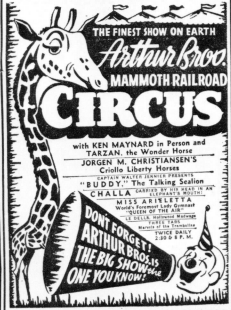

Opposition tactics frequently broke into newspaper print as well. In 1945, Cole Bros. Circus and Arthur Bros. Circus were a few days apart in Wisconsin. Arthur countered the gambling reports that Cole had planted. Cole predictably said "Wait for the big one!" **Authors' Collection.**

Sandusky, Ohio, on the same day in 1935, no paper was pulled or covered, both shows paraded without incident from the other, and at the afternoon shows, each ringmaster urged the audience to see the other circus at night.

For all the fighting, there was continual question about the value of opposition. If its advertising disappeared, a show was not likely to get an audience. But if two show dates were close together and the "circus war" came to public notice, the chances were that both did better business. The rat sheets were intended to discredit the other fellow, but one wonders if they did not firm up a public impression that all showmen were scalawags. Covering paper was a lesson in advertising but perhaps not the one that an opposition brigade thought it was teaching.

In 1945, Harrisburg, Pennsylvania, was treated to a billing war. Clyde Beatty Circus was due in town May 20; while Ringling would not arrive until July 2. The brigade was busy putting up "wait" paper. **John Van Matre Collection.**

Grand master of the word crafters was Richard F. (Tody) Hamilton. The New York Times said, "He jingled words like bells." And he inspired millions to buy circus tickets. **Kathrine E. Chenoweth Jenkins.**

CHAPTER 10

Bill Writers and Press Agents

Behind the heralds and lithographs, the couriers and the newspaper ads—behind all of the elaborate wordage that hailed the approaching circus—there was the man who created the copy—the bill writer. It was his handiwork that resulted in the boastful phraseology in circus advertising. It was his craftsmanship that turned out the circus publicity stories that press agents brought to editors. Often, the bill writer who drafted the printing in the winter was the same man who appeared in the editor's office as advance publicist for the circus in the summer. However, press agentry and bill writing were separate skills, and one did not necessarily excel at both.

There were few by-lines for bill writers, few credits to press agents. But the names of many are recalled, and the feats of some are known. John Tryon was among them. Noted for "highest intellect and most scholarly acquirements," he handled advertising copy and "wrote up all the descriptive matter for different shows" in the days of the Flatfoot circuses, the 1830s. Perhaps that "highest intellect" helped set the pattern for using ostentatious verbiage.

Hyatt Frost became a press agent for Raymond & Waring in 1847. His greatest reputation, however, was as press agent and manager of the Van Amburgh Menagerie for many seasons. Frost sprinkled his copy for Van Amburgh couriers with Biblical quotations about animals to calm the opposition from churches, pointing

out the difference between worldy circuses and his educational and moral menagerie. Not just publicity, but also the steering of opinion was a circus routine long before public relations agencies came to the field.

W. T. Van Orden was press agent for the Spalding & Rogers enterprises, especially the Floating Palace. He wrote copy and placed ads but also met the press and conducted its tours of that fabulous circus boat. Van Orden's help in writing parodies of Shakespeare's works made Dan Rice a leading Shakespearian clown. When Rice and Spalding became bitter enemies, each hired a writer to compose the vitriolic rat sheets with which to attack the other. Each hired a specialist in the scurrilous, but neither knew that they had hired the same writer. Clarence Chester Moore wrote the rat sheets for both sides.

Richard P. Jones handled publicity for Welch, Lent, Rice, and one Adam Forbach, whom he renamed Adam Forepaugh and called 4-Paw—an early classic in manufacturing an image and a logo. But Jones gave it all up to become a doctor. Charles Stowe was not satisfied to work for simply the Sells Bros. Circus. Instead, he made it known as the Sells Bros. Seven Elephant Show and later the Sells Bros. 50-Cage Menagerie, all as part of his tenure as press chief there. He included recipes and farming tips along with circus material in couriers that he wrote for Sells.

A later Forepaugh promotion was a national beauty contest

and presentation of the winning queen, all the work of Charles H. Day, one of the greatest early press agents. It was Day, too, who kept Forepaugh in competition with the Barnum show and conducted Forepaugh's share of the publicity war over white elephants—which discredited white elephants forever and helped put all circus publicity to question.

P. T. Barnum, of course, was the creative genius of most press agentry and publicity concepts, but his fame came from management of the American Museum. W. C. Coup saw the publicity value in Barnum's name and induced him to join in a new circus. Barnum himself had little to do with actual publicity work on the Barnum circus. That chore was in the capable hands of Richard (Tody) Hamilton, perhaps the greatest single press and publicity figure in circus history. He earned that status by creating the Jumbo campaign, if no others. He was a principal factor in making the Barnum circus the Greatest Show on Earth, passing up the larger Forepaugh show and others that were well established. His handling of publicity and his skills as a bill writer were sufficient to keep up with James A. Bailey, the circus wizard who created Barnum & Bailey.

Bailey and Hamilton as early as 1881 brought many editors from around the country to see the Barnum & Bailey opening in New York and to enjoy a three-day press party—a device used now by pro sports, the military, industry, government, and show business. Tody Hamilton proclaimed that "to state a fact in ordinary language is to permit a doubt about the statement." So he never let ordinary language creep into his talk or type. He was renowned for the use of long words—sesquipedalianism—which became a regular practice, a circus landmark in itself. Hamilton caused editors to see the circus as a source of news and succeeded in getting his circus covered in the uppity dramatic notes and reviews. He was followed by Willard Coxey, who became a leader in placing circus features, even full-page stores, with responsible editors. James J. Brady learned from Coxey about promoting big space in the papers.

John M. Burke holds a place of distinction among the publicity giants. He took over where the dime novel authors left off to make Buffalo Bill a world celebrity. He was press agent for Cody and the Wild West show through most of their combined existence. To help get the job done, this Easterner took on the appearance of a character as Western as those about which he wrote. He became "Arizona John" and, by right of self-created commission, "Major" John Burke. He had shoulder-length hair, as did most western personalities, but Burke put his up in a bun with three hairpins when away from the public.

Dexter W. Fellows was a giant among press personalities. He worked on the Cody show and others but mainly Ringling Bros. and Barnum & Bailey. Newspaper people loved him, in part because of his ability to remember their names from year to year. No matter that he worked hard at this and studied a little booklet of names before unleashing his overpowering presence on another newsroom.

Fellows dressed the part—even wearing checkered vests in his earliest seasons. He handled Ringling-Barnum in the heyday of nationally known stars such as Lillian Leitzel, the Flying Codonas, the Zacchinis, and the Wallendas. He experienced one of a press agent's greatest hazards when he began to get newspaper coverage about himself as much as about his circus. His successor in kind was Frank Braden, once of little Gentry Bros., then ahead of the 101 Ranch, and next working with Fellows on Ringling. Braden, too, was beloved by editors and copyboys across the country and could get circus publicity where others failed. Braden was a story man, one who could write circus copy but who shined brightest in pointing out the stories that reporters themselves would do well to write before someone else beat them to these natural by-line pieces. Veteran newspapermen in the 1980s still harked back to memories of that notable day when as cub reporters in long-ago newsrooms they looked up and fell victim to the winning personality of Dexter Fellows or Frank Braden.

No one practiced the press agent's arts with more aplomb than Francis Beverly Kelley. Urbane and polished, he filled a newsroom with his presence just as did Dexter Fellows. It was Fellows who told the young Kelley that a press agent never carries a briefcase—"You would look like a school teacher!" Fifty years later, Bev Kelley still carried show publicity material only in a manila envelope.

It was Kelley who convinced the *National Geographic*—twice—that the circus was a study in geography and worthy of major coverage therein. He manufactured circus news when he took a baby elephant to a Republican convention and a steam calliope to the Truman inaugural parade. He wrote numerous books and inspired more. Between circus assignments, he handled national press for the March of Dimes, and he was agent for dozens of Broadway productions. True to his circus experience, Kelley was best in taking shows on road tours rather than sitting out the New York runs. Perhaps Kelley's most important contribution was influencing Ringling-Barnum public relations after the Hartford fire. This began just hours after the blaze and continued for years. His judgment and delicate touch prevailed over a less-studied approach and did much to save the circus, both as Ringling and as an institution.

But while Bev Kelley was scoring national publicity, he also was succeeding greatly in a circus press agent's first duties—the care and treatment of editors while his show approached their towns and the handling of local reporters at the show grounds on circus day.

With most circuses, the press agent visited editors ahead of show day and sought advance publicity. The Ringling-Barnum show, however, developed a system that allowed a press agent to appear in a given town both ahead of time and on the circus day as well. There were enough men on the staff so that each agent was assigned certain towns and was allowed to handle the whole publicity program in his assigned spots. This all-star cast included not only Dexter Fellows, Frank Braden, and Bev Kelley, but also Allen Lester, Bill Fields, Sam Stratton, Bernie Head, Frank Morrissey, Tom Killilea, and many more, including Eddie Howe, trainee under the GI Bill of Rights after World War II.

The procession of press agents has been nearly as impressive as the circuses they heralded. Yet, only some among them have been bill writers as well. These trades overlapped, but usually a man is better known for one skill than the other. Among the bill writers was Alf T. Ringling. One of the original brothers, his contribution to their partnership was the writing of publicity material. The bill writing abilities of Tody Hamilton, Charles Day, and Hyatt Frost have been acknowledged. In more modern times, three additional names stand out.

One is Justus Edwards, press agent for Clyde Beatty Circus and Polack Bros. Circus in the 1940s and 1950s. Edwards was a skilled writer and an original thinker insofar as circus ads, programs, and bills were concerned. His work included excellent layout and artwork. Edwards, like many of his fellow press agents, held an undying and unlimited love for the circus as an institution. He knew his subject and delighted in recalling its lore and adding to its history. He respected circus people and marvelled at their accomplishments. Thus, it was second nature to write publicity material about them.

Another bill writer was that jack of all trades, Floyd King, who was at his best as agent and bill writer. He, too, loved the institution and revelled in its excesses. King was excited about being a circus man when he first joined Cherokee Ed's Wild West and when he left the Memphis Commercial-Appeal's police beat in favor of the Al G. Barnes Circus press job. He was equally excited about being with the circus nearly seventy hectic seasons later.

Floyd King delighted in creating new circus bills with the old formula of expansive language, unmitigated exaggerations, and elaborate illustrations. It was what came to be expected, if not demanded, from circuses; the public likes it as a unique style of advertising and journalism, counting it unthinkable to call up anything so pointless as consumer protection. Floyd King was the final practitioner of old-school bill writing. His heralds reeked of the lessons taught by Tody Hamilton and other pioneers.

The epitome of bill writers came in the person of Roland Butler. From the Sparks Circus, he moved up to the top post in the Ringling Bros. and Barnum & Bailey press department in the 1930s, and for twenty years his artwork and verbiage marked all Ringling publicity material. He engineered the campaigns for the Ubangi Savages, Giraffe-Necked Women, and Gargantua the Great. An artist by trade and talent, Butler created a style for illustrating circus ads that has not been equalled. His ability for crafting powerful slogans in a few simple words leaped out from every billboard and newspaper ad—"the world's most terrifying living creature" or "tribe of monster-mouthed Ubangi savages" among them. Butler was the all-time master at drawing clown faces. He combined artistry with readable type to contrive the best circus title logos ever. His advertisements seemed to stand apart on a newspaper page, demanding attention over all else.

Roland Butler was violent in his speech as he was extravagant in his ad copy. He lavished adjectives and superlatives on his circus subjects. But for himself he reserved a title that to the public seemed uncharacteristically modest. He called himself a bill writer. And Roland knew that this superlative put him in honored company.

If the Barnum show ripped Forepaugh, then Adam's agents were not left speechless. Forepaugh's master bill writer, Charles H. Day, could recapture the initiative. Writing special bills like this one, however, came only after the bill writers already had turned out the expansive wordage for the show's day-after-day ad campaigns. **Authors' Collection.**

Routine ad copy for circuses was something apart, and the men who composed it were creative writers who first identified many of the questions and answers that face agency and marketing people today. Cooper & Bailey's bill writer demonstrated the art with this copy in 1879. **Authors' Collection.**

"JUMBO," the Gigantic Elephantine Monster

Purchased at the Zoological Gardens in Regents Park, London, England, at a cost exceeding $25,000.

THE BIGGEST ELEPHANT EVER SEEN IN OR OUT OF CAPTIVITY!

For many years a TREASURED AND ROYAL FAVORITE. **Her Majesty** the Queen, and her children and grandchildren have ridden on his back. With manually...

HIS ENORMOUSLY DEVELOPED STATURE

is even ill temper and ferocity as is always the case with African males of his series, and the Directors of the "Zoo," against the

Remonstrance of the People and Press

of Great Britain, disposed of him to the Showman Prince and his associates in beat...

This Miraculous Moving Mountain of Flesh, this Most Prodigious Towering Animate Wonder, is the most COLOSSAL AND COSTLY FEATURE ever presented to any audience.

On Exhibition EVERY AFTERNOON and NIGHT.

ment. To get him to the vessel at the dock it was necessary to BUILD A TREMEN-DOUS LOW-WHEELED VEHICLE, which he was gradually induced to enter, after weeks of delay, when

FORTY STRONG DRAUGHT HORSES HAULED HIM TO THE SHIP, the hatchway of which had been cut away and the upper deck raised to receive him.

His mighty ears are as large as a folding parlor door, and he is

LARGER than any TWO ELEPHANTS in Existence.

Oh, That Precious Baby!

BIRTH OF THE BABY ELEPHANT   BORN IN CAPTIVITY!

Oh, that Darling Baby!
Only nursing Baby Elephant ever exhibited in New York.

Oh, that Cunning Baby!
As full of Playful Pranks as a Mischievous Kitten.

BABY ELEPHANT WAS BORN AT BRIDGEPORT, CONN., FEB. 2d, THIS YEAR.

Its weight was 145 pounds, height 35 inches and length 36. The length of trunk and tail, each 7 inches. It stood erect and firmly on its feet in 30 minutes, and in two hours nursed the breasts of its colossal mother. There were present at the birth and soon afterward

Eighty Learned Doctors and Savants,

who for the first time in history were enabled to accurately establish the period of gestation at about twenty months. Its eventful and important was this occasion, that more than

One Hundred Columns Published in the Daily City Press

consumed the evening of the previous stronger, describing its habits and nursing ways...

A prominent showman, when it was sixteen hours old, offered

$200,000 for the BABY and its MOTHER,

which was promptly declined. Private parties in New York and Hartford

INSURED ITS LIFE ONE YEAR for $300,000,

paying a premium of $1,00 weekly, aggregating $50,000.

The Mother of the Distinguished Scientific Baby

is a "other elephant called "queen," formerly the property of James A. Bailey, who took her as one of his most noted features in his celebrated...

THREE YEARS' JOURNEY AROUND THE WORLD

"Queen," is 25 years old, and weight 4,800 pounds.

The Father is the Lordly Elephant "Chieftain,"

of the London Circus had prior the the consolidation with the Barnum Show. He weight 8,800 pounds, and his age about 30 years.

PAGES OF GRAPHIC, TRUTHFUL PORTRAIT VIEWS
IN THE ILLUSTRATED NEWSPAPERS OF AMERICA AND EUROPE.

Father, Mother and Baby Elephant

WILL BE SEEN AT EVERY PERFORMANCE WITHOUT EXTRA CHARGE, TOGETHER WITH THE TENS OF THOUSANDS OF OTHER RARE NOVELTIES.

A CONTENTED AND HAPPY ELEPHANT FAMILY!

Hamilton created the Jumbo campaign. It captivated the emotions of two nations and added a word to the language. **Authors' Collection.**

Richard P. Jones set the Sells Bros. Circus apart as a major enterprise through his "50 Cages" campaign, which included these bills in 1884. Integrity and credibility for the show were among his goals in an era when rat sheets had devastated the circus business. **Authors' Collection.**

Louis E. Cooke handled landmark advertising campaigns and bill writing for W.W. Cole, Buffalo Bill and Barnum & Bailey. **Circus World Museum.**

Willard D. Coxey helped make the Ringling Bros. Circus known in every household. **Circus World Museum.**

Dexter Fellows was considered by many to be the master among press agents. He was recognized more for creating stories to be covered by others, rather than as a writer himself. **Circus World Museum.**

Frank Braden was highly respected in newsrooms throughout the nation and engineered outstanding circus publicity coups. **Authors' Collection.**

Roland Butler set the modern standards for both bill writing and circus artwork. **Authors' Collection.**

Allen Bloom, Ringling's senior vice-president for marketing and sales, maintains close supervision over all advertising—logos, art work, newspaper layouts, TV tapes, posters, bill writing, allocation of budget shares to each advertising medium, and more—for Ringling Bros. and Barnum & Bailey's twin circus units plus the ice shows and other entertainment operated by the company in the 1980s. **Ringling Bros. and Barnum & Bailey Circus.**

PRESS BOOK No. 2

Howe's Great London Circus

To The Publisher:

The notices enclosed in this book are not duplicated in your circulation territory. These stories have been compiled with care and the promises to the public will be fulfilled.

You will please bear in mind that under no conditions are these notices to be considered as an advertising contract.

City _____

Day _____

Date _____

BERT RUTHERFORD,
General Agent.
General Press Agent.

DEPARTMENT OF PUBLICITY
ADVERTISING CAR No. ONE

Dear Sir:—

We are taking the liberty of enclosing a small amount of advertising matter for our Big Five Ring Wild Animal Circus, which is to exhibit in

_____

CHRISTY BROS BIG 5 RING WILD ANIMAL SHOWS

The Newest Big Show In All The World

5 Continent Menagerie

1250 People — 600 Horses — 50 Cages Animals
30 Lions — 2 Cars of Elephants and Camels
5 Bands — 2 Calliopes — 2 Complete Electric Light Systems—30 Double Length Steel Cars
6-Pole Big Top — 5 Mammoth Rings —
2 Steel Arenas — Wild Beast Hippodrome

1000 Character Bible Spectacle

Noah and the Ark

The Longest, Costliest and Most Magnificent Open Den

Free Street Parade at 12 O'Clock Noon Daily

2 SHOWS DAILY 2 and 8 P.M.

Christy Bros. Circus travels on its own special train of 30 double length steel cars, and carries the largest collection of trained wild animals in the world. You will not regret your visit to our show, and we know that you will carry home with you pleasant memories of a happy holiday spent with us.

Won't you please co-operate with us by displaying our printed matter as conspiciously as possible in your establishment?

We are enclosing Two Reserved Seat Tickets for your personal use as an appreciation of your efforts in our behalf.

Sincerely,
CHRISTY BROS.

Advertising and publicity at the grass roots level was a special knack for circuses. Despite crudeness of the material, the system worked. Press agent for Howes' Great London **opposite page, left:** misplaced his own apostrophe but the little press book garnered publicity for the show. **Opposite page, right:** Christy Bros. Circus traded tickets for advertising space in feeder towns. **Above:** Cole Bros. Circus contracted for ad space with a form simplified to the extreme, but calling for editorial support as well as ad linage. At other times, other circuses created highly sophisticated press manuals, inventive promotion plans, and original ad tie-ins. **Authors' Collection.**

COLE BROS. CIRCUS
(INCORPORATED)

$_____ _____, 1943

This is to certify that the undersigned Publishers of_____
have this day entered into an agreement with the Agent of the above named Circus to run advertisements as specified below:

Daily (Paper)_____   (Sunday) _____

_____ Adv. on_____   _____ Adv. on_____

_____ Adv. on_____   _____ Adv. on_____

_____ Adv. on_____   _____ Adv. on_____

_____ Adv. on_____   _____ Adv. on_____

Together with liberal display cuts and reading notices to be furnished by the Agents. In consideration of which we have received an order upon the Treasurer of the above named Circus for $_____.

Treasurer's check, bearing even date herewith, will be paid upon presentation at the show grounds between 2 and 3 p. m. on the date of exhibition. It being understood that the publishers will furnish copies of papers containing advertisements or news stories of the Circus, together with all pictorial and display ad cuts which may have been furnished.

_____ Agent.   _____ Publisher.

COLE BROS. CIRCUS
(INCORPORATED)

$_____

TREASURER, Cole Bros. Circus: _____, 1943

Upon presentation of this order, together with copies of papers containing advertisements and reading notices, as well as all cuts furnished, please pay_____or order, $_____.

Daily (Paper)_____   (Sunday) _____

_____ Adv. on_____   _____ Adv. on_____

_____ Adv. on_____   _____ Adv. on_____

_____ Adv. on_____   _____ Adv. on_____

_____ Adv. on_____   _____ Adv. on_____

_____ Press Agent.

Payable between 2:00 and 3:00 P. M. on date of exhibition, at
the ticket wagon on the show grounds.

Form No. 19—500—3-43

The contracting press agent gave each newspaper a numbered booklet of prepared stories ready for use and complete with mats of the illustrations. This is one of Ringling's 1924 press books. Each local editor had to be assured that other papers in the area would not turn up with identical stories, since that embarrassment would reveal he was using material prepared by the circus rather than his own staff. **Authors' Collection.**

The puffy material written by circus press agents, such as this example from the Seils-Sterling Circus, was hardly great journalism. But it was used. In a string of nineteen Kansas towns played by the Floto show in 1905, fourteen papers carried a particular story from the press book, while ten used another and ten used a third. One newspaper printed fourteen stories from the press book, and in all the show scored about sixty-three hits in the nineteen towns. Several editors even printed the standard review written in advance by the press agents and left with the editors before the show for use after the local performances. **Authors' Collection.**

Roland Butler's logos for the Ringling-Barnum title long outlasted his own tenure with the show, and his drawings of cats and clown faces have been borrowed by several other shows. **Ringling Bros and Barnum & Bailey Circus.**

Ringling Bros.- Barnum & Bailey Combined Circus

Town Cancelled July Rome Subst--

CITY. Binghamton, New York.   DATE Thursday, July 11th   193-

NAME OF PAPER	Space Contracted	Amount	Tickets	BUS. MANAGER	MAN'G EDITOR	CITY EDITOR
Leader - Press, PM 6 days	74 in	$137.75	Op	R.E.Bennett	Tom Hutton	S.A.Weller.
				See Mr Hutton, took book # 51 and story.		
Sun,AM 6 days.	74 in	$129.50	op	*miss* H.M.Ayres.	Walter J. Lyons "Bud"	S.W.Nash.
				See Mr Lyons, took book # 61 and story .		

No publications 4th of July either papers

Town Cancelled July 9 on account of floods

ROLAND; Youngstown in Saturday, July 20th, mail roto today Mr Ward.
Pat Valdo's - Binghamton town - (Patrick F. Fitz

Roland, As you enter Mr Huttons office you will notice a photo of Clyde Beatt-
that his weakness, that along with the propaganda put out by De Roselli along
with his admiration of Bev Kelley. He has to be handled just right.

Binghamton 1935

ADV. SCHEDULE -	June 29	Sun. 30	July 1	2	3	4	5	6	Sun. 7	8	9	10	11	Space	Rate	Amt
Leader-Press-P.M.	11		8½	8½	8½		8½	11		4½	4½	4½	4½	74 in	2.50 1.75	137.7=
Sun — A.M.	11		8½	8½	8½		8½	11		4½	4½	4½	4½	74 in	1.75	129.5-
															Total 26-	

Over what railroad does show arrive? Lackawanna R.R.   Lot Location Stowe Park

from Utica Leave on Lackawanna for Syracuse

DOWN TOWN TICKET SALE Edw. A. Johnson Weeks & Dickenson Music Store, 39 Chen-
Dickenson   St,12 tickets

| 58 | OUTSIDE PAPERS | Press Agent Edw. A. Johnson | Date June 27, |

TICKETS OVER

The contracting press agent's report for Binghamton, N.Y., in 1935 indicated his schedule of ads in the two papers at a cost of $267.25. The agent, Edward Johnson, gave Press Book 51 to one paper and Book 61 to the other. He arranged for a music store to sell circus tickets on show day. Then he warned Roland Butler, who would come in later, that one of the editors was partial to rival showmen on another circus. All of this and other work by the advance was to no avail; at the last minute the town was cancelled because of floods. The press agents then had to scramble to get as much attention as possible for the substitute town in a slim two days. **Circus World Museum.**

And get it they did. Butler dashed to Rome, N.Y., the substitute stand, and bought this double-truck advertisement in The Daily Sentinel. "Like a thunderbolt!" he declared. The paper pushed aside news of Italian mobilization and TVA votes in Congress to put three circus pictures on Page 1. There was not time for posters, no power in broadcasting yet. The single newspaper edition was the sole announcement. Despite the short notice, 10,000 people came to the show in Rome the next day. **Authors' Collection.**

Perhaps influenced by the great Walter Winchell at the time, Ringling's F. Beverly Kelley wears his hat as he speaks into the radio microphone. Kelley was a pioneer in the use of broadcasting for show promotion. With Ringling, Hagenbeck-Wallace and other circuses, he perfected early radio publicity techniques and went on to explore television as well. **Authors' Collection.**

The working press came to include radio and television. Broadcasters frequently did remote pick-ups from high wires and tiger cages. **Authors' Collection.**

RINGLING BROS AND BARNUM & BAILEY
1956 TV-RADIO Working Pass
To Restricted Departments of The Circus
NOT GOOD FOR SEATS

Issued to _____

Place _____ Date _____

Signed _____

NOTE: THIS WORKING PASS IS NOT A PERMIT FOR TAKING AMATEUR OR PROFESSIONAL MOTION PICTURES. It is not transferable and will not be honored if presented by an unauthorized person. Nor will it admit more than one person unless so specified. Please cooperate with us in protecting the status of radio and television representatives entitled to the use of this pass in pursuit of their work.

NORMAN CARROLL, TV-Radio Director   **RALPH ALLAN, Ass't.**

CHAPTER 11

Radio and Television

Broadcasting is the rookie in circus advertising—unless one counts the clown who, in the time and style of a town crier, went to the village square and called out the news that the circus was in town. For more than 125 seasons, the circus got along without radio and television, and for several more it did not know what to do with them.

Some of the first uncertain steps came in the 1920s. Sells Floto made a pass at radio in Chicago in 1922. Lew Graham, whose powerful voice filled the huge Ringling-Barnum big top with announcements, talked more softly on guest appearances with radio stations in a few principal cities during 1923. Johnny Agee is said to have told circus bedtime stories over radio to promote his own circus that year. As if Lew Graham's decibels were not enough of a challenge to the new medium, the Sells Floto steam calliope was turned loose for a concert over WOAW, Omaha, in 1925.

The Sells Floto show continued to pioneer in the field. In 1929, it hired Klara K. Knecht as educational director. Her main job was to get schools dismissed on circus day, but another role was making guest appearances and setting interviews on radio stations. Each spring, she made about thirty radio shows in Chicago on behalf of the circus. In 1930, Klara appeared on about four stations a week as Sells Floto moved through Ohio and Pennsylvania during May. She told listeners about the show's great star, Tom Mix, who himself was to be a radio star as well. With Hagenbeck-Wallace in 1934, she was on radio 210 times, more remarkable when it is known that the show played 174 cities but sixty of these places had no radio station. Radio was just getting well started, but it had learned one thing about circuses—eleven stations and one network in Chicago gobbled up 366 free tickets during the engagement of Cole Bros.-Clyde Beatty Circus in 1935.

About that time, the great circus press agent, Dexter Fellows, was asked to say a few words at a banquet of the Advertising Club in New York, so he told a yarn about the profane old showman, Adam Forepaugh. Too late, he learned that the quoted profanity went out over the entire NBC network.

That interview and scores of others were set by F. Beverly Kelley, the master of broadcast publicity and one of the best press agents ever to represent a circus. He was with the John Robinson Circus as a free-lance author a year and then wrangled a post with Ringling-Barnum in 1930. There he joined Clinton Connell— "Uncle Toby"—in making school, radio, and service club appearances in the style of Klara Knecht. After Uncle Toby got crosswise with management over an impromptu press party that he staged at Niagara Falls, Kelley continued as a one-man radio department through 1932. In that time, his biggest hit was placing Clyde Beatty on the powerful Lowell Thomas network news show.

After serving as chief of all publicity on Hagenbeck-Wallace in 1933, Kelley resumed radio work for Ringling in 1938. He presented the circus as a news event and stressed interviews. Only rarely did the show buy commercial time in that period. The heart of Kelley's material was a series of forty recorded programs in which he narrated circus stories, punctuated with both circus music and the imitation of wild animal sounds by Bradley Barker. These were recorded as quarter- and half-hour radio shows by the World Broadcasting Company. Barker came to the assignment after making the sounds of animals for the Frank Buck movies and even the MGM lion. Buck himself, featured on the circus in 1938, was a frequent guest on radio programs arranged by Kelley. The biggest score in this period, however, was getting the Ringling band on the popular Fitch Bandwagon radio program. It brought more mail than any other program ever done by the strong Sunday night network feature. For routine interviews, Kelley's favorite was Felix Adler, king of the clowns. Kelley continued with the circus as head of the combined radio and press department from 1945 to 1947.

When Kelly came back to Ringling in 1954, television was a reality. Times had changed since Klara Knecht and Hagenbeck-Wallace had played radio-less towns. Now it took both Kelley and Charles Schuler to keep up with publicity chores on radio and television alone in Ringling's towns. Now, they noted, there were more radio and television stations than newspapers, much more of a surprise then than now.

Circuses used broadcasting largely as a publicity vehicle, and radio-television people liked to do broadcasts from the high wire or the lion trainer's arena. But commercials were sure to come. The shows did a little and then more advertising on the air. First, there were spot announcements to be read by the local announcer. Then there were radio transcriptions, and finally tape recordings in ten-, twenty-, thirty-, and sixty-second versions.

Television stepped up the pace in the 1950s, but still the users were uncertain about how to use this medium. There were interviews, and news cameramen came on the show grounds for film footage. But even in the 1960s, circuses were so unfamiliar with television that when they provided a still photograph for a voice-over, their photo slides often were vertical shots rather than the horizontal ones required by television.

Newspaper advertising dominated circus ad budgets until the 1970s. By then, shows had passed through the era of thirty-five-millimeter filmed commercials and were using video tape. And the budgets reflected a progressively greater turn to television. Promoters debated annually about whether to buy television. One year, a promoter would lean toward television and the next he might exclude it entirely. Ultimately, television usually took more than half of the ad budget for a typical city, while newspapers held on and both radio and direct mail struggled to keep a share.

Color television took the place of most circus posters, with nearly no one realizing why this was the trade. Each served the same purpose in its turn, depicting the color and the panoply of the circus. Once men and boys stared at dazzling lithographs, a rare exposure to color. Now families saw the pretty costumes and amazing activities promised by the circus via television. Until color television came along, nothing could do this quite as well as posters. With television in hand, there was little role for posters.

Most of this was strictly a Ringling-Barnum story. The other indoor circuses, usually under the auspices of a Shrine temple or other clubs, found it more difficult to pay for television commercials. The tented circuses also found it difficult and too expensive for the most part. By the 1980s, however, circuses such as Clyde Beatty-Cole Bros., Carson & Barnes, and Circus Vargas were making frequent use of effective television commercials.

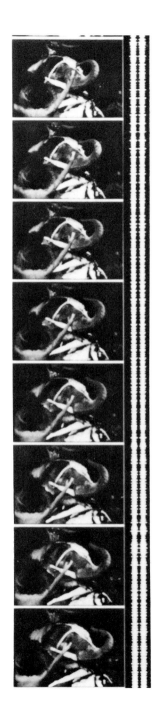
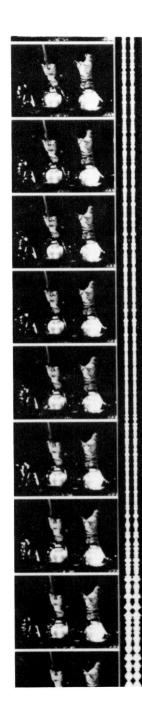

Venturing into television advertising, the Ringling show first used a few 35mm slides, then annual combinations of 10-, 30-, and 60-second spot announcements on 16mm movie film. Each of these would be tagged with local information about the circus date. Now the show uses a sophisticated television campaign with video tapes for each edition of the circus. **Ringling Bros. and Barnum & Bailey Circus.**

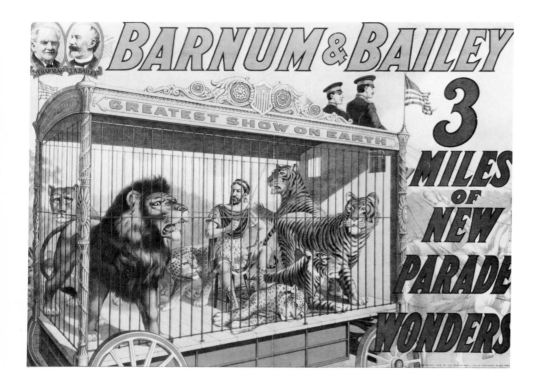

First there were the lithographs to advertise street parades. Whether it was the giant Barnum & Bailey or the latter-day Diano Bros., circuses put great emphasis on their street parades. **Authors' Collection**.

CHAPTER 12

Street Parades

In modern advertising, nothing quite compares with the grand, free street parade of a big circus. Posters and heralds have their counterparts. Radio and newspapers are easy to understand. But street parades? Here was a unique medium, something that few could do at all and none could do as well. It was like a massive moving show window. It surpassed coming attractions at the movies or a free sample at the candy store.

The circus put together a fantastic procession of bandwagons, mounted people, clowns, cages, and tableau wagons. Horses' heads bobbed with red plumes; shiny harness was trimmed in brass. Wagon wheels rolled with a sunburst effect. Elephants were decked out in rich velvet blankets. Red-coated bandsmen played their hearts out. At just before noon, this parade moved through the principal streets of the town. Curbs were lined with excited townspeople. A circus parade was not to be missed and not to be underrated.

The show was its own best advertisement. Posters had promised wonders, and here they were. Five elephants! Real Arabs, Indians, and Chinese right here in town. Clowns and pretty ladies and zebras and calliopes! The parade showed off the circus wares and built demand that resulted in sales.

Philip Lailson's circus, America's second, appears to have been first with a parade. It was advertising in the purest, simplest form. The several performers rode horseback through the streets of Philadelphia each day during the early summer of 1797 to announce another performance.

By the late 1830s, circuses were using tents and moving daily. As the string of wagons neared the town of the day, the show owner called a halt for employees to don uniforms and costumes. The caravan of wagons became a procession of floats—flags flying, performers smiling, musicians tooting. The arrival of the show also was its street parade; it was a grand entry into town showing off all that the circus had to offer.

Howes Great London Circus brought from Europe several massive wagons decorated with gorgeous wood carvings that depicted mythology, art, and history, wagons designed solely for parade purposes. Soon, every major circus was compelled to buy comparable parade features. The Howes wagons were a problem on the crude roads and weak bridges of the 1860s and 1870s. Moreover, some were built like nests of boxes, and inner parts could be elevated, rising even thirty feet when in use during parades. The introduction of telephone and electric wires overhead in most cities in the 1880s meant there no longer was adequate clearance for the higher wagons. By then, the bigger shows had forsaken overland moves in favor of the glories of railroad transport. Heavier loads and longer moves were routine. People and horses were more rested. It was a golden age for circuses. Shows were larger, and competition was intense. Advertising expanded—and it included bigger and better parades.

Spalding and Barnum had forty-horse hitches. Buffalo Bill himself rode parade. Ringling Bros. had one giant wagon carrying a pipe organ, another with a chime of bells. John Robinson's calliope was drawn by twenty-four ponies. Sells Bros. and others showed fairy-tale floats for the children. A series of tableaux representing the nations was paraded by the U.S. Motorized Circus, then Robbins Bros. and Cole Bros. Later Christy Bros. acquired surplus Barnum wagons and displayed an elaborate parade.

No longer was the parade also the show's arrival. Instead, people crowded the railroad yards to watch the show unload. Then they thronged the circus grounds to see the big tent put up. The preparations became further enticements; the makeready was like so much more advertising. Then came the parade. It was prsented on the biggest screen of all—live. It was an 1800-second spot announcement—a three-D wonder in living color, stereo sound, and exotic aromas. It was a capper, a climax to the show's saturation campaign.

First came the owner in a carriage, then trumpeters and flag-bearers on horseback. The bandwagon was drawn by six or eight, maybe even twenty-four or forty beautifully matched draft horses, and other wagons were pulled by similar teams of four, six, and eight. Townspeople marveled at the stock that a good circus carried. It was as if someone today were to display the finest luxury sports cars, the most powerful off-the-road diesel tractors, and a private jet plane.

The paraded cages usually had the sideboards in place, but they were emblazoned with the amazing inventory that each wagon carried—maybe Royal Bengal tigers or a "blood-sweating behemoth from the River Nile." The panels might promise an emu or an eland or a vlaak vaark, but one had to come to the circus to see all of that. Yet, some cages were opened to view. In one, a trainer sat calmly among his black-maned lions. In a glass-sided den full of writhing serpents, a pretty girl caressed the biggest of them all. With that to be seen in the parade, imagine what was under the big top!

The parade brought more music—a clown band, Scotch bagpipers, and the sideshow's Dixieland minstrels. Mounted units included armored knights or fox hunters or fashionable equestriennes. Sometimes there was cavalry and always a Wild West section with cowboys, Indians, and a stagecoach or covered wagon. Mysterious Arabs guided camels. Then came the elephants, trunk to tail, shuffling along with their self-important handlers.

Last was the steam calliope, a wonder lost on late generations. When the player manipulated the keyboard, steam powered the set of whistles—tuned or partially so—and they emitted an awesome melody. A steam calliope had to be the loudest thing in show business until the advent of human cannonballs and rock concerts.

Printed advertising featured the marching advertisement. Couriers and posters encouraged everyone to see the parade—ads to advertise the advertisement. For the biggest and best parade of all, the Barnum & Bailey 1903 edition, more than twenty different styles of posters were devoted to the parade alone. Nearly every show's standard order to the printer called for a heavy proportion of parade lithographs. Showmen felt that getting people to see the parade was the surest way to get them into the big top as well. At least, it was like other show advertising campaigns in that one never knew which aspect actually induced the customer to buy a ticket, so none was overlooked.

But bigger parades meant that a show had to carry more horses than otherwise and more wagons. They meant more cars on the train and correspondingly higher railroad costs. Other problems set in. First it was the electric wires, then the trolley schedules, and next the auto traffic. Some cities insisted on parades for the extra business that they brought to town, but others grew protective of asphalt streets that became rutted under heavy wagons on summer days. The performers uniformly hated parades; those with enough influence managed to be excused.

Show owners began to question the process and the value. Street parades were at their best from about 1880 to around 1910. Right on the heels of its best parade, Barnum & Bailey eliminated the whole concept in 1905. Public demand and competition brought it back, but the trend was there. The Great Wallace Show proposed to the Ringlings that parades be discontinued. That time, Sells Floto insisted on continuing, and others felt that they had to be competitive.

Ringling Bros. and Barnum & Bailey did quit after 1920. The big shows of the American Circus Corporation planned to drop parades in the middle 1920s, but rowdy competition from the 101 Ranch Wild West, which paraded, delayed all that. It took the Great Depression to knock out more parades and those largely because the shows themselves collapsed—Christy, Robbins, Gentry, Sparks, and more. The 1934 Hagenbeck-Wallace parade and the 1935 Cole Bros. march were regarded as revivals. Cole quit after 1939. King Bros. had a creditable revival in the 1950s. Clyde Beatty Circus tried it a year.

By any measure, the circus street parade was a unique and effective advertising medium for nearly a century. People who saw it were likely to go to the circus as well. Parents who thought that the children would settle for the parade alone often found themselves caught up in the excitement, and all went to the show. Circuses spent lavishly on parade equipment and on posters to advertise the parades. It was good advertising.

When the circus itself turned up, the trainload of wagons displayed advertising—or packaging—of its own kind. These were the cages of Christy Bros. Circus in 1928. Earlier in show history, parade and arrival were one and the same. **Gene Baxter.**

Couriers picked up the theme. This page from a Ringling Bros. courier advertised circusdom's most unique form of advertising. **Authors' Collection**.

Massive wagons built solely for parade purposes constituted features the shows could advertise. **Circus World Museum and Cincinnati Art Museum.**

Then came the street parade itself. It was an advertisement just as much as those banners on a wall above the main street of Decorah, Iowa, for Forepaugh-Sells in 1911. **Circus World Museum**.

Throngs jammed the streets to see the parade, another testament to the advertising. This was Ringling Bros.' first visit to Cincinnati, 1905. **Missouri Historical Society**.

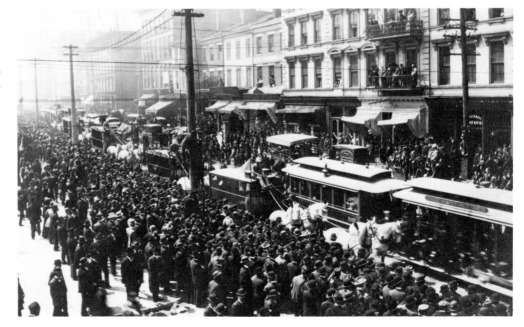

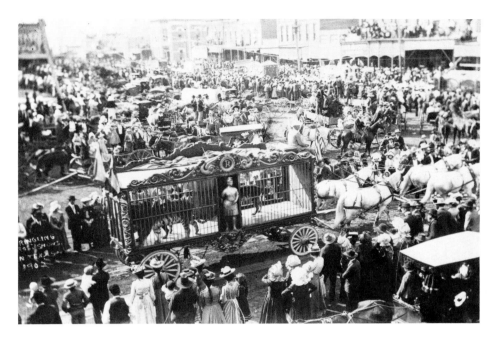

It was the same in the town square of a Texas stand on Ringling's 1902 route. In Salt Lake City in 1897 or New Orleans later the same season, huge crowds lined the streets to see the circus parade. **Utah State Historical Society, Circus World Museum**.

Residents of Manhattan, Kansas, turned out to see the Sells & Downs street parade of 1904, thanks in part to wall work of the billposters and banner men. **Kansas State Historical Society.**

Flowery bonnets were the style when people gathered to watch Campbell Bros. Circus parade. One family has a good view from the back of a wagon, while their team seems to be looking at the billposting. A scowling Cossack is the passing parade feature of the moment. **Jim McRoberts.**

Horses paid special attention when elephants scuffed past them in Providence, R.I. Each circus had an outrider to sound the warning, "Hold your horses. The elephants are coming!" Not a few teams spooked and ran, but these seem content to put ears and noses at attention. **Providence (R.I.) Public Library**.

As if lithographs in the pool hall and camels on Main Street weren't advertising enough, the Great Wallace Show saw another opportunity. It sold ad space on the camel blankets for Parry Buggies, Yucatan Chewing Gum and Oliver plows. Thus, people in Boonville, Mo., saw advertising at three echelons. **Missouri Historical Society**.

Even the sophisticates of Yale University paused to watch the Ringling Bros. parade pass through New Haven, Conn., in 1907. **New Haven Colony Historical Society**.

Cole Bros. Circus paraded with great success during the 1930s. **Circus World Museum**.

Bringing up the rear of the traditional circus parade was the steam calliope. The Two Jesters calliope was with Hagenbeck-Wallace for this 1934 scene. Escaping steam indicates the player was pounding out some ear-busting tune at the time. **John VanMatre.**

With the sound of calliope whistles still ringing in their ears, the populace turned to the next item on the circus day agenda. The afternoon performance would start before long. **Authors' Photo**.

Circus advertising has had its effect; throngs jam the midway of the Clyde Beatty Circus at Los Angeles, or nearly any other show, other city. **Authors' Collection**.

CHAPTER 13

The Circus Midway

Inevitably, circus day comes around. It may be after a traditional two-week campaign for a tented show or a month's advertising by an indoor circus. The advertising has had its effect. The posters have aroused curiosity and the urge to see. The newspaper ads and publicity have spiced up that interest and honed it even more. Heralds and couriers have generated excitement. Radio has pushed both urgency and the appealing sounds. Television has transmitted some of the circus color and pageantry. The street parade has displayed a free sample. In all, the campaign has worked its magic; advertising has performed as well as any circus star.

Customers are thronging to the box office of the arena or to the ticket wagon on the teeming show grounds. Customers—the final test of advertising. But the circus has not quit yet. Especially not if it is an outdoor extravaganza. Those customers still will traverse the midway—and that has got to be one of the greatest point-of-purchase sales alleys in all the world. No supermarket's checkout counter—draped with gum and batteries and geegaws though it may be—can equal the last-minute sales shot taken by any self-respecting circus.

There are balloon venders, lemonade hawkers, pit shows, and free acts. They sell hot dogs and birds-on-a-stick and elephant rides. One works his way to the ticket wagon as best he can; there are temptations and bargains all along the way. Most of all, there is the sideshow—and particularly, its own form of advertising, the garish sideshow bannerline with oil paintings of all the wonders to be seen inside. The museum of curiosities, the emporium of human oddities, the collection of strange and wonderful animals from all around the world—by any name, it is of something less than premiere status in society, but it holds an unending appeal to human nature. Just as any point-of-purchase concept should. The circus will work that appeal over well as the customers approach the big show. Sales efforts are rampant. Thus, after a hawker puts a balloon in the hands of a child so that no father dares refuse, that susceptible parent comes face to face with the sideshow banner line. Now that's advertising!

At the dawn of merchandising, it must have been on a circus that man first realized the importance of color. Sideshow banners are painted in reds, oranges, and yellows. And for product enhancement that dwarfs television efforts to make hamburgers seem juicier, that even puts automobile photo retouchers to shame, the sideshow banner stands supreme.

The family portrait of a midget clan shows them not in a scaled-down world, but alongside a massive puppy that makes clear their tiny dimensions. Or perhaps one Lilliputian is standing in the palm of a giant's hand. The "world's ugliest woman" is even more graceless as depicted on the banner. A snake enchantress is shown with coil after coil of venomous vipers, none seeming to be

On the midway are added enticements for point-of-purchase action—novelties, cotton candy, and the side show, where garish paintings capture everyone's attention. **Clyde Beatty-Cole Bros. Circus**.

The banners are gaudy and unbelievable and not to be taken seriously, on the John Robinson Circus of the 1920s or any other outfit or occasion. But they capture crowds and prompt spontaneous ticket sales. **Authors' Collection**.

There are talkers to describe the wonders, or sell the tickets. Theirs is a fantastic tale, but it works for Ringling and all the others. **Ringling Bros. and Barnum & Bailey Circus**.

There are free samples—in this case the tiny Doll Family—on the bally stand in front of the banners. Or minstrel dancers and a Dixieland band in that John Robinson view. Many people buy tickets and see the side show. **Ringling Bros. and Barnum & Bailey Circus**.

Then it is on to the marquee and into the big top for the big show. Circus advertising in all its excesses and variations has fulfilled its mission. The public is going to the circus. **Authors' Photo**.

charmed at all. One really ought to find the ticket man and see that shocker inside. Any portrait of a fat lady is likely to indicate that she is even too gross to be painted in such a restricted area, just twelve by twelve feet. Or perhaps one is attracted to the rhythmic old Alabama minstrels, the diabolic magician, the fakir immune to nails and fire and cannon shot. It was the circus that discovered the most sensuous sirens, not on the Rhine, but from the Nile, where they danced surprisingly. Not so surprising, one of them is depicted on the bannerline. Moreover, she is ready to dance here and now on the bally stand, that platform in front of the bannerline where some attractions make brief appearances as enticing proof that everything promised is inside and alive.

It is all point-of-purchase at its best. The circus-goer who came to buy a ticket to the three-ring big show now is told by the sideshow talker that there is plenty of time to do both, so the visitor succumbs to appeal of the instant—and buys a sideshow ticket, too.

Those sideshow banners have done it again. The color, the contrasts, the appeal to curiosity and surprise have taken effect. Another time, one shops carefully but then falls victim at the rack of packaged calories, or in disbelief snaps up a scandal sheet alongside the cash register. This time the same impulse buyer takes in the sideshow. The bannerline is the circus way of extracting that same last coin for the same sort of forbidden luxury, the same kind of proscribed extravagance, the same unmindful jolt to the budget.

From there, it is only a few exhilarating steps to the main entrance, the circus marquee, which opens the way to the big top wherein await those wonders. The animals and acrobats and aerialists promised in all the brilliant posters are now at hand. They are just beyond, under those massive tents, as depicted in the couriers and heralds. The clown from the newspaper ad is cavorting there, too. The anticipation is delicious, and advertising has delivered for both the buyer and the seller.

INDEX

263

XYZ

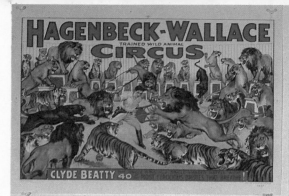

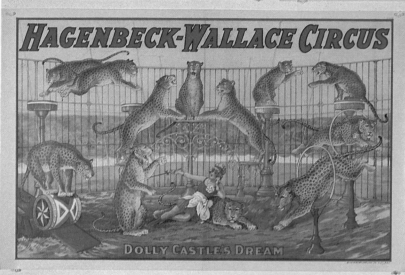

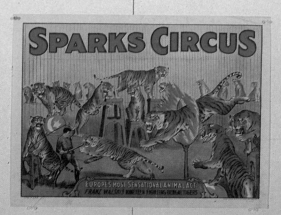